I Can Do Math

90 interactive minibooks that promote independence in young math learners

Fun exercises and pictures to color that build skills in counting and numbers, addition and subtraction, problem solving, and geometry

Desirèe Rossi

Developmental Editor:

David Costello

Pembroke Publishers Limited

Pembroke Publishers
538 Hood Road
Markham, Ontario, Canada L3R 3K9
www.pembrokepublishers.com

Desirèe Rossi is a specialist in Educational Sciences and Clinical Psychology. She has extensive experience working with children in both pre-school and the primary grades. Ms. Rossi is the author of many educational books, kits, games, and digital systems to help young children have fun while they learn.

Library and Archives Canada Cataloguing in Publication

Title: I can do math : 90 interactive minibooks that promote independence in young math learners / Desirèe Rossi ; developmental editor: David Costello.

Other titles: Matematica con 90 minilibri. English

Names: Rossi, Desirèe, author. | Costello, David (Professional learning facilitator), editor

Description: Translation of: Matematica con 90 minilibri. | Includes bibliographical references.

Identifiers: Canadiana (print) 20240420268 | Canadiana (ebook) 20240420276 | ISBN 9781551383699 (softcover) | ISBN 9781551389691 (PDF)

Subjects: LCSH: Mathematics—Study and teaching (Early childhood)

Classification: LCC QA135.6 .R67 2024 | DDC 372.7/044—dc23

Cover Design: John Zehethofer
Typesetting: Jay Tee Graphics Ltd.
Editors: Joanne Close, David Kilgour, Alison Parker

Printed and bound in Canada
9 8 7 6 5 4 3 2 1

Hi! I am Leo!
And these are my friends
of Cheerful Meadow!
We are running to the **mini library** to build and
read our favourite **minibooks**.
What are you doing? Are you coming too?
Come on, fill out your personal card
and join us!
Name:

Here is your mini library!
Isn't it beautiful? Every time you complete
a minibook, color it here so you can see
your progress.
1 2 3 4 5 6 7 8 9 10 11 12 13 14
15 16 17 18 19 20 21 22 23 24 25 26 27 28 29 30 31 32 33
34 35 36 37 38 39 40 41 42 43 44 45 46 47 48 49 50 51 52
53 54 55 56 57 58 59 60 61 62 63 64 65 66 67 68 69 70 71
72 73 74 75 76 77 78 79 80 81 82 83 84 85 86 87 88 89 90

CONTENTS

Activate Learning with Minibooks

A child, a teacher, a book and a pen can change the world.
Malala Yousafzai

Given the chance to create, children are more likely to engage in the learning process. When doing and thinking are connected, they may be motivated to learn and persevere in an activity despite the cognitive fatigue and the inevitable errors that will likely occur.

Minibooks are small thematic booklets of eight pages, each dedicated to a concept. Children can build the minibooks by using creativity and fine motor skills: folding, cutting precisely, mentally rotating and predicting the result, experimenting, making mistakes and learning from those mistakes, comparing ideas, learning through modeling, and peer education. Inside *I Can Do Math* there is a page with illustrated instructions for assembling the minibooks and a QR code to access the video tutorial.

With minibooks, first the hands are "set in motion" and then cognition is stimulated. Book after book, children enrich the "shelves" of their mini library, represented on the final page of this book. We advise that you photocopy the page and then invite the children to color the spines of the minibooks as they complete them. At the end of this book, there is a self-assessment where children express the degree of commitment, difficulty, and emotions felt during the activity.

I Can Do Math is dedicated to the development of student mathematical understanding and consists of activities that gradually progress from early mathematical concepts to addition and subtraction and problem solving. The 90 minibooks are divided into six sections:

- Foundational Knowledge
- Counting and Numbers to 20
- Addition and Subtraction to 20
- Numbers Beyond 20
- Problem Solving
- Geometry

Each section begins with an overview of a particular mathematical concept. *I Can Do Math* is filled with a variety of activities that support a range of instructional and learning goals. Inquiry-based workshops and lessons included in this book scaffold and reinforce skills being highlighted in the minibooks. These workshops and lessons are closely connected to the contents of the minibooks and provide children with opportunities to further explore the math concept by applying different skills and perspectives.

NOTES FROM THE CLASSROOM

As a primary teacher (K–2), you may sometimes find yourself searching for activities that engage students and provide meaningful opportunities for students to practice and build understanding of key math concepts.

You can assign the minibooks for independent and guided practice, review, consolidation, and formative assessment. They can also become a key component in a student's learning portfolio, referenced throughout the year to make connections among concepts and leverage and build on previous learning.

It is important that we have manageable, sustainable methods for monitoring student learning in relation to key math concepts. In these pages, you'll find reproducibles you can use to record student learning in relation to the six sections in the book. The first provides a tracking sheet that highlights the six key math concepts, and will offer an opportunity to indicate whether students have mastered that particular concept.

In addition, you'll find individual tracking sheets for each of the six key math concepts that focus on the individual concept and its foundational aspects. These six trackers allow the teacher to monitor student learning in relation to the various foundational aspects of each key concept.

Minibooks can be used to

- introduce a topic
- delve deeper into content explored in class
- review content
- explore a concept through a different perspective

I Can Do Math has a friendly guide character, Leo, who acts as a companion for the entire group of minibooks. Leo encourages and motivates children and acts as a tutor who, through images, supports children in understanding which skill will be most required in completing a particular minibook.

There is a minibook dedicated to the character, Leo the Caterpillar, at the beginning of this book. Here, Leo illustrates the basic words of instructions, including look, listen, say, read, write, color, circle, and mark with an x. In this way, the child who looks at the image of Leo the Caterpillar will already know which activity will be highlighted in the minibook they are about to build. During the construction of the minibook, which precedes the completion phase, children can review the pages and try to predict what they will have to do.

Most of the pages in the minibooks include written instructions, which you can read aloud or can be read by the children, depending on their skills. Having this option provides you with opportunities to differentiate based on the various learning needs in the classroom. Activities are designed to start and finish during a lesson. This flexibility allows you to schedule working on the minibook at the *just right* time. Illustrations are black and white so that each child can personalize their pages, coloring them as they wish.

In addition to individual students completing the minibooks, students can work in pairs or small groups where they can engage in peer assessment with classmates. In some cases, this interaction between classmates is explicitly stated in the minibooks.

Once assembled and completed, the minibooks can be attached to a notebook, collected in a display case, hung on a poster, or stored in a small box that acts as a traveling mini library. The creativity of children may lead them to generate their own special minibooks, which may have little to do with the math content, but which indicate how "taking away an idea" or a tool and using it in other areas is a valued learning objective.

The minibooks can be used as part of any instructional model—guided math, workshop model, centers, three-part lessons, or direct instruction—and can be leveraged at any point during the lesson to support and extend student understanding of the math concept.

In addition to the minibooks, *I Can Do Math* offers various classroom resources that can be used by the teacher and the student to support mathematical understanding. Reproducible classroom resource materials can be used by the teacher during direct instruction and guided practice, and by the student during centers and independent practice. These eleven sheets will complement the minibooks, and can be used at any point throughout the student learning experience.

IT'S EASY TO CREATE A MINIBOOK FROM A PRINTED SHEET:

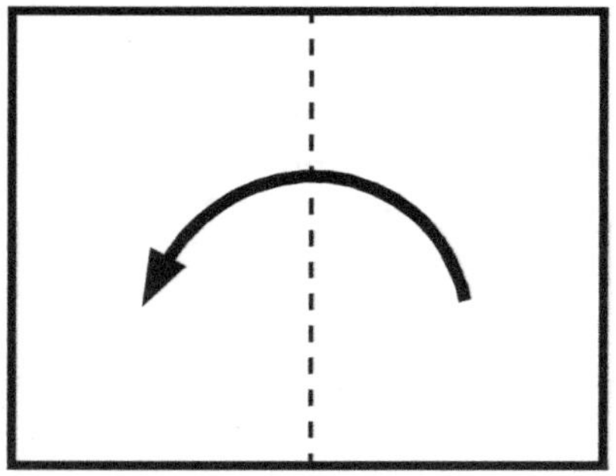

1. With the printed side down, fold the paper in half, the right edge over the left.

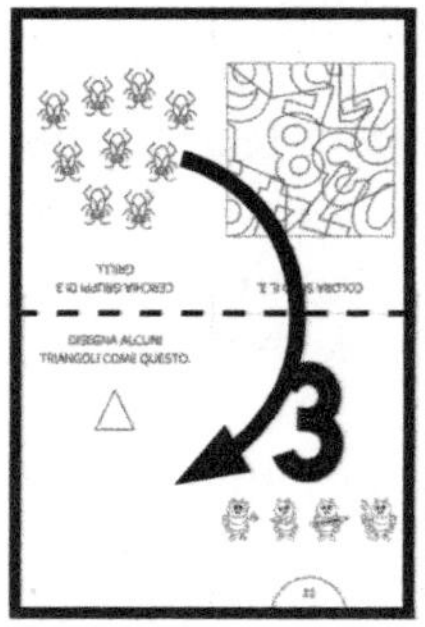

2. Fold it in half again.

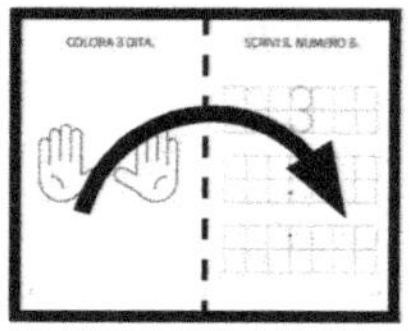

3. Fold it in half one more time.

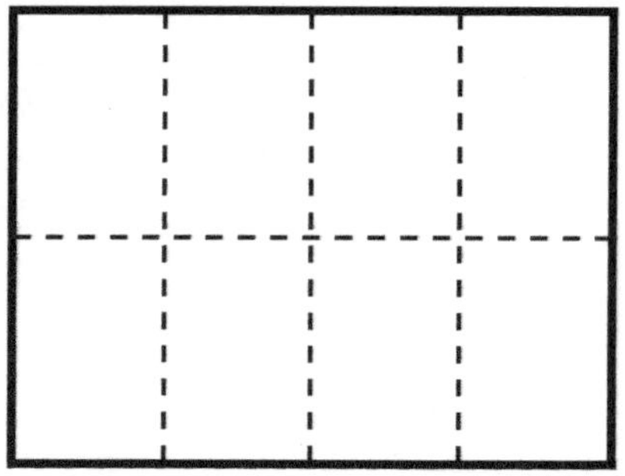

4. Open the sheet with the blank side facing up.

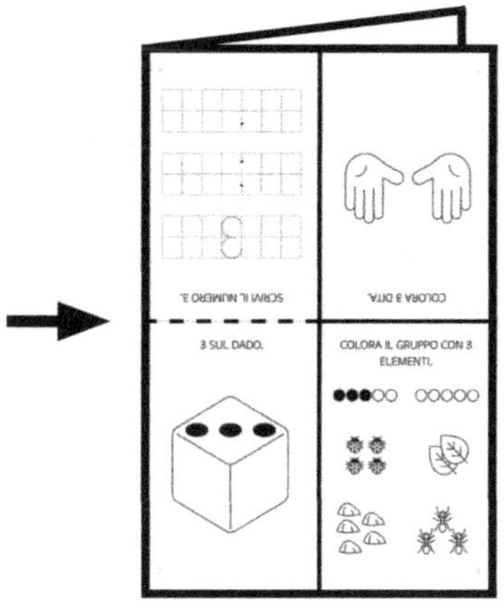

5. Fold it in half and cut the long side between pages 2 and 5.

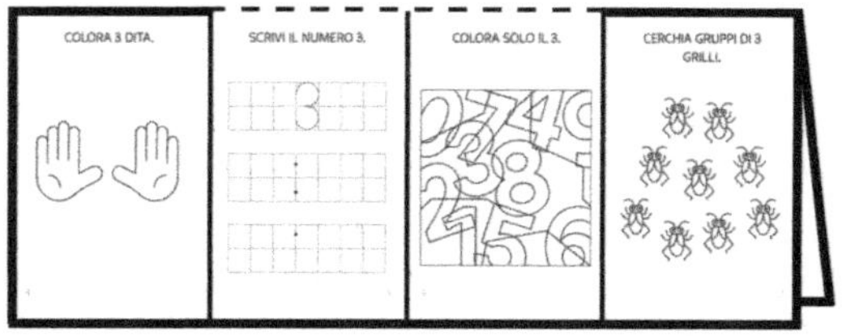

6. Open the sheet so you can see pages 4, 5, 6, and 7.

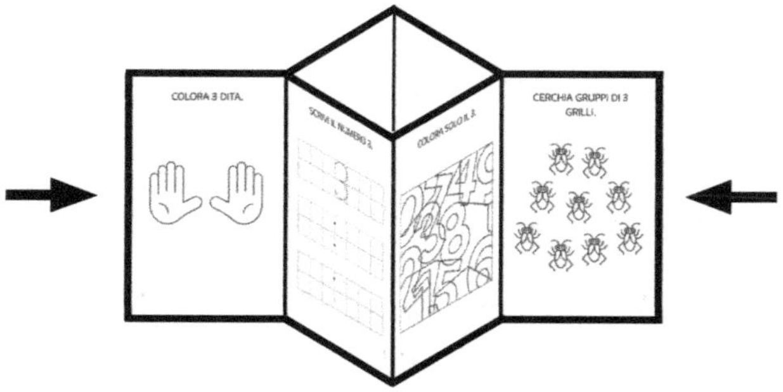

7. Fold as shown and you have your minibook!

Watch the tutorial on how to build a minibook.

LEO'S INSTRUCTIONS

Count: Count totals.

Listen: Listen carefully to the instructions you are given.

Look: Look at the pictures or read the numbers.

Delete or circle: Remove the intruders or circle what you want to highlight.

Color: Color the drawing according to instructions.

Draw: Draw items according to instructions.

Write: Write the numbers.

Six Learning Concepts Checklist

STUDENT	LEARNING CONCEPTS					
	Foundational Knowledge	Counting & Numbers to 20	Addition & Subtraction	Numbers Beyond 20	Problem Solving	Geometry

© 2024 *I Can Do Math* ISBN 978-1-55138-369-9 www.pembrokepublishers.com

FOUNDATIONAL KNOWLEDGE

Foundational Knowledge

Research has shown that we are born with the ability to identify/visualize and differentiate small quantities from one another. This is referred to as **subitizing**. As children age, their ability to subitize continues to develop as they are provided opportunities to engage in math activities.

Calculation skills develop from the age of 2 and 3 as children discriminate between a collection of items by comparing and/or combining. Despite not yet possessing counting skills, children begin to perform simple addition and subtraction through subitizing and visualization. Therefore, it is important to stimulate and develop these skills in children as these are building blocks for more complex processes.

It is important that children have opportunities to experiment, reason, interpret, and grow their understanding of number and quantity. Gardner, in his work on multiple intelligences, defines **logical-mathematical intelligence** as the ability to think and process information in numerical terms and abstract relationships. The basis of numerical competence includes skills such as comparing, ordering and classifying objects, estimating quantities, creating and solving problems, analyzing situational and variable components, using abstract symbols, and discovering and using algorithms and logical sequences.

Numerical competency is closely linked to the development of language. Every quantity has a name that can be expressed through verbal language. As indicated by Piaget, a child's ability to produce a correct verbal sequence of numbers is not an indication of an ability to count according to quantity. To count, children must be able to demonstrate the following counting principles (Gelman & Galistel, 1978):

- Stable Order: Numbers have a name and are said/written in a sequential order.
- One-to-One Correspondence: When saying the names of numbers, each item receives one count.
- Cardinality: The last number spoken in a counting sequence names the quantity for that set.
- Abstraction: It does not matter what you count, how we count stays the same.
- Order Irrelevance: The order in which items are counted is irrelevant.

Research shows that children can begin to develop numerical competence at a very young age, based on their experiences in their environment. The more experiences children are immersed in, the stronger the numerical foundation. These skills are then further developed once children begin school.

As children progress through school, they strengthen their numerical competence. During their early school years, they rely on working with quantities (e.g., counting, comparing, combining). Over time, they transition to the written symbolic system and the ability to operate with increasingly abstract content. Counting strategies that were key in early years are abandoned in later years when students have automatic retrieval of facts.

NOTES FROM THE CLASSROOM

Children need to understand the foundational aspects of mathematics. As a teacher, your feedback highlights the importance of requisite readiness skills so that they can access grade-level curriculum. In this section, you will find hands-on tasks that will help students develop readiness skills (e.g., sequencing, relationships among items) they will leverage throughout the year.

To further support foundational knowledge, you can use the included tracking form (pg 14) that highlights the key learning areas within foundational learnings: differentiate numbers and letters; comparison; recreate the scenario; patterns; categories; sequencing; and prepositions. You can use this form to monitor student learning within the key learning areas and can use the information gathered to guide instruction.

In addition to this tracking form, there are reproducibles (pg 24) to support both teacher and student when working within the foundational knowledge section of *I Can Do Math*. The visuals can be used by the teacher to model learning and as examples when working with the whole class, small groups, or individual students. They can also be used by the student to support learning of the key areas within foundational knowledge.

Bibliography

Fuson K.C. (1991), *Relations entre comptage et cardinalité chez les enfants de 2 à 8 ans,* "Les chemins du nombre", pp. 159-179.

Gelman R. and Gallistel C.R. (1978), *The child's understanding of number,* Cambridge, Harvard University Press.

Lucangeli D., Poli S. and Molin A. (2003), *L'intelligenza numerica (3 volumi),* Trento, Erickson.

Wynn K. (1990), *Children's understanding of counting,* "Cognition", vol. 36, pp. 155-193.

Wynn K. (1992), *Addition and subtraction by human infants,* "Nature", vol. 358(6389), pp. 749-750.

Foundational Knowledge

STUDENT	FOUNDATIONAL KNOWLEDGE						
	Differentiate Numbers & Letters	Comparison	Recreate the Scenario	Patterns	Categories	Sequencing	Prepositions

EYE ON THE DISGUISE

Goal

Stimulate attention, discrimination, and visual memory.

Materials

- Clothes to dress up in (e.g., pants, skirts, sweaters, shirts, coats, dresses, wigs)
- Accessories (e.g., glasses, handbags, earrings, ties, hats, caps, scarves)
- Box to hold the materials

Directions

Divide the children into two groups. All the children sit down, except one, who goes to dress up and can be helped by a partner. The child can use the clothes and accessories as part of their disguise. When ready, the disguised child stands in front of the two groups. The other children observe and can ask them questions relating to the disguise (e.g., where they come from, what their name is, what they are doing dressed like that).

After answering questions, the disguised child leaves the room and, with the help of their partner, quickly changes three elements of the disguise—clothes and accessories can be replaced, accessories can be moved or added.

The child then returns to the room. The two teams observe their classmate in silence for a maximum of one minute and, after a brief consultation between team members, try to identify the differences. The team that guesses the greatest number of differences wins the round. The game resumes with a new partner in disguise and a new helper.

NUMBERS THAT INCREASE AND DECREASE

Goal

Recall the number sequence (count up and down from 1 to 10 with direct reference to the quantity).

Materials

- Numbers from 1 to 20 printed on a card with a colored background
- Scotch tape
- At least 10 steps, inside or outside the school building

Directions

Print the numbers and ask each student to color the background of a number card. The same color can be used for the numbers with the same number of ones (e.g., one color for 1 and 11, another color for 2 and 12). Once you arrive at the stairs, starting from the lowest step, place the number 1 in the center of the riser, so that it is clearly visible. Continue in the same way with the other numbers, up to 10. If possible, proceed to 20. Then go up the stairs with the children while counting the steps out loud; then go down, counting from 10 to 0 (or from 20 to 0). To introduce the notion of quantities, it is possible to have as many children climb as indicated by the number.

Variation

If there are no stairs in your school (or they are shorter than 10 steps) or there is an accessibility issue, modify the activity by placing the numbers, in order, along a hallway wall. The starting point would be zero and you would place 1 at the point of the first step. Then, when using cards, students can count moving forward then backward.

SUPERMARKET IN THE CLASSROOM

Goals

- Estimate the number of objects in a set (more and less regardless of the size of the objects).
- Select objects based on certain attributes.
- Promote easy recognition of quantities using an orderly arrangement.
- Counting: working with quantities.

Materials

- Shelving, a mobile object rack on wheels, or a recycled cardboard display
- Cardboard or plastic containers of various items (e.g., pasta, rice, pudding, chocolate, biscuits, salt, tea, ice cream containers, yoghurt cups, milk containers, detergent and shampoo bottles, toothpaste, toothbrushes, bubble bath).
- Baskets
- Hula hoops

Directions

In a space that can remain in use indefinitely, organize the "supermarket." Involve students in collecting the materials listed above to create this space. While it can also be an area delegated to symbolic play, its use must be well regulated.

After all the materials have been collected, propose classifying objects into departments as the first activity (e.g., food, personal and house cleaning products, pet products, games, school supplies). Divide the class into small groups: each group will take care of a "department," arranging the products and applying labels on the shelves.
For the second activity, divide the class into 4–5 groups and give each group their own space, near the "supermarket." Give each group two hula hoops. Groups fill their hoops with items from their department. Groups indicate which hoop contains more items. Ask them to compare objects of different sizes in the hoops. Does the size of objects influence children's concept of quantity in the collection? Students return the items to the supermarket shelves.
Finally, have students work with a partner. Give each pair a shopping basket and a list of different items. The pairs go "shopping," placing items in their bag and sitting down only after they "purchase" the products on their list.
Ask each pair to check the shopping list of another pair of students. Once all lists have been checked, have students work with you to create a graph of the collected items using the departments as categories.
The "supermarket" can also be used at a later stage, assigning prices to the items and equipping the store with a cash register to provide students with practice in adding and subtracting numbers to 20.

A LITTLE ORDER EVEN IN NATURE!

Goal

Use natural material to build sets to arrange and count.

Materials

- Natural materials collected by children (e.g., stones, sticks, pinecones, acorns, leaves of the same type, shells of the same type)
- Paper collection bags, containers, or wooden boxes
- Cloth sheet or large sheet of wrapping paper
- Camera, phone, or tablet to take photos

Directions

Organize some class outings in the garden or schoolyard to collect natural materials. Outline the types of materials to choose; it is important that children gather objects that belong to a group or category to allow comparison of sizes (e.g., leaves from the same type of tree).

Back in the classroom, in a space free of chairs and desks, have the children sit in a circle around a cloth. They take turns to carefully empty the contents of their bags. At this point, the materials will all be mixed. Discuss the objects and the groups that could be created from what students have gathered. Divide the children into small groups according to the quantity of sets they

want to create, give each group a container, and indicate the type of object to collect.

Once the material is sorted, you can begin the next phase of the activity—arranging and ordering. Check that there are approximately 10–15 items to be sorted and that there are not too many similarities between the items. Give each group a white poster on which to place the items and indicate which attribute to arrange by: length, height, weight, width, size, or thickness, as examples. Finally, ask them to number in ascending or descending order. Let the children have time to look through their items, compare each item, and try to arrange through a process of trial and error. Give each group time to change their arrangements until they obtain a good result. Finally, share all the work: students can ask questions of other students if they think there is another way to organize the objects. Once the activity is completed, photograph and display pictures of the posters.

After the Activity...

Use the natural material collected for artistic experiences, such as the creation of mandalas on the ground, for numerous counting activities that take place daily in the classroom.

With stones, it is possible to propose the "date with natural materials" activity. Choose a place in the classroom where, every day, you can ask the children to mark the day and month by arranging the materials in an orderly manner in groups of 5, for example 4 leaves for April and 16 stones for April 16 (16 stones are organized in 3 groups of 5 and 1 extra stone).

EVERYTHING IN ITS PLACE!

Goal

Categorize into sets.

Materials

- Gardening tools (e.g., watering can, shovels, jars, small rakes, seeds, bags)
- Boxes and food packaging (see the activity "Supermarket in the Classroom")
- Different types of clothing (e.g., shirts, jackets, sweatshirts, socks)
- White posters, pencils, and markers
- Large box

Note: Instead of concrete objects, students can use images.

Directions

Place some of the objects listed above (Materials list) in a large box. Have the children find the box in the classroom. Tell them that it is necessary to do some tidying up and that they must decide as a group where to put each object. Together, identify three categories to which the objects belong and three possible places in which to store them (e.g., clothes in the wardrobe, food in the refrigerator, gardening tools in a chest of drawers). Then prepare three posters together with students and draw on each one a "reorganization space" among those identified. Children color and embellish them.

Hang (or lay out on the floor) the three posters in three different places in the classroom. Then call one child up at a time, ask them to close their eyes, select an object from the box, and place it in on the matching poster, getting help from classmates if necessary. Continue in this way until all objects are in place!

WHERE DO I PUT IT?

Goal

Exploring spatial awareness.

Materials

- White and blue cardboard tags, measuring 5 x 10 cm
- Two cardboard boxes
- Colored pencils, markers

Directions

The first phase involves creating game material.

Give each student a white tag. Ask them to illustrate and label a part of the body (e.g., right hand, left hand, eyes, nose). As the children complete and label their illustrations, write a directional word on each blue card (e.g., front, back, top, bottom, inside, outside, center, side, near, far).

Have children place their cards in one box while you place the directional cards in another box. Ask the children to stand up. Choose a child and ask them to select a card from each box and say out loud what they have selected (help read the cards as needed). For example, if the child draws two cards "right hand" and "under," they can decide whether to say, "Right hand under the notebook" or "Right hand under the chin," as examples. All the classmates will have to make the indicated gesture. Whoever makes a mistake or gives an impossible task is eliminated (eventually another child will be chosen to give the tasks). The game ends when only 2 children remain in the game.

Subitizing

Suggestion for 1

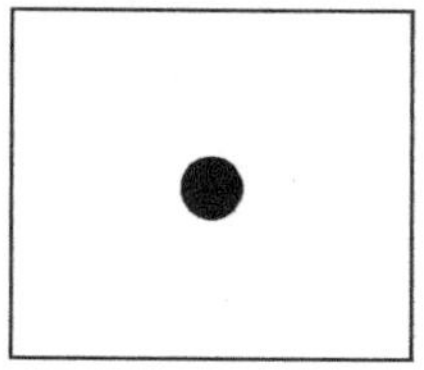

Suggestion for 2

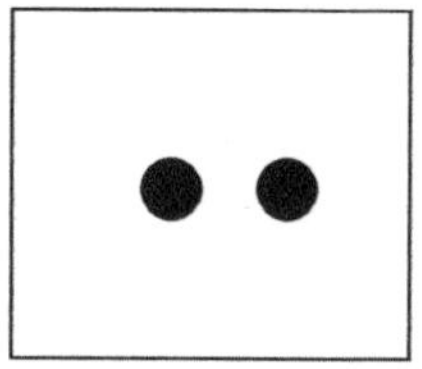

Suggestion for 3

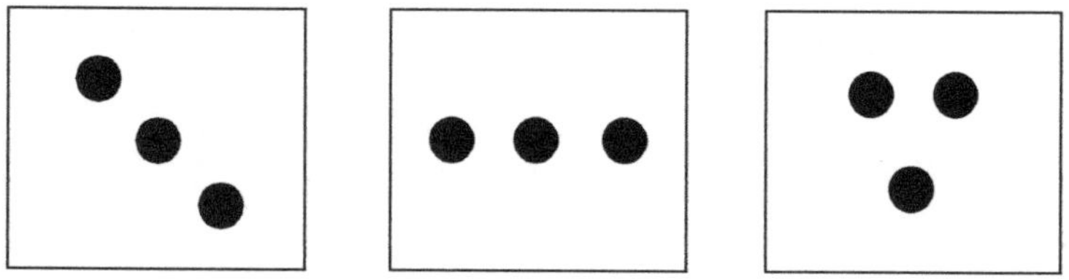

Suggestion for 4

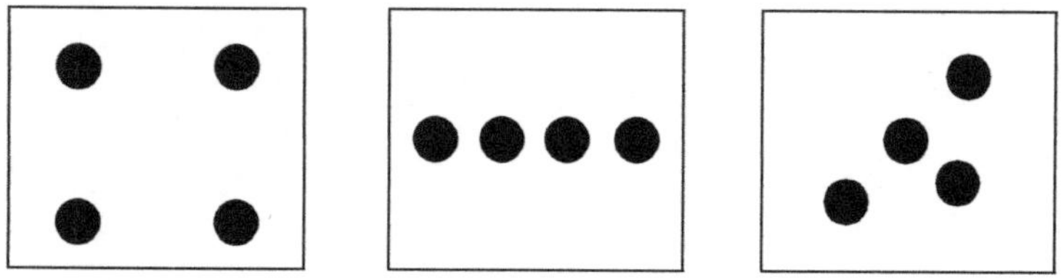

Suggestion for 5

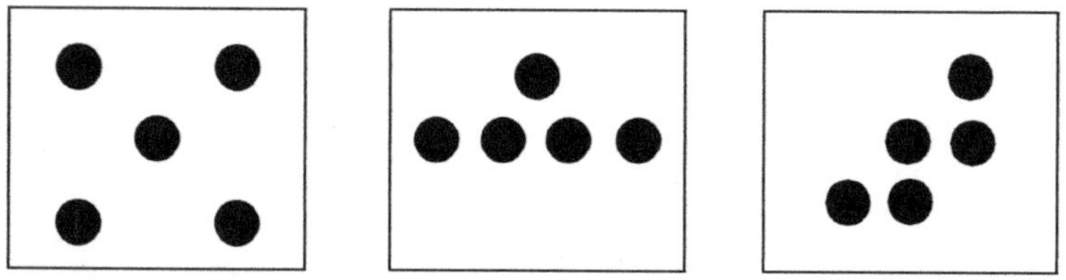

Suggestion for 6

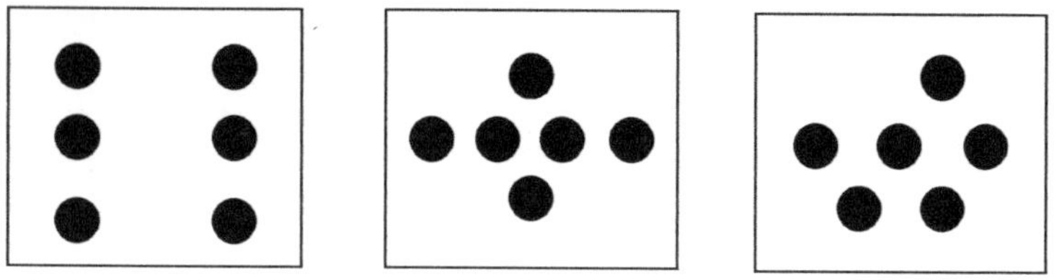

Five Frame

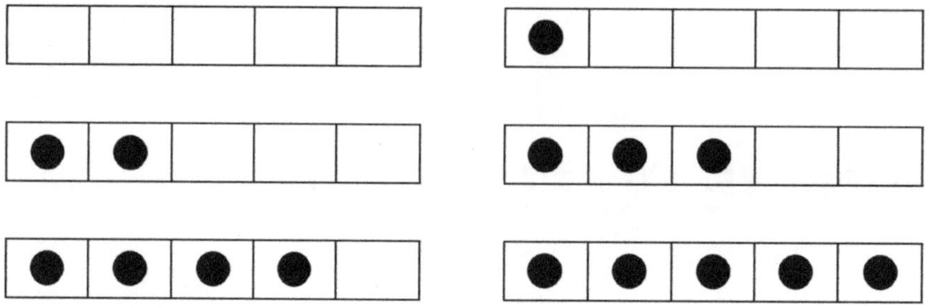

Ten Frame

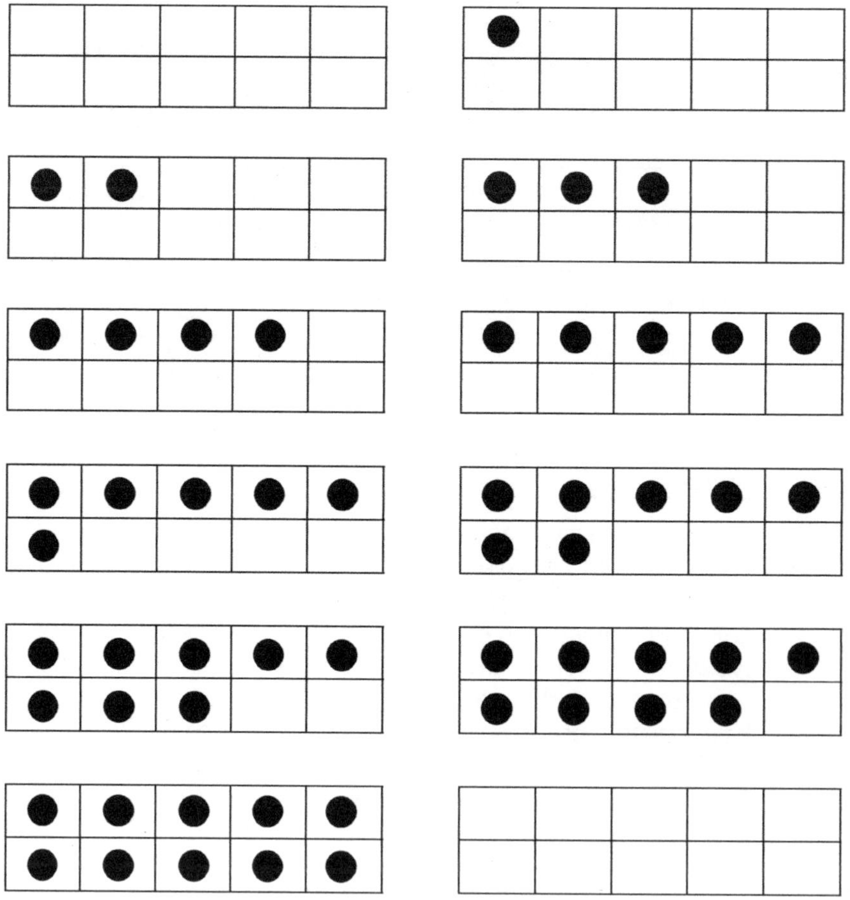

I am __ years old

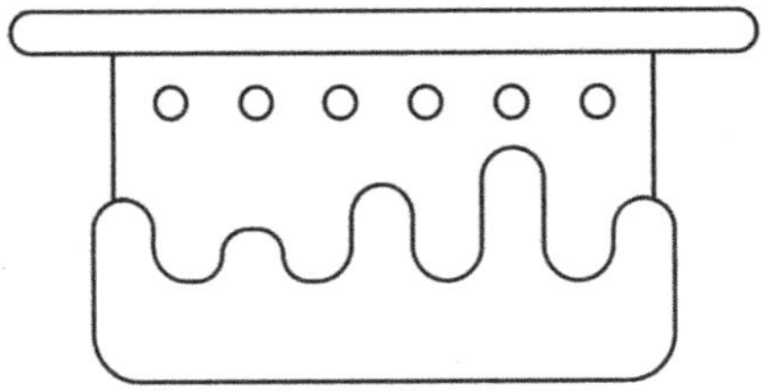

Draw candles on the cake to show how old you are.

My face

Draw and color your face.

Today's date is...

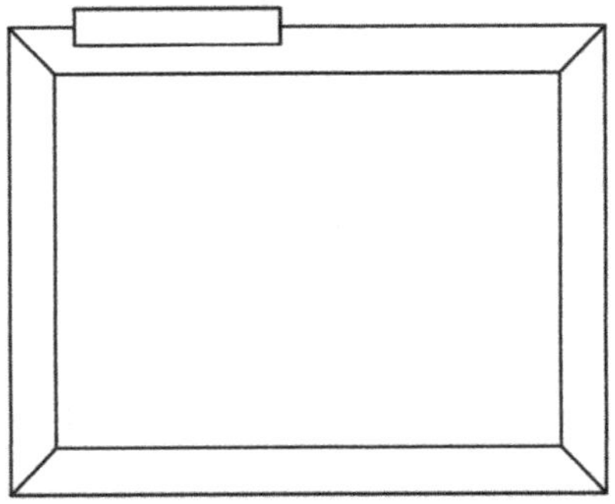

Use numbers to print today's date.

The numbers of my life...

1 2 3 4 5 6 7
8 9 10 11 12 13
14 15 16 17 18 19
20 21 22 23 24 25
26 27 28 29 30 31

1 2 3 4 5 6
7 8 9 10 11 12

Circle the numbers of your birthday.

Numbers I know

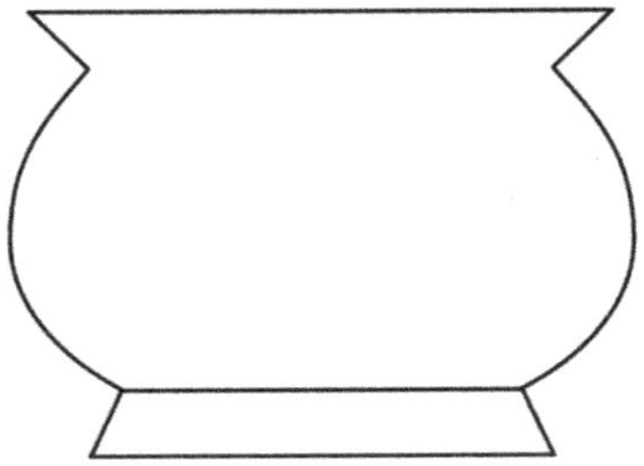

Print the numbers you know.

MY WORLD IN NUMBERS

The people in my life

Draw the people important to you.

Identify

∑	∞	A
	6	
2	R	1

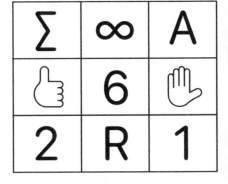

Color only the boxes with numbers.

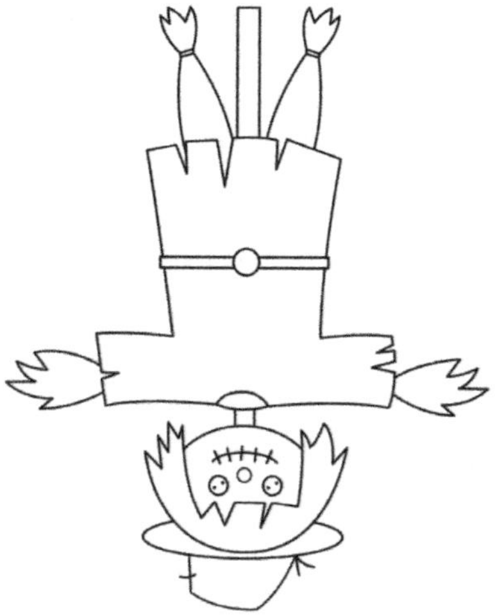

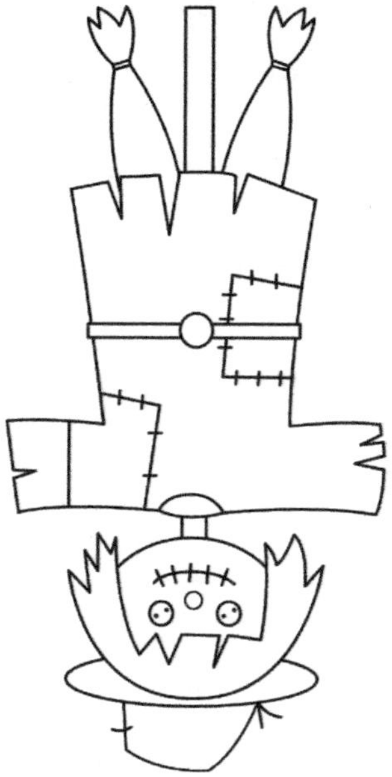

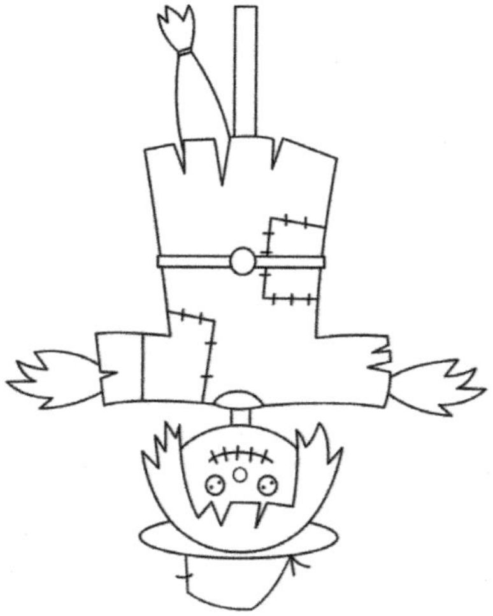

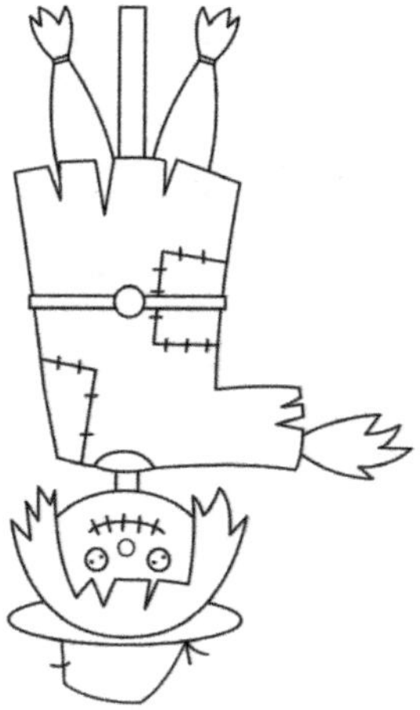

THE STRAW MAN

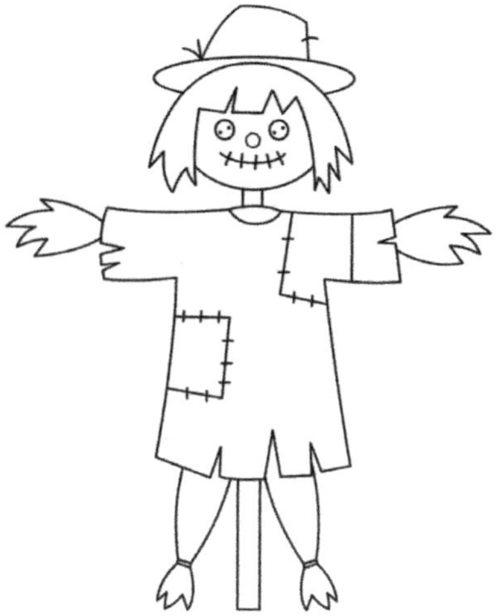

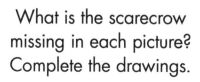

What is the scarecrow missing in each picture? Complete the drawings.

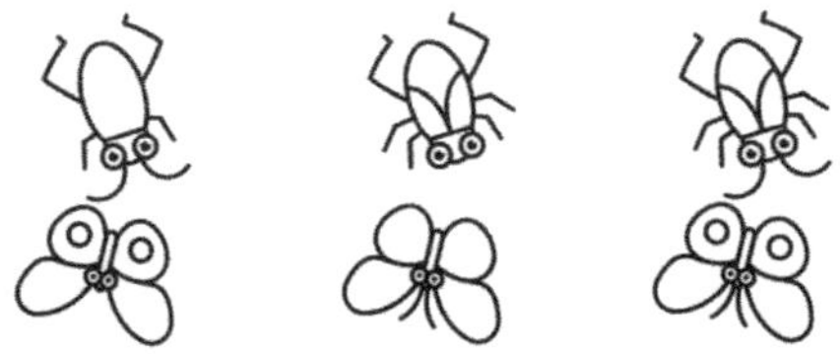

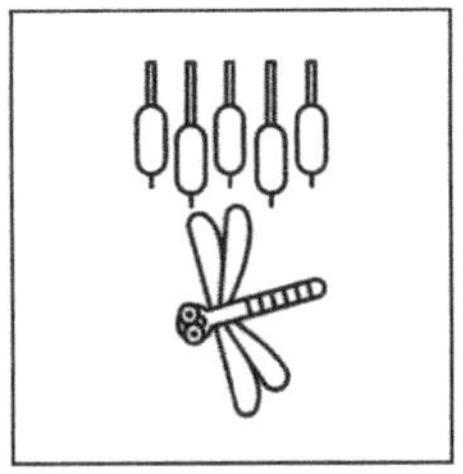

Now compare your work with a classmate's. How did it go?

SHARPEN YOUR VIEW!

Circle or color the drawing below that is the same as the one above.

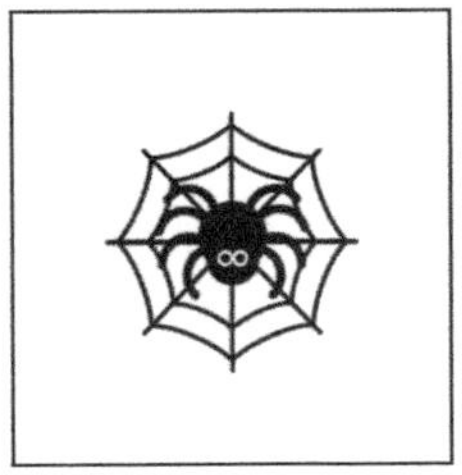

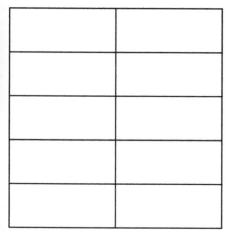

WHERE ARE YOU, YOU LITTLE PESTS?

Play with a friend. While you watch, ask him/her to count to 7.

2

This is a memory game. Look at the positions of the insects for a few seconds, then turn the page and draw them in the same positions.

3

Look at the positions of the flies in the grid.

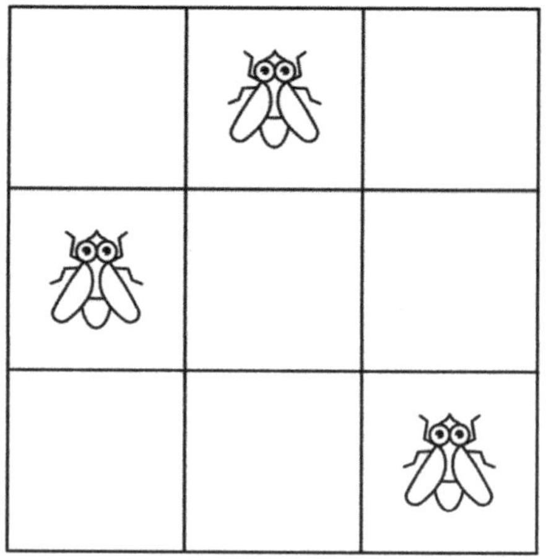

4

Now draw the flies in the same positions as in the grid before.

5

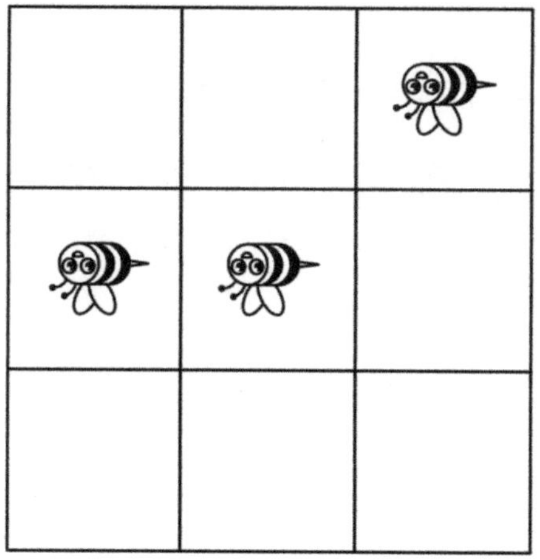

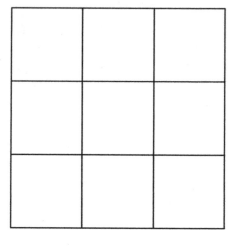

Look at the positions of the bees in the grid.

6

Now draw the bees in the same positions as in the grid before.

7

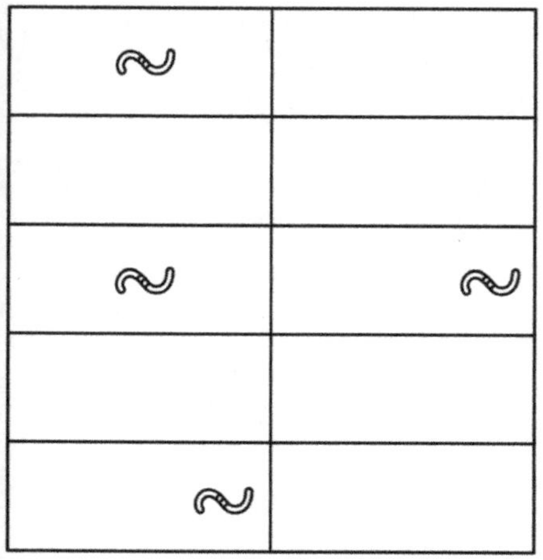

Look at the positions of the worms in the grid.

8

Now draw the worms in the same positions as in the grid before.

7

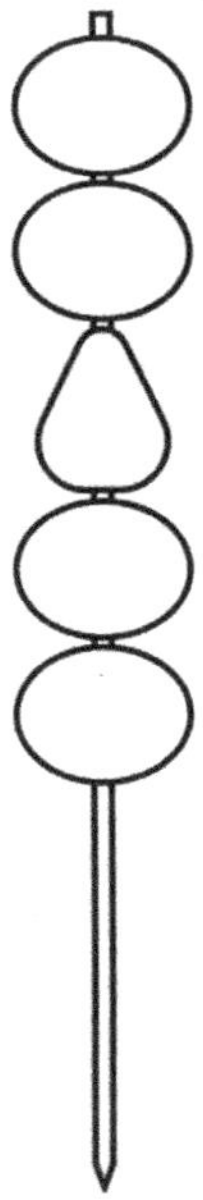

6

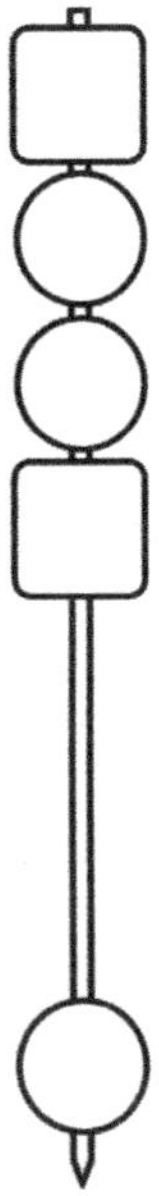

5

4

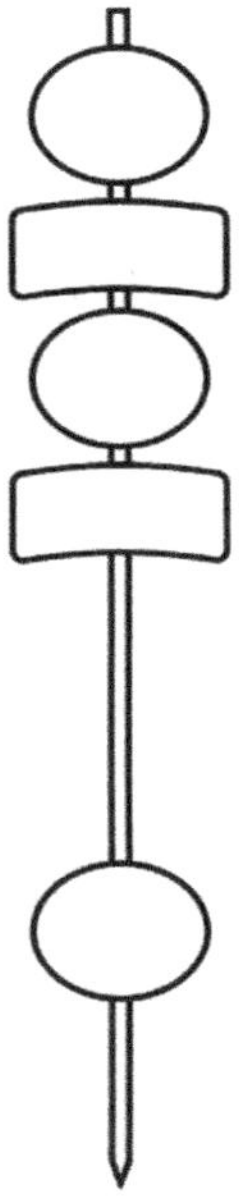

8

FRUIT ON A STICK

On each page look at the fruit on the stick and complete the pattern, then color.

6

2

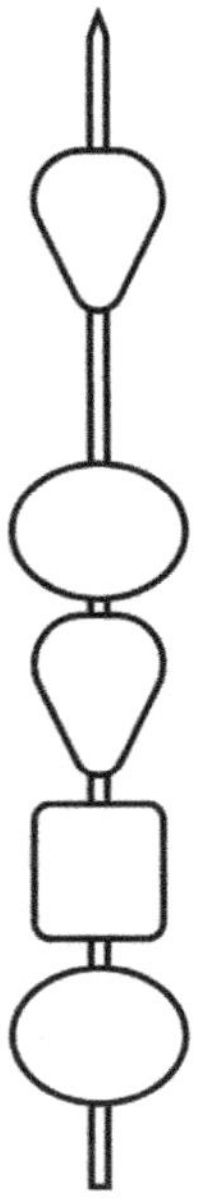

3

WHERE DO I DRAW?

Listen to the directions, look at the image, and draw.

Draw an apple **inside** the basket.

Draw a banana **outside** the basket.

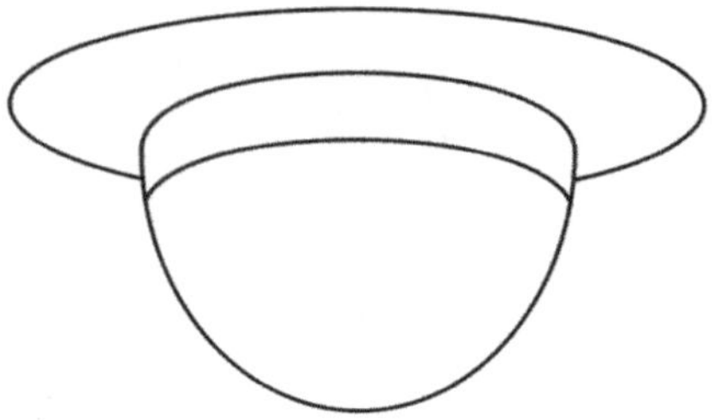

Draw a face **over** the hat.

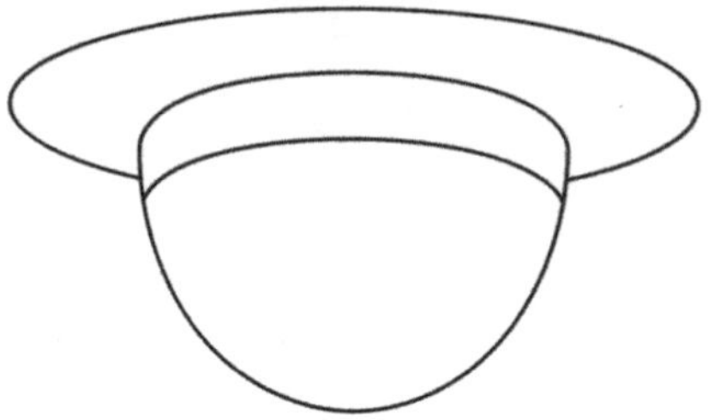

Draw a face **under** the hat.

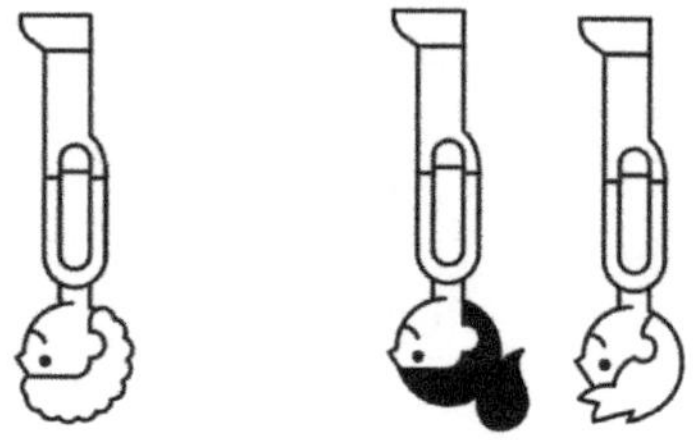

Draw a child in the **middle** of the line.

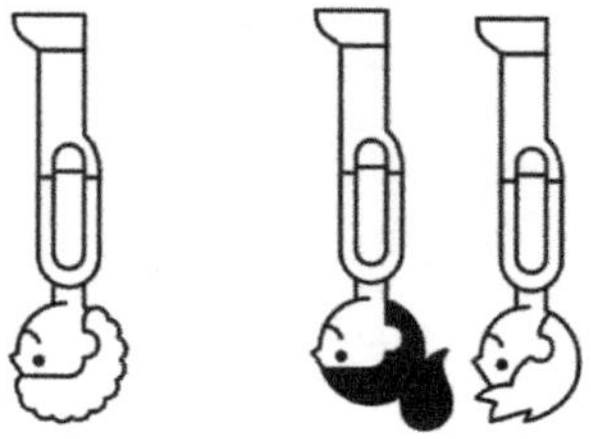

Draw a child in **front** of the line.

Draw a kitten **behind** the first person in the row.

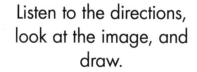

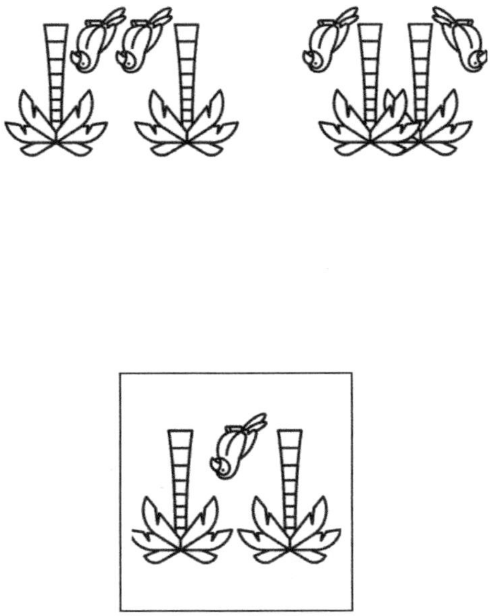

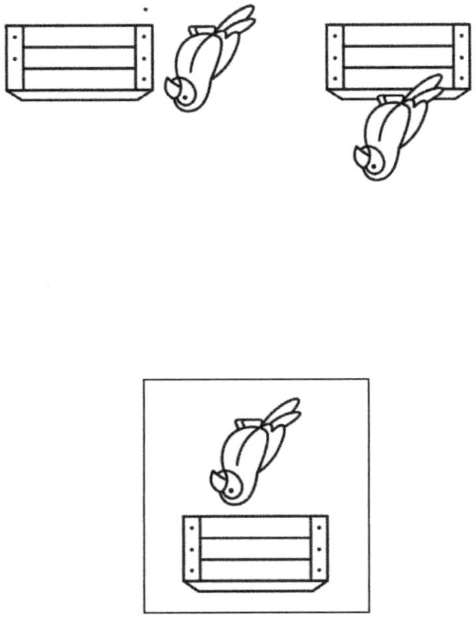

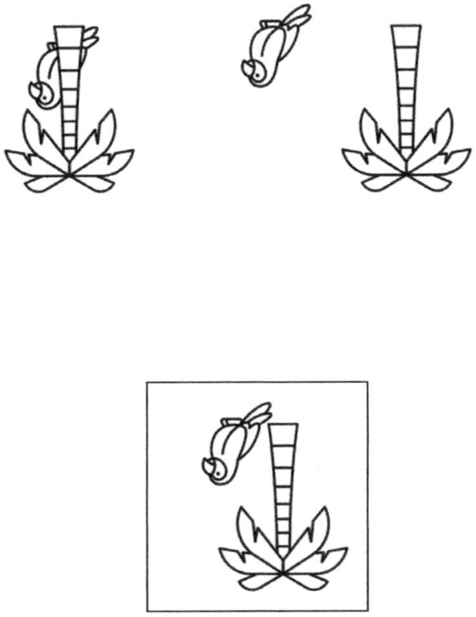

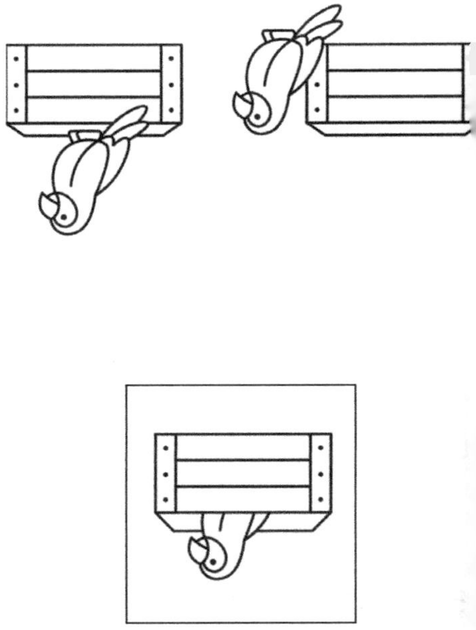

Now compare your work with a classmate's. How did it go?

WHERE DID YOU GO?

Look where the parrot is in the above image and color the opposite image below.

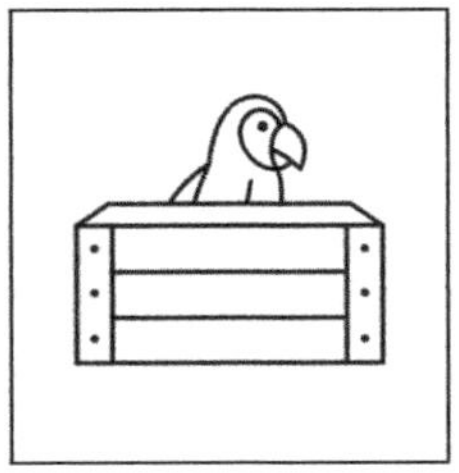

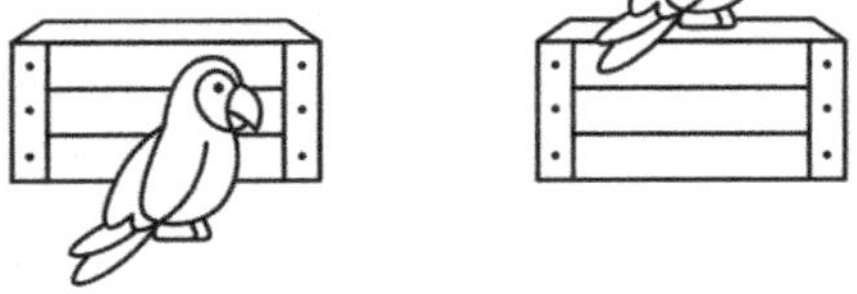

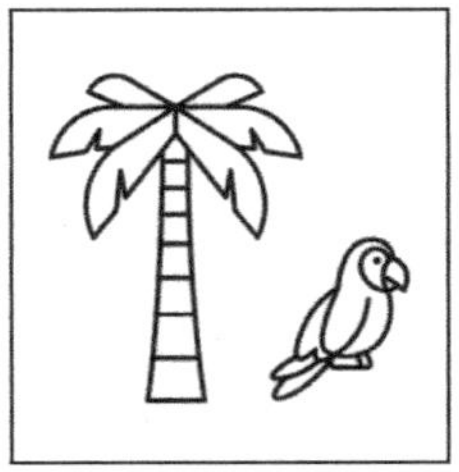

CHANGE YOUR POINTS OF VIEW AND FIND...

Look at the item drawn below and circle it in the image above.

6

Look for the carrots in the garden.

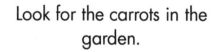

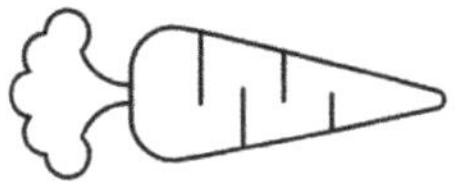

Look for the hat at the swimming pool.

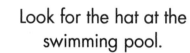

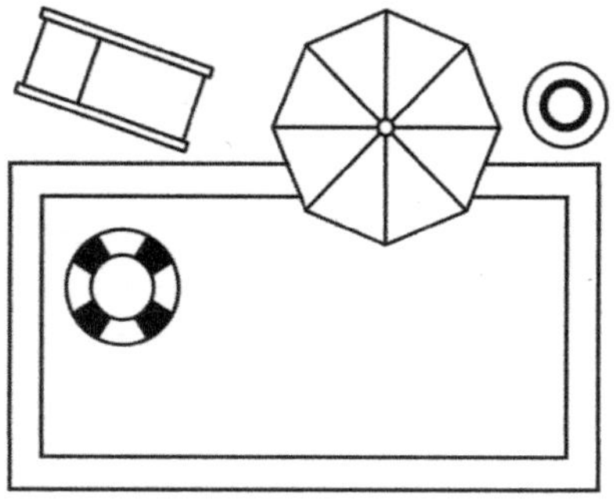

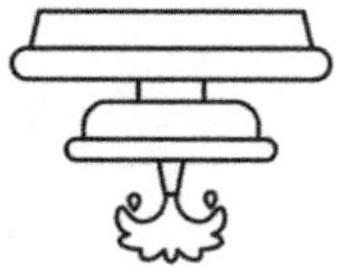

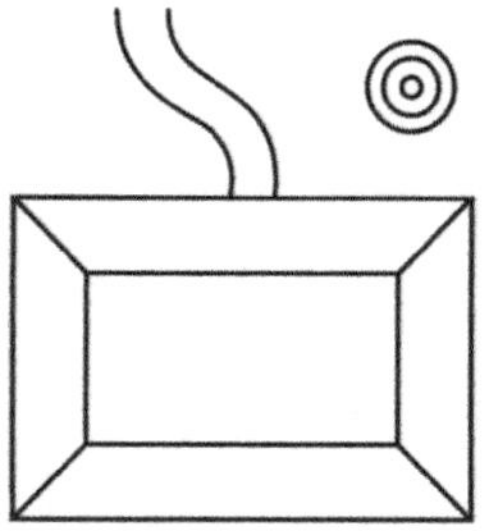

Look for the fountain in the garden.

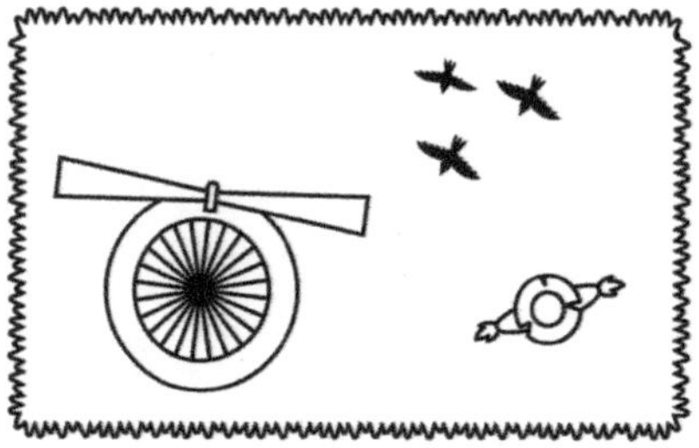

Look for the scarecrow in the field.

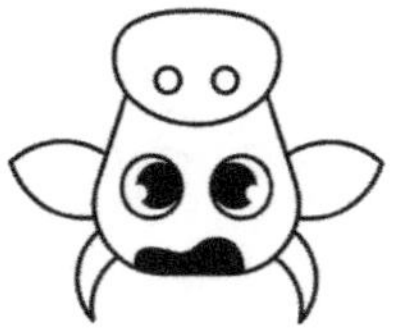

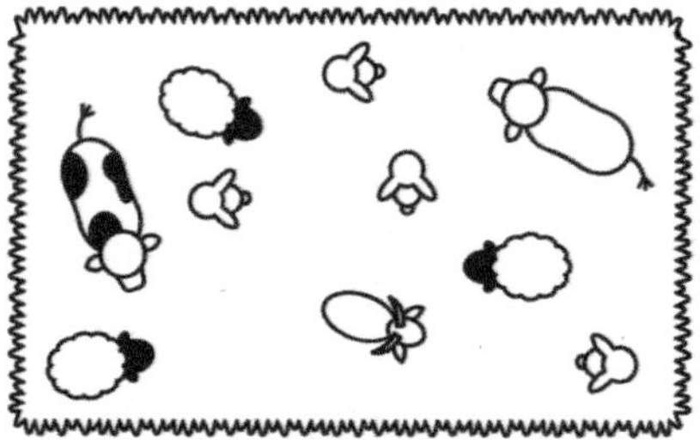

Look for the cow in the field.

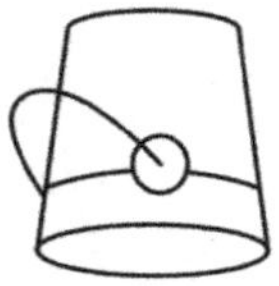

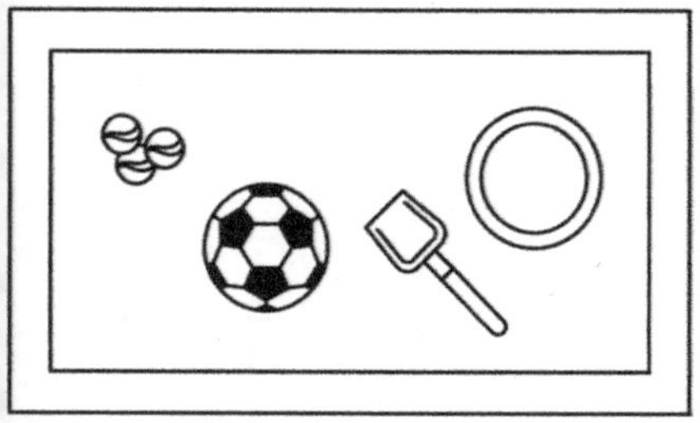

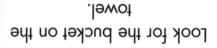

Look for the bucket on the towel.

Look for the car in the parking lot.

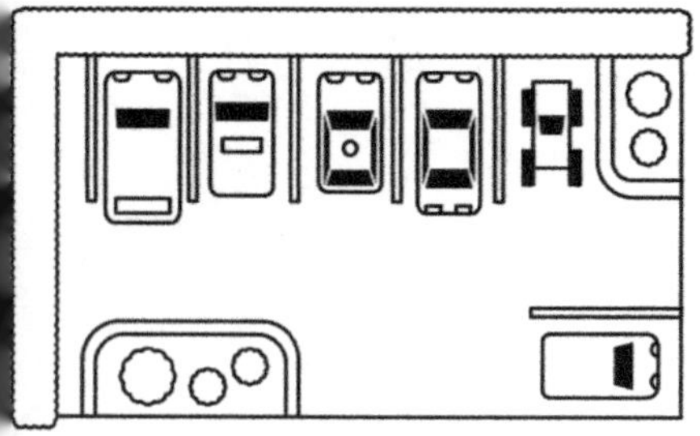

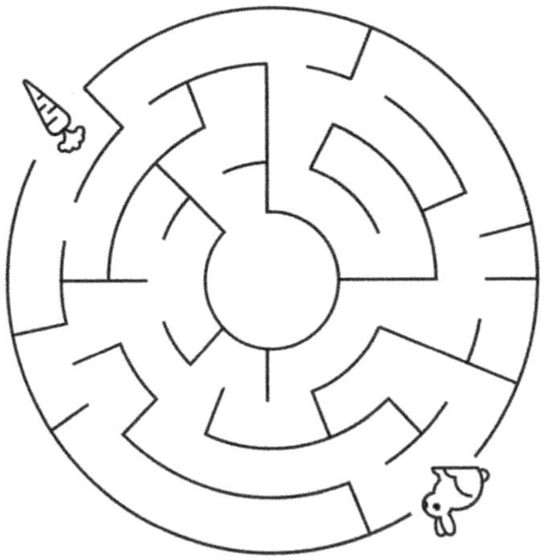

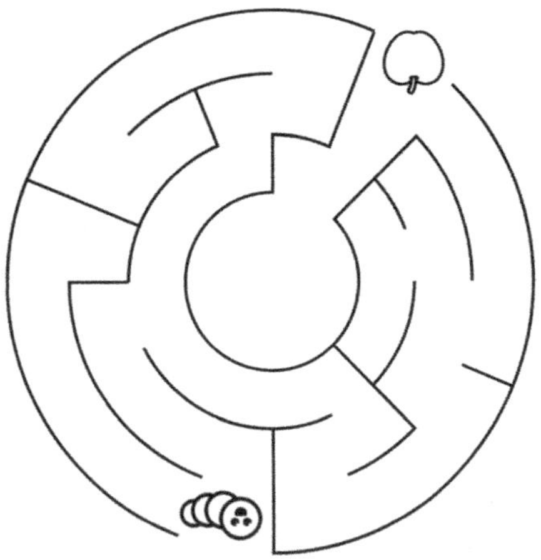

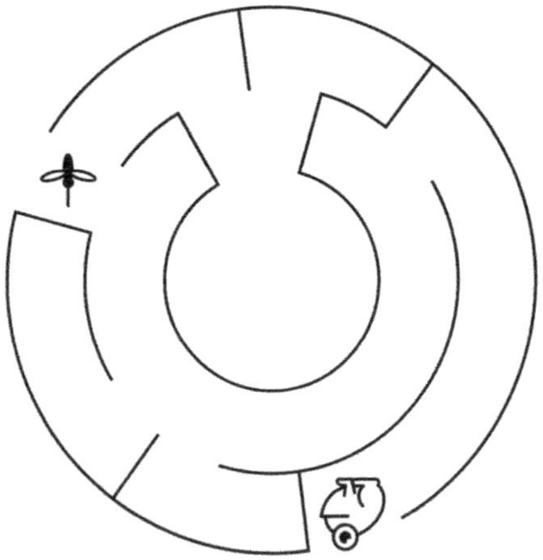

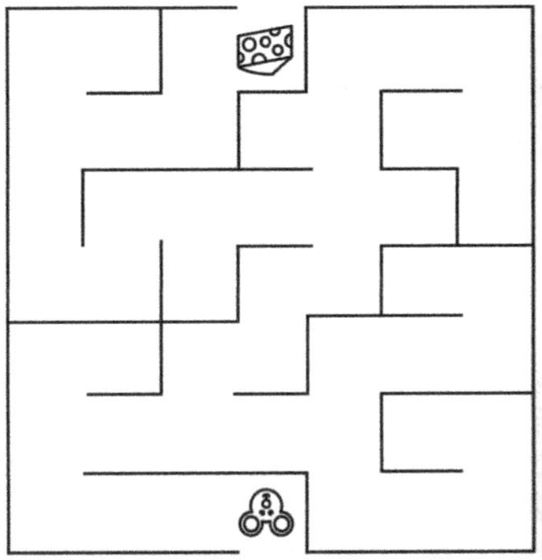

THE RIGHT WAY

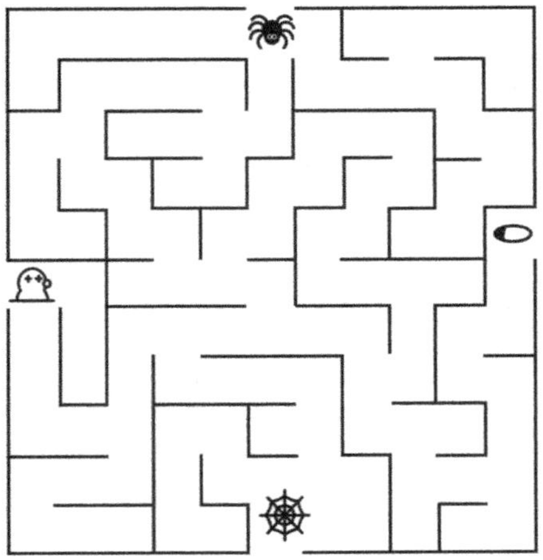

Look at the maze on every page. Use your finger to find the path for each animal to get to the food, then trace the path with a pencil.

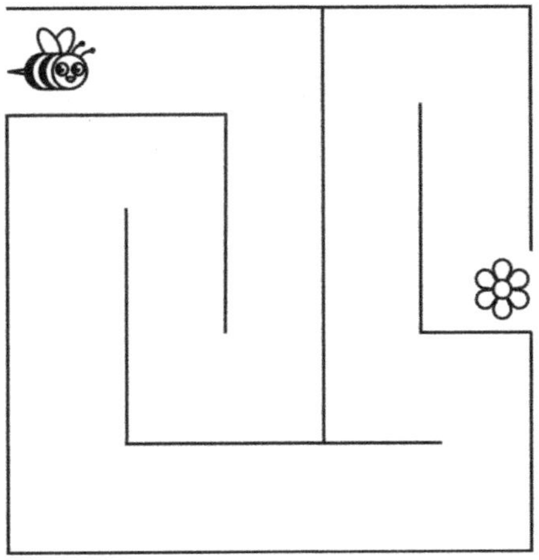

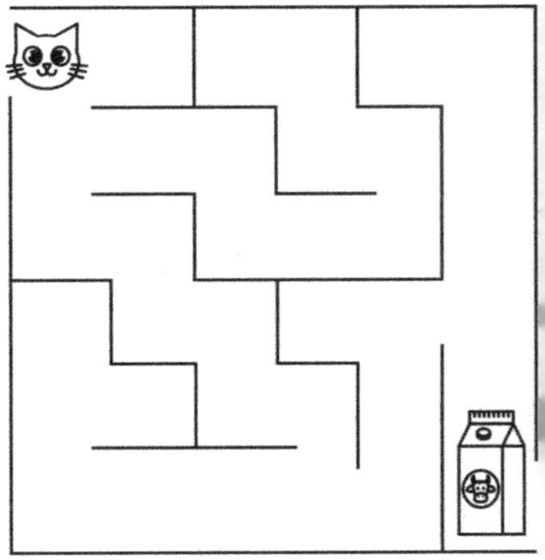

TIC-TAC-TOE

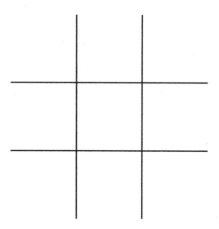

To win tic-tac-toe
you need to line up
3 objects in a row
vertically, horizontally, or
diagonally.

Where can you add a bee to win tic-tac-toe?

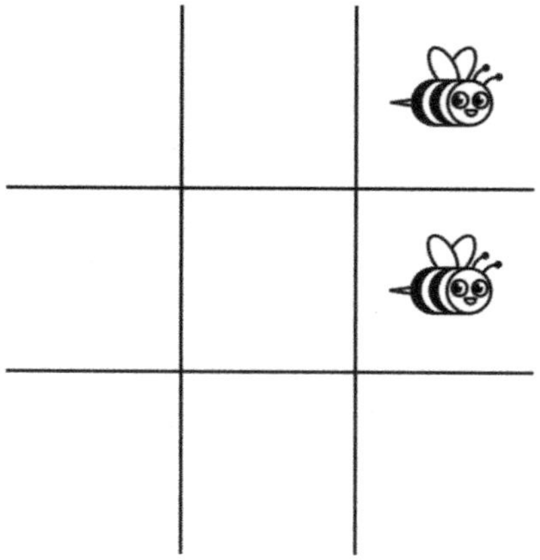

Add a flower and win tic-tac-toe!

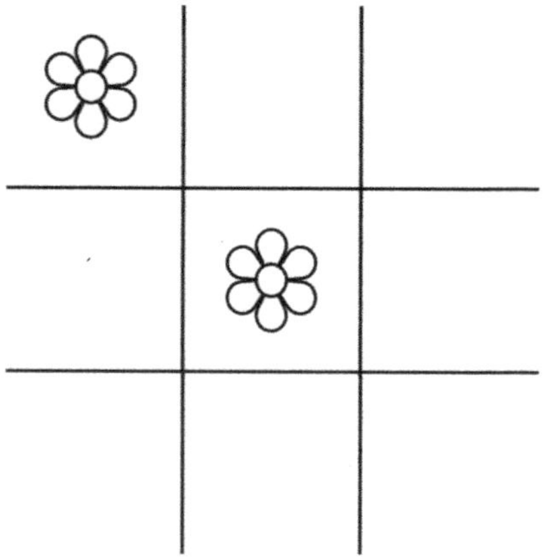

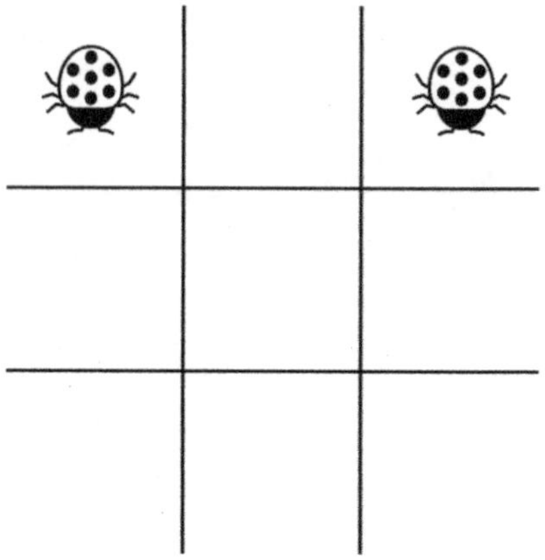

Draw a ladybug to win tic-tac-toe!

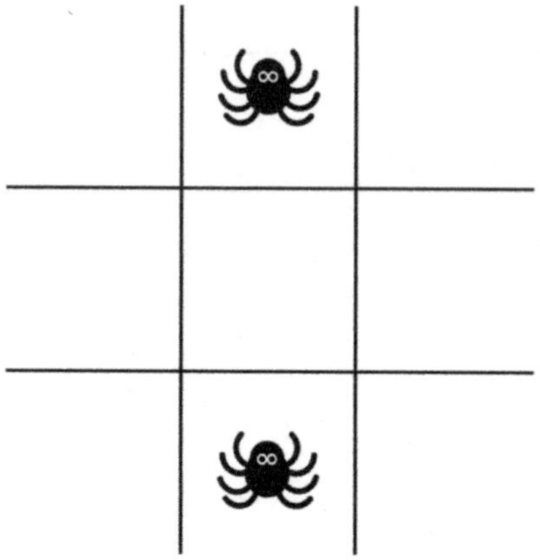

Play tic-tac-toe with spiders.

Now play with a classmate. Take turns drawing one item at a time.

Now play with a classmate. Take turns drawing one item at a time.

Now play with a classmate. Take turns drawing one item at a time.

ALL IN A ROW...

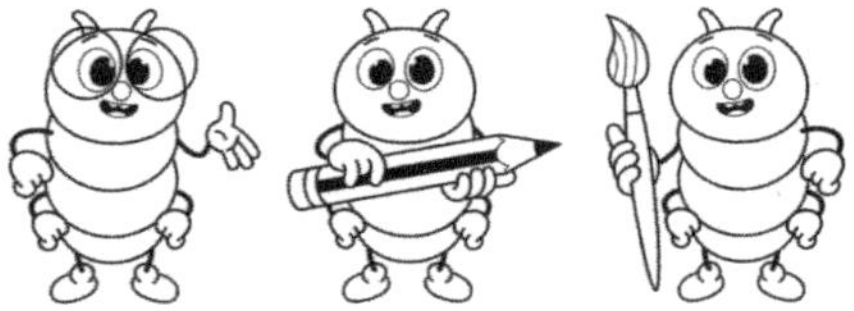

The items on each page are sorted as indicated. Draw the missing items.

from tallest to shortest.

from lightest to heaviest.

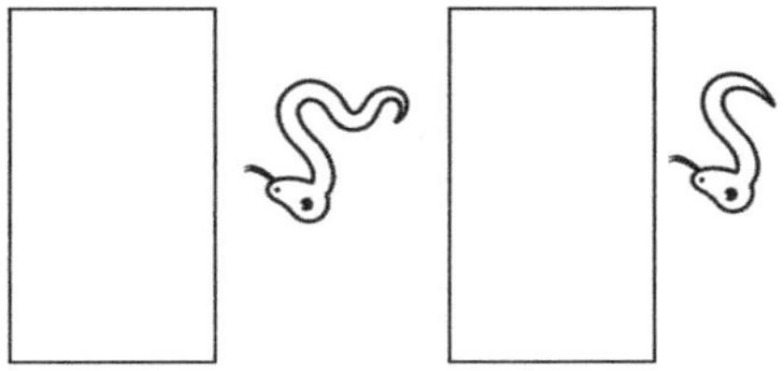

from shortest to longest.

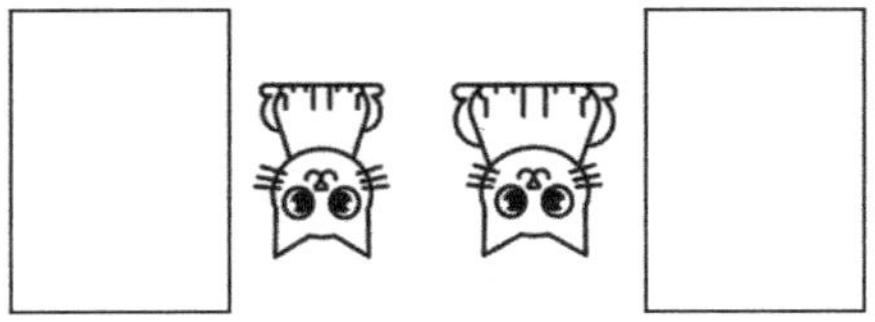

from biggest to smallest.

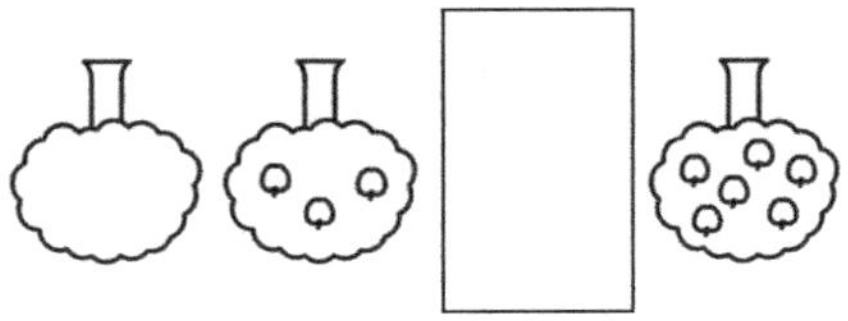

from the most apples to the least apples.

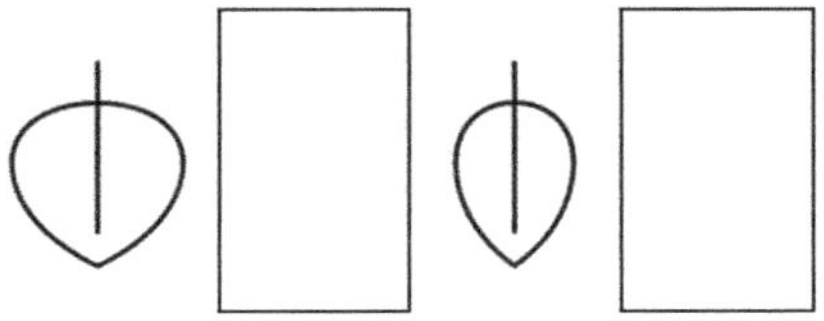

from thinnest to widest.

from full to empty.

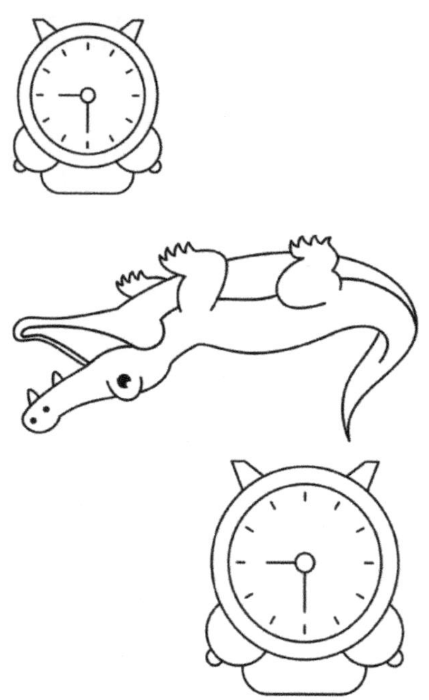

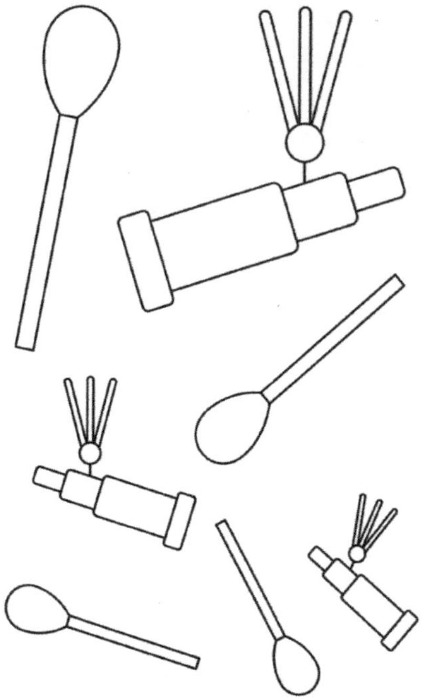

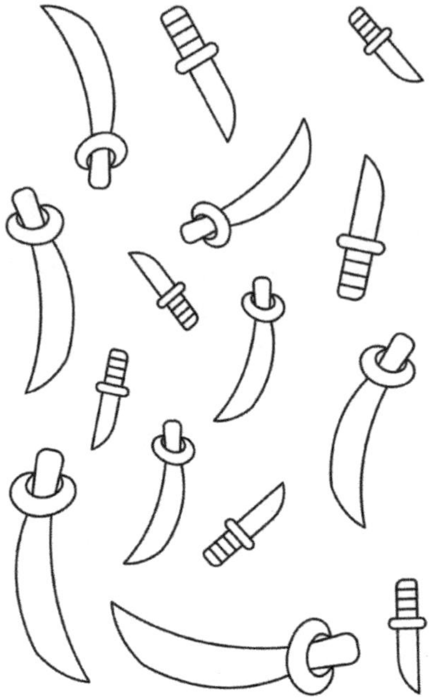

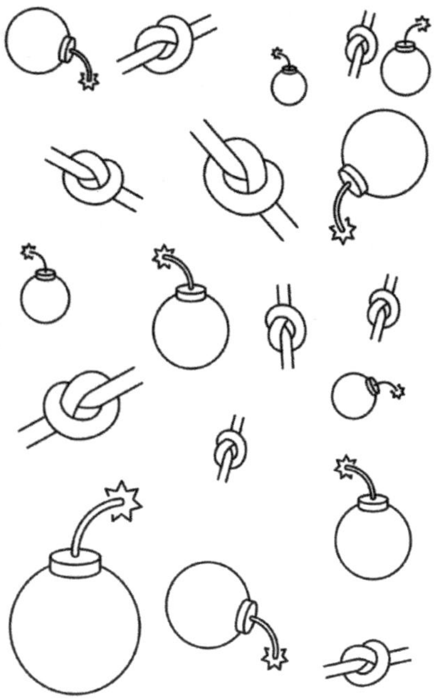

ONE MORE...

Count the items on each page and color the group of objects that has one more item than the other group.

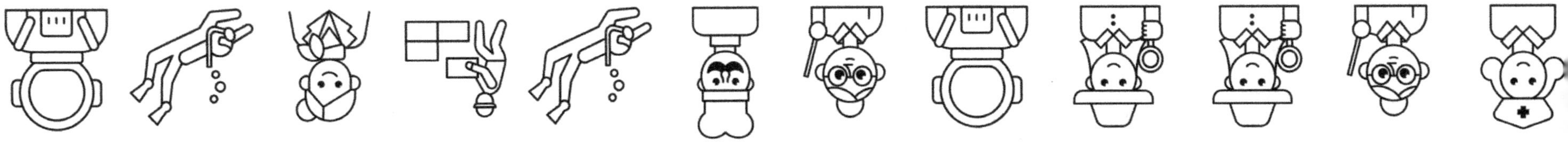

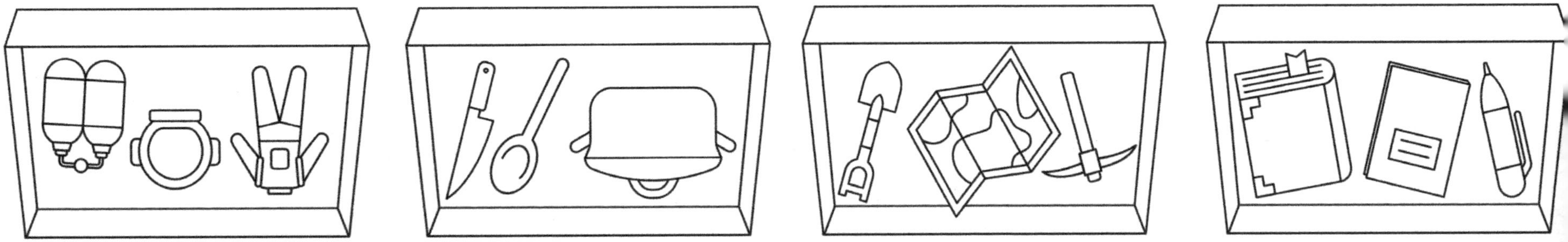

WHO USES THESE OBJECTS?

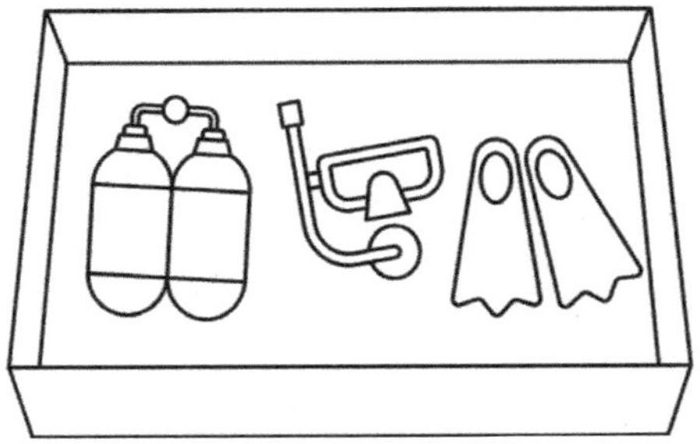

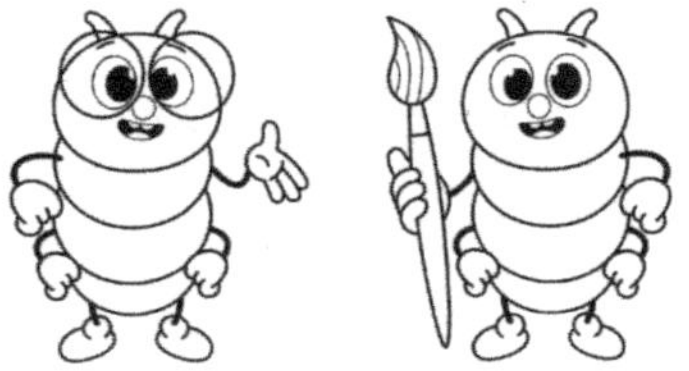

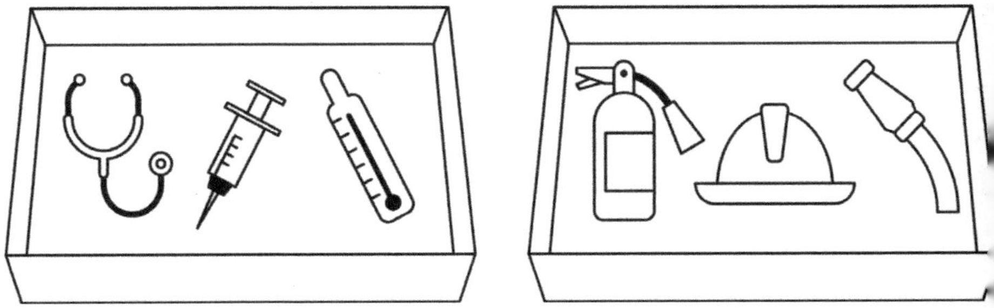

Look at the items in the box on each page and color the person who uses them.

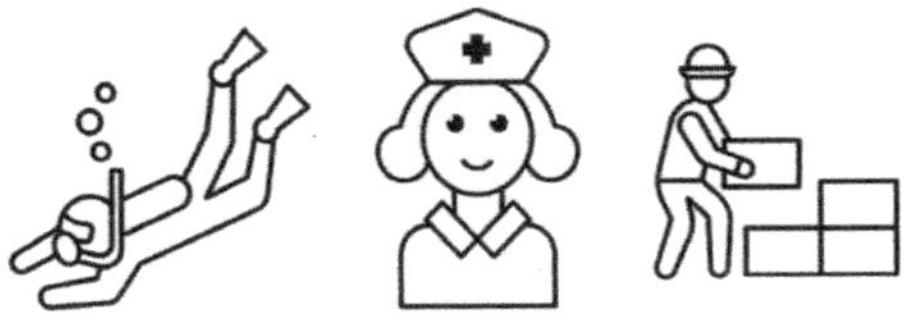

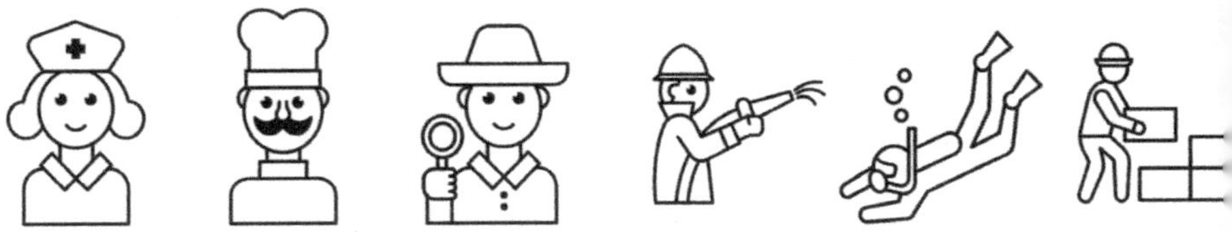

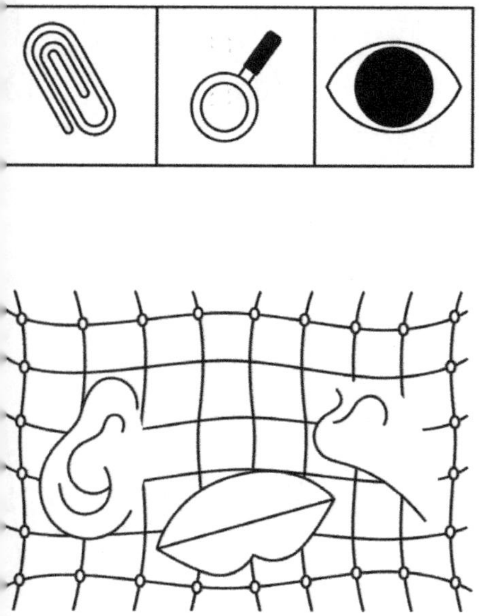
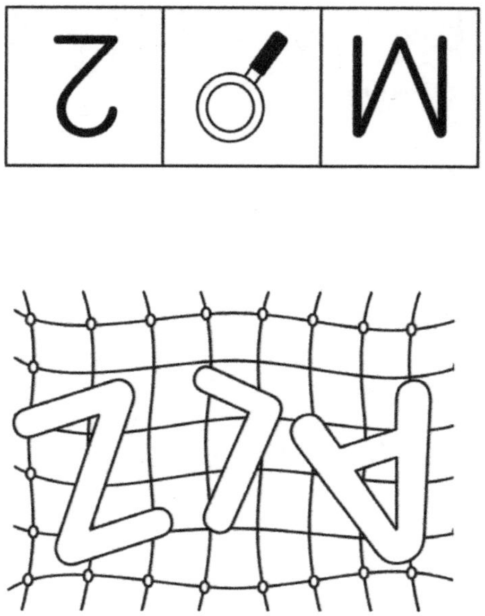
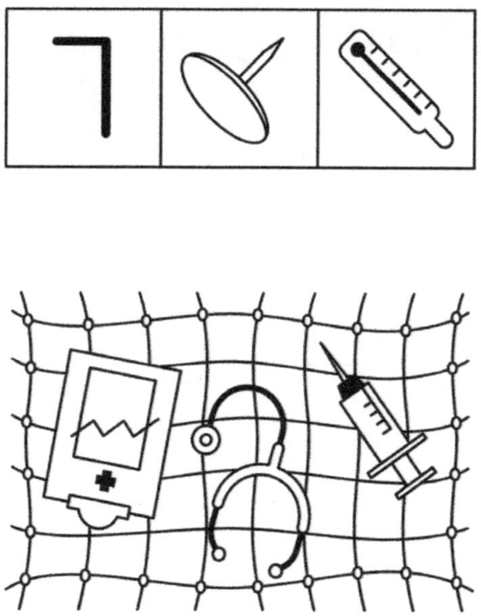
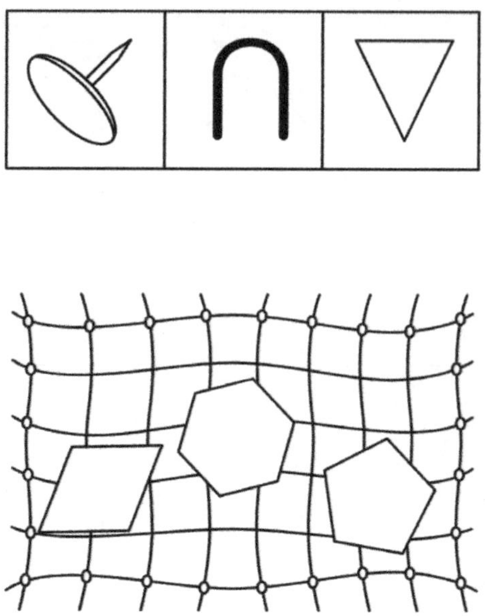

WHERE DO YOU PUT IT?

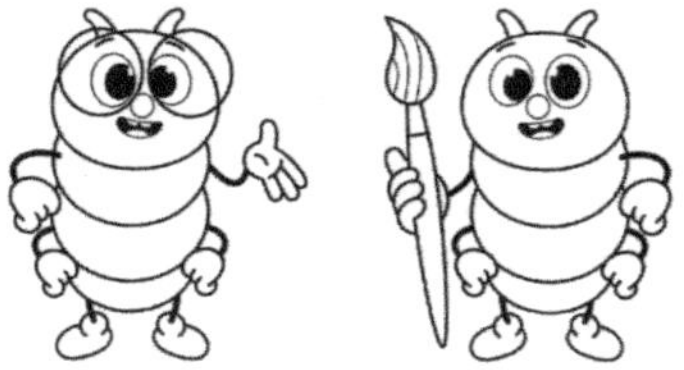

Look at the items in the net and color the item below that belongs in that group.

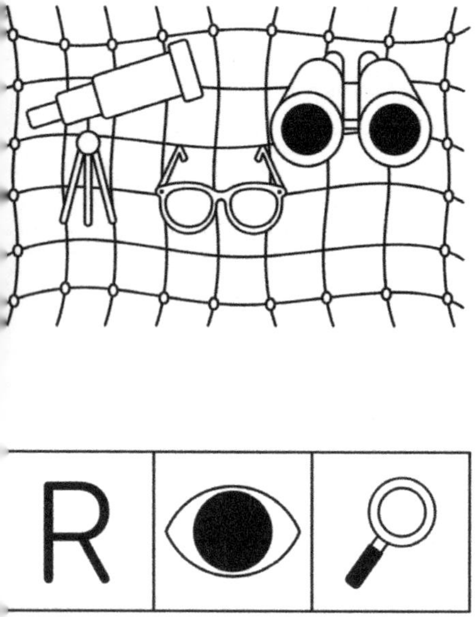

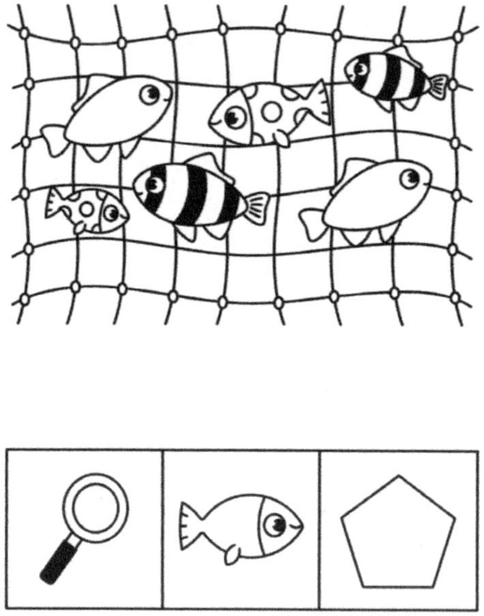

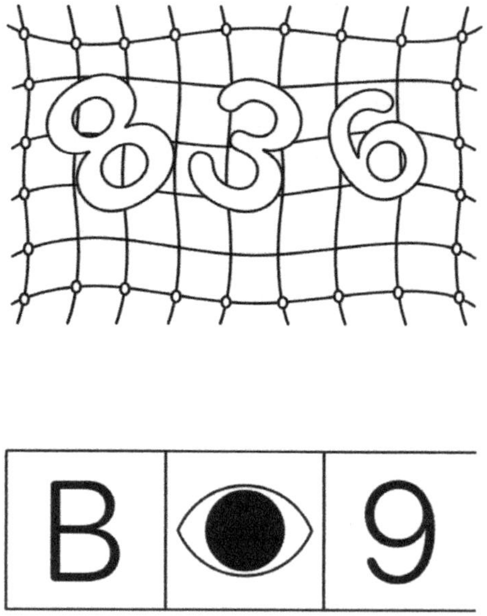

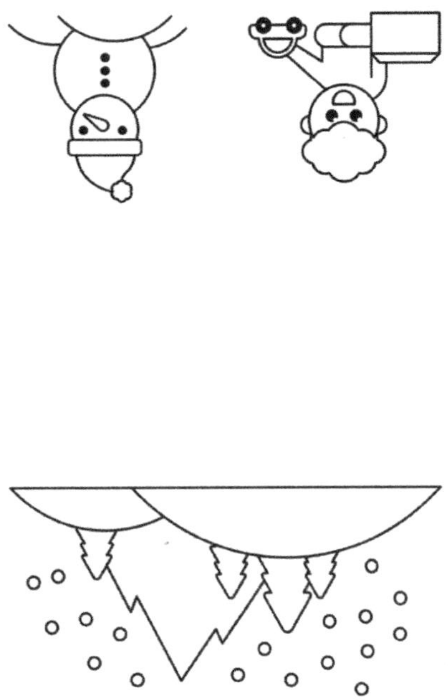

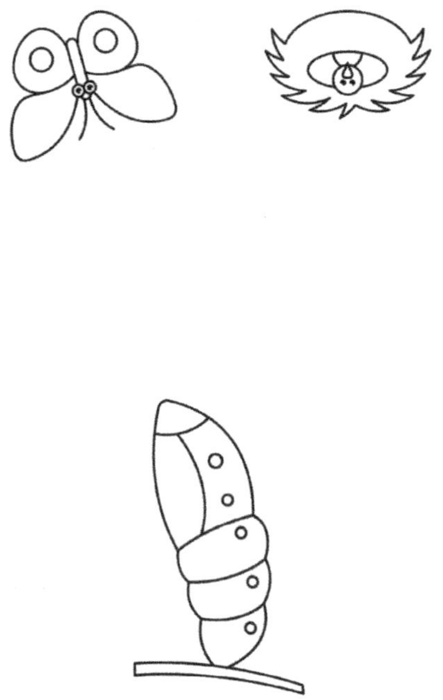

WHAT HAPPENS NEXT?

Look at the image at the top of the page and color the picture at the bottom of the page that shows what happens next.

Counting & Numbers to 20

STUDENT	COUNTING & NUMBERS TO 20					
	Counting Principles	Number Sequence	Comparing Numbers (<, >, =)	Ordering Numbers	Make Ten	Groups of Ten

COUNTING AND NUMBERS TO 20

Counting and Numbers to 20

As mentioned, children can visually count and discriminate small quantities from a very young age. When the quantities increase, we need to support children's developing ability to count through intentional activities. When counting, attention must be directed, by moving the eyes from one object to another, towards the items that are part of the quantification. As a reminder from the opening sections, to count children must be able to demonstrate the following counting principles (Gelman & Galistel, 1978):

- Stable Order: Numbers have a name and are said/written in a sequential order.
- One-to-One Correspondence: When saying the names of numbers, each item receives one count.
- Cardinality: The last number spoken in a counting sequence names the quantity for that set.
- Abstraction: It does not matter what you count, how we count stays the same.
- Order Irrelevance: The order that items are counted in is irrelevant.

The workshops and minibooks that follow aim to strengthen and solidify these principles, which can serve as a basis for building knowledge of the abstract and symbolic system that characterizes more advanced numerical skills.

Building calculation skills with access to the solution are part of algorithmic and executive practices that include the ability to retrieve numerical facts. For example, consider the number 5. You can decompose 5 into:

2 and 3
3 and 2
4 and 1
1 and 4
5 and 0
0 and 5.

As students become capable and confident in breaking apart and building numbers to 5, they will then move to working with numbers to 10. Decomposing numbers is a fundamental stage for working with operations, and this skill is developed through repeated activities acquired mainly during the early years of school.

Comparing quantities, first in a concrete way and then accompanied by the comparison on the number line, requires understanding of the mathematical terms greater than, less than, and equal. Subsequently, a correspondence between these words with the graphic symbols >, <, and = are necessary. The same thing happens for the mathematical terms "before" and "after", which first require an understanding of the meaning to then become very simple mechanisms with which to identify the number that comes before and the one that comes after a given number. Children cannot be rushed through this progression—they must understand the concept, whether it is comparing or identifying before and after, and they must be able to use the terminology and symbols when working with the concept.

Children must therefore be encouraged to carry out experiments of quantification, comparison, and composition and decomposition of numbers using different approaches that are as active and engaging as possible. The workshop proposals, together with the minibooks, aim to support and extend students' mathematical understanding through activities that connect concepts and symbols.

NOTES FROM THE CLASSROOM

As teachers, we recognize the importance of number and how it permeates many mathematical concepts and strands. Counting principles are a crucial aspect in numeracy and one that far too many students struggle with in Kindergarten through Grade 2. The workshops and minibooks in this section will support students in being able to accurately count a collection and will provide you with plenty of choice to address students' individual learning needs.

In addition to counting, students must have opportunities to work with numbers. This work can be in the form of comparing and ordering numbers and determining how numbers can be constructed and deconstructed, which form the basis of place value as well as addition and subtraction.

Counting and Numbers to 20 encompass many key learning areas. To support this learning, you'll find a tracking form (pg 40) that highlights the key learning areas: counting principles; number sequence; comparing numbers (<, >, =); ordering numbers; make ten; and groups of ten. Teachers can use this form to monitor student learning within the key learning areas and can use the information gathered to guide instruction.

Bibliography

Lucangeli D., Poli S. and Molin A. (2012), *L'intelligenza numerica Abilità cognitive e metacognitive nella costruzione della conoscenza numerica dai 6 agli 8 anni, vol. 2,* Trento, Erickson.

NUMERICAL COURSES IN THE GYM

Goal

Recognize and differentiate numbers from other types of symbols.

Materials

- Gym equipment (e.g., hoops, cones, balance poles, clubs, ropes, balls, scarves, obstacles)
- 40 cardboard cards numbered from 1 to 20, 10 different symbols, and 10 letters of the alphabet

Directions

Take the class to the gym and prepare a maze together with obstacles and objects that encourage the children to move in a variety of ways—jump, crawl, run, roll, balance. Place two signs at each crossroad, one sign with a number and the other a letter or another symbol. To get out of the maze, children must follow the route indicated by numbers. To make the activity more challenging, the road leading to the exit can be twisted, go back, move horizontally/obliquely, or follow curved lines.

Divide the class into three groups and start one at a time. After two laps, change the route, increasing the level of complexity.

NUMERICAL PAINTINGS

Goals

Know how to read a numerical legend that associates a number with a color; discriminate numbers.

Materials

- Reproduction of the card illustrated below
- Ruler, pencil, markers or different types of paint
- Black and white print of very simple paintings, landscapes, or animals without details

Directions

Prepare and distribute a card like the one on the side to the students.
Point out that the legend explains which colors to use.
After this first training phase, the children are ready to repeat the experience with different types of drawings.
Take one of the images you chose previously (a landscape, a painting, or an animal; it can also be a drawing taken from a coloring book). Using the ruler, draw a few lines on the sheet with the pencil and insert a number in each space, to which you will associate a color (to be indicated in the legend); you can use a maximum of 5 colors.
Then photocopy the sheet and distribute it to the children, placing the sheets close together and checking whether the children have carried out the activity correctly.
You can use this material for group work or as an activity to carry out in free time.

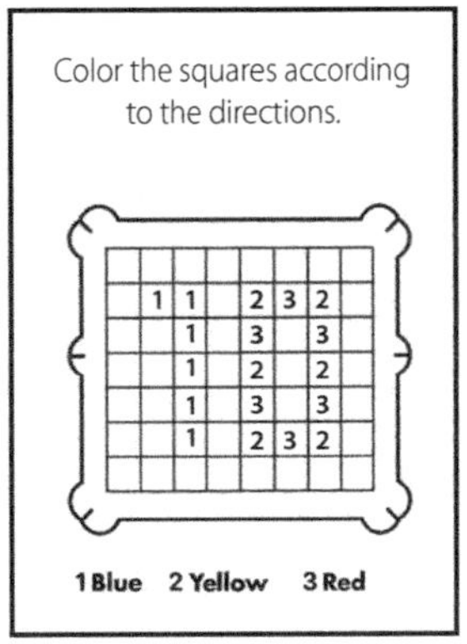

RIDDLES WITH NUMBERS

Goals

- Know how to identify a certain number of elements possessed by a specific animal in an image.
- Think and try to give an answer based on the clues given.
- Ask questions using low quantities to identify a living thing.

Materials

- Images on cardboard/card of different types of animals with recognizable numerical characteristics (e.g., number of legs, tentacles, wings, antennas)

Directions

Arrange the children in a circle and choose a child to start the game. Ask them to select a card, look at it carefully without letting others see it, and describe the animal on the card to their classmates. They can say, for example: "This animal has 8 legs and a hairy head." The classmates take turns trying to guess the mysterious animal. Whoever gets it wrong is eliminated from the game while whoever guesses correctly takes the place of the game manager and selects a new card.

ATTENTION! It is important, under penalty of exclusion from the game, that the riddle always and only involves numerical characteristics associated with other qualitative characteristics (e.g., 6 legs, 2 wings, 8 tentacles).

FLAGS AND FRIENDS OF 10

Goals

- Activate selective attention to an assigned number.
- Match quantities to make 10.
- Remember the friends of 10.
- Respect the rules of the game.
- Follow directions.

Materials

- Cards with numbers from 0 to 10 (two cards for each number)
- Scarf

Directions

Move to a spacious area (e.g., the gym, schoolyard, garden, multipurpose room) and divide the class into two groups. Arrange them in two rows, facing each other, and place a card with a number at the feet of each child. Give the same number to the children who are facing them (i.e., the number 1 in one row will face the number 1 in the opposite row).

Position yourself between the two rows, with a scarf (the "flag") in your hand. Then call a random number (for example, 1); the two children who have that number will have to leave the lines and run to "steal" the flag, taking it and bringing it back to their starting place without being touched by the other. To make the game more challenging, you can indicate a path to follow to return to base and add rules to block whoever has the flag in their hand. Play many times so that all the students understand the rules and have a chance to play the game (at least two calls each).

Variation

Offer the "Flag" game as a "Friends" version of 10. Before organizing this change in the game, it is advisable to discuss it in class before trying the variation.

Arrange the children in two rows. The first row has the numbers 0 to 10. The second row is considered friends of 10. When you call a number, the child in the first row with the number called will start. The child from the second row with the friendly number to 10 corresponds.

For example, say you call the number 1. The child with the number 1 in the first row will start towards you. The child with the number 9 in the second row will start towards you. Before taking the flag, the children will have to show their card and check that the sum of the two numbers is 10.

If teammates notice a mistake, they can intervene and correct it. Repeat the game several times to consolidate learning.

LISTEN AND DRAW

Listen closely to what you are told to draw. Draw it. Color it.

2

Draw 1 yellow ball.

3

Draw 1 yellow-and-blue ball.

4

Draw 1 yellow ball and 1 blue ball.

5

Draw a yellow-and-red ball.

6

Draw 1 yellow ball, 1 blue ball, and 1 red ball.

7

Draw 1 ball that is yellow, blue, and green.

8

Draw 1 yellow ball with blue dots.

PICTURE SUDOKU

Look at the sample sudoku: the figures appear only once in each column and each row.

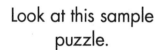

Look at this sample puzzle.

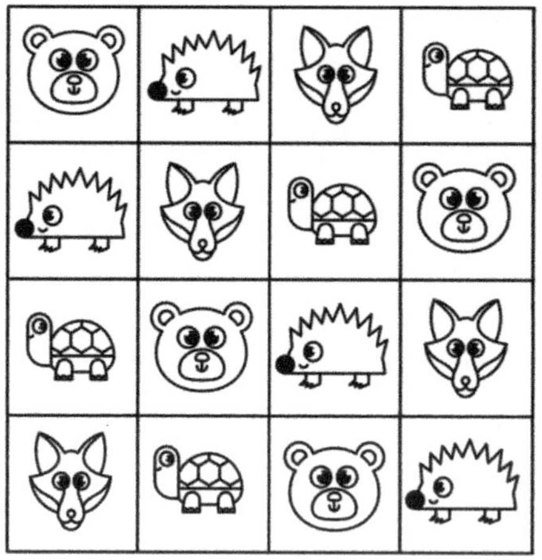

Complete the puzzle.

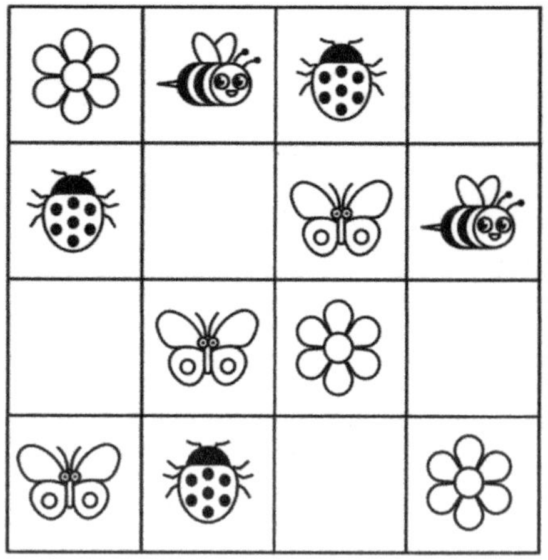

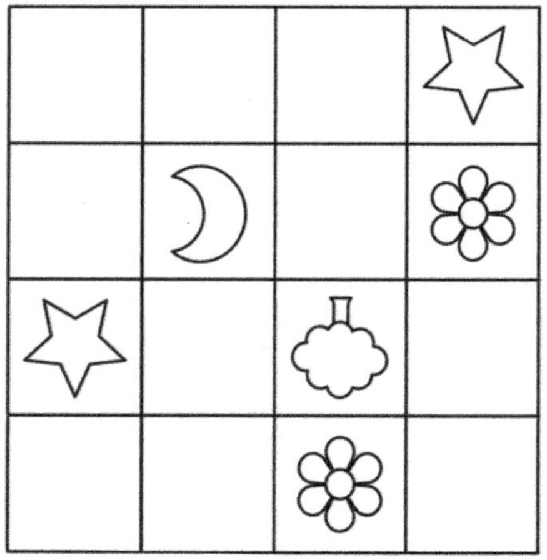

Complete the puzzle.

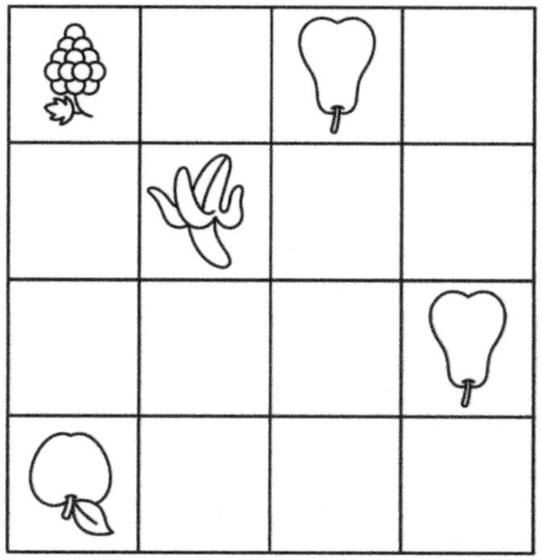

Complete the puzzle.

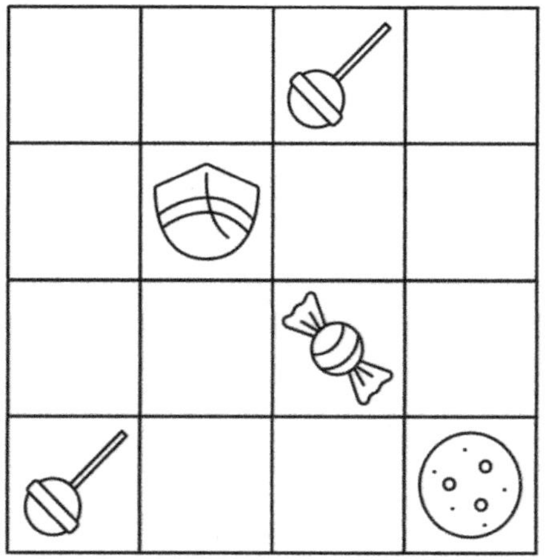

Complete the puzzle.

Complete the puzzle.

Complete the puzzle.

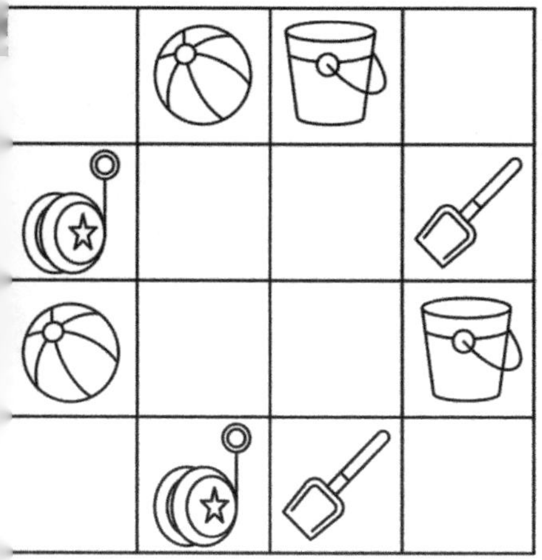

2

1 on the die.

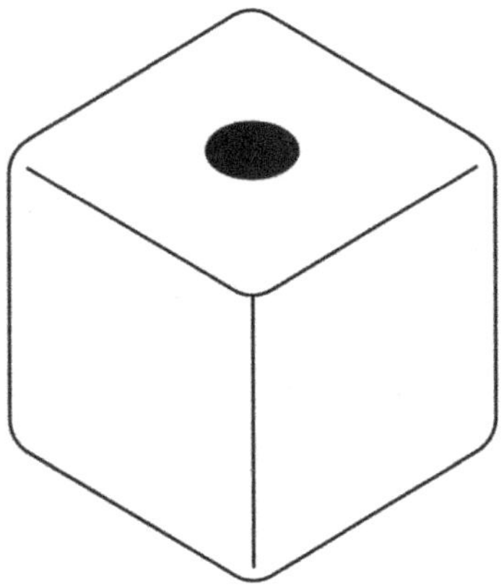

3

Color the groups with only 1 item.

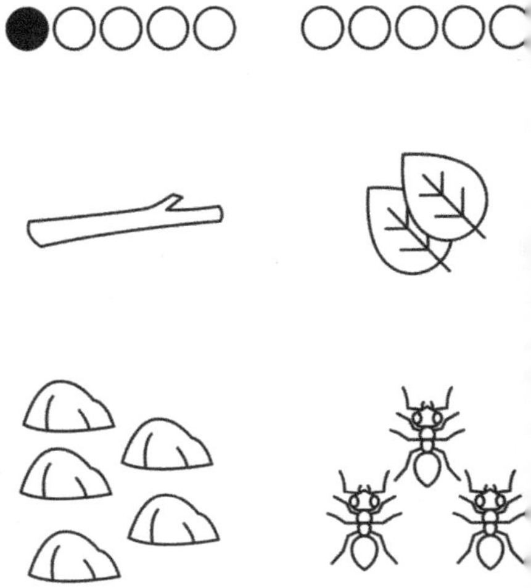

4

Color 1 finger.

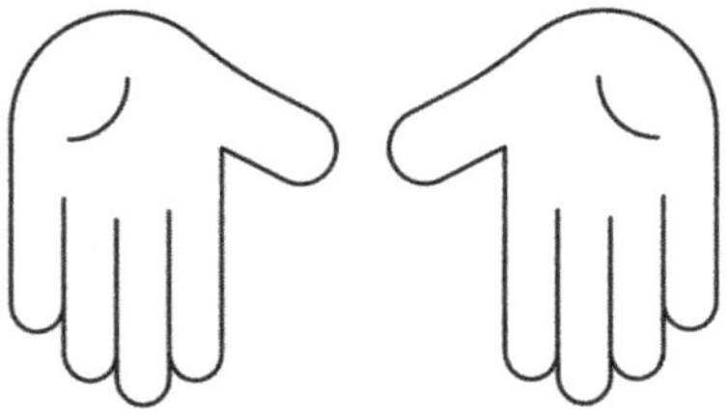

5

Write the number 1.

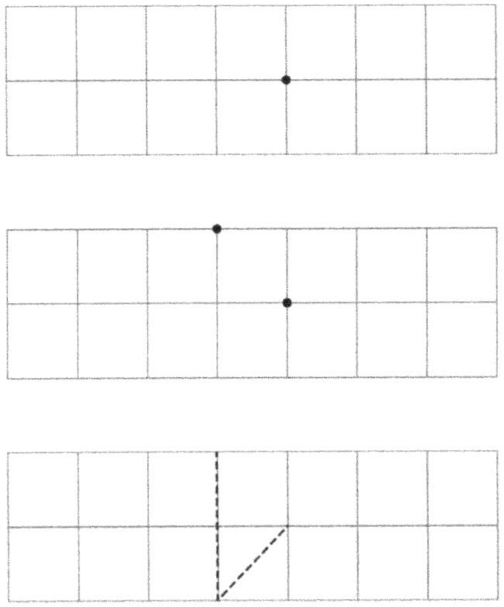

6

Color the number 1.

7

There is 1 sun and it's yellow.

8

Draw 1 line.

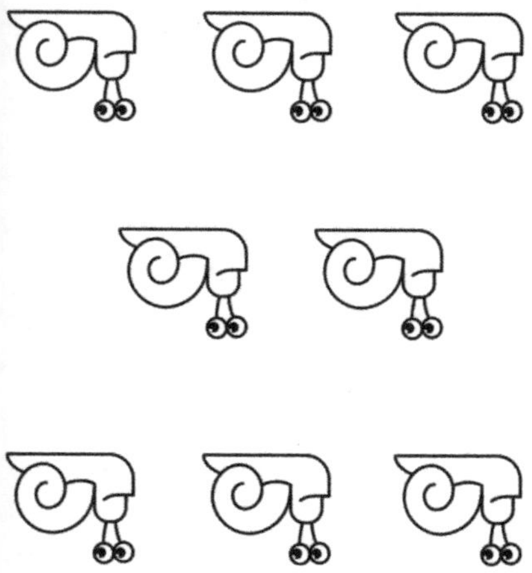

Circle pairs of 2 snails.

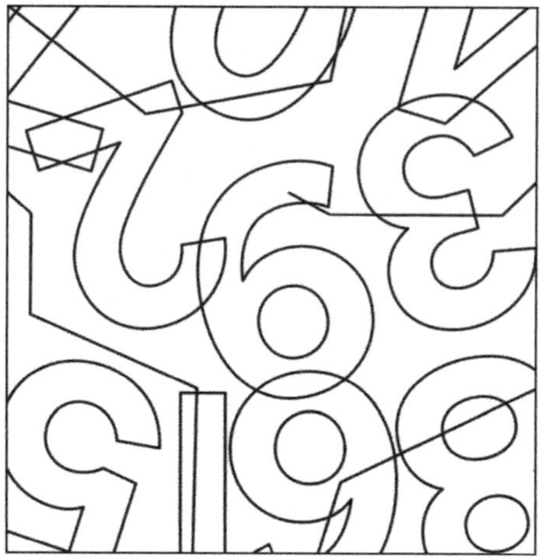

Color the number 2.

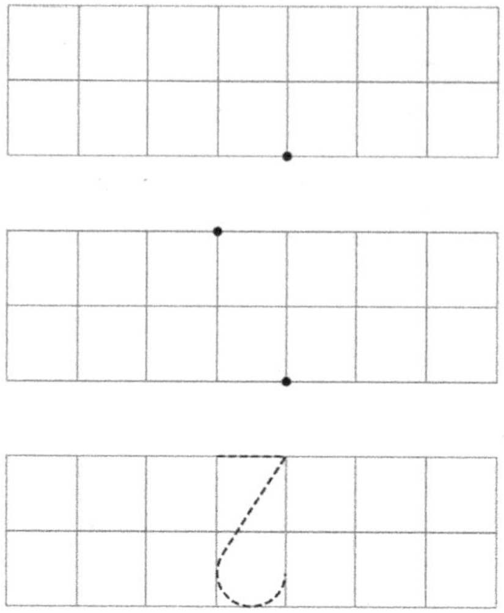

Write the number 2.

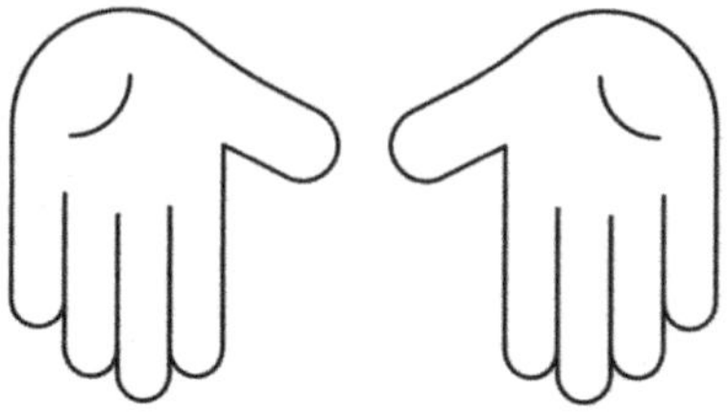

Color 2 fingers.

Use a ruler to draw 2 lines starting from the same point.

2 on the die.

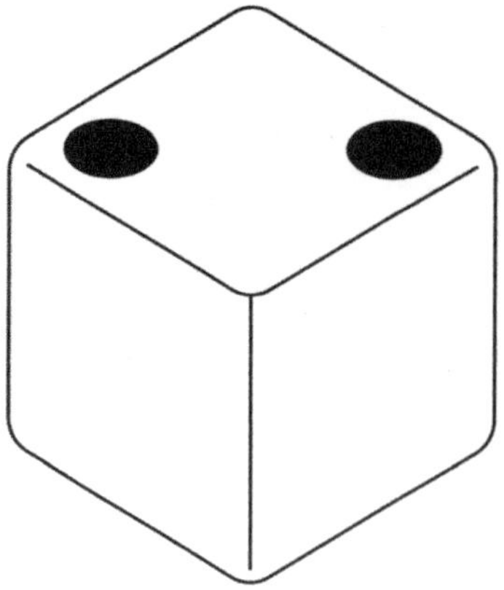

Color the pairs with 2 items.

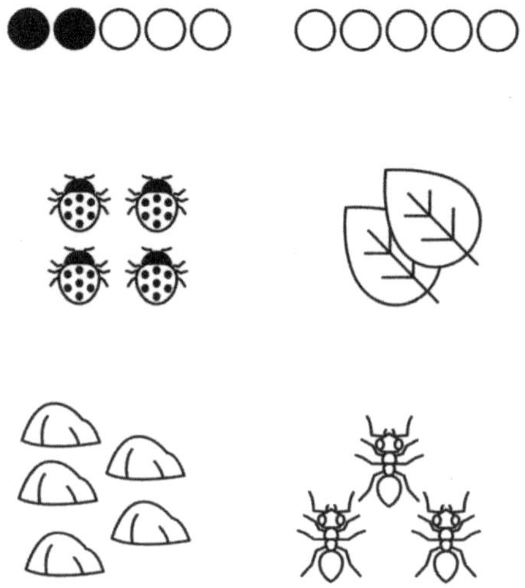

2

3 on the die.

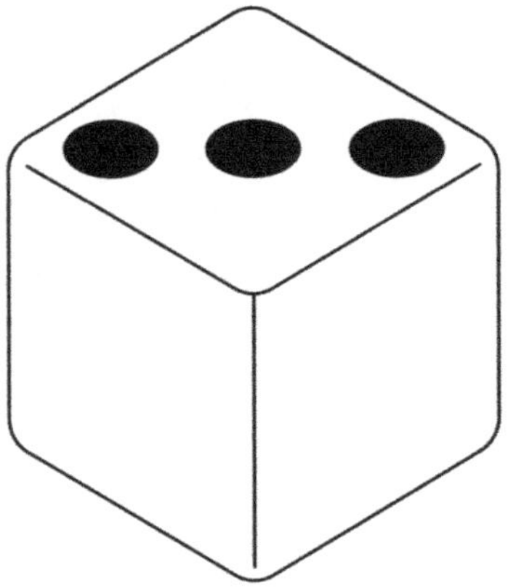

3

Color the groups with 3 items.

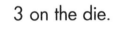

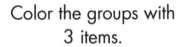

4

Color 3 fingers.

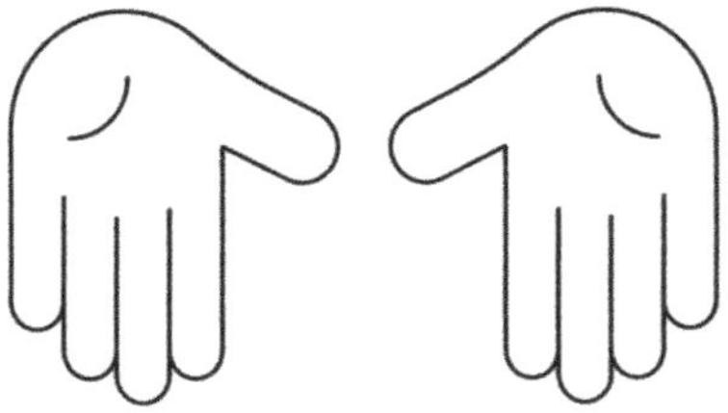

5

Write the number 3.

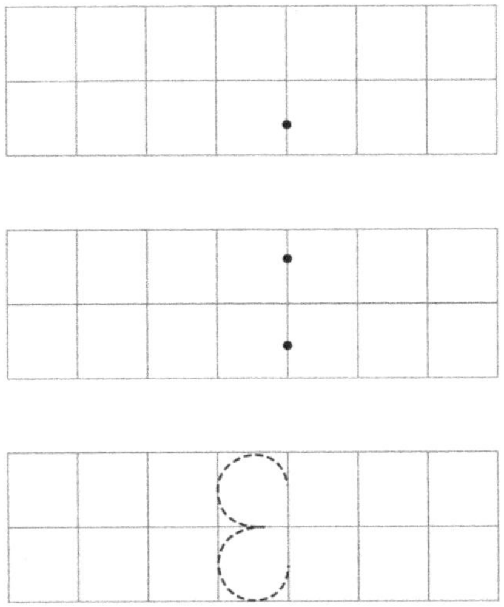

6

Color the number 3.

7

Circle groups of 3 crickets.

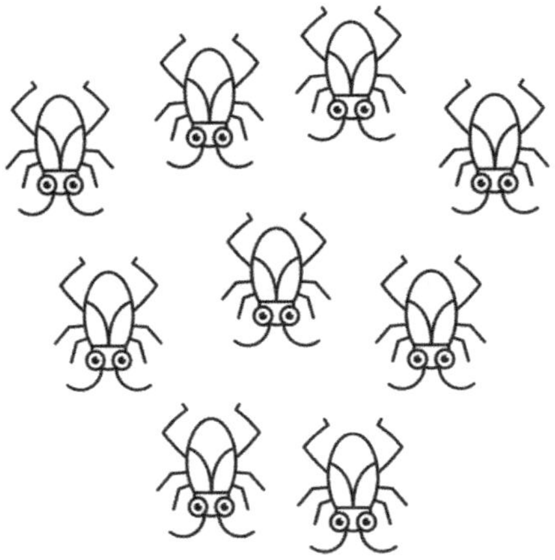

8

Draw some triangles like the one below.

4 on the die.

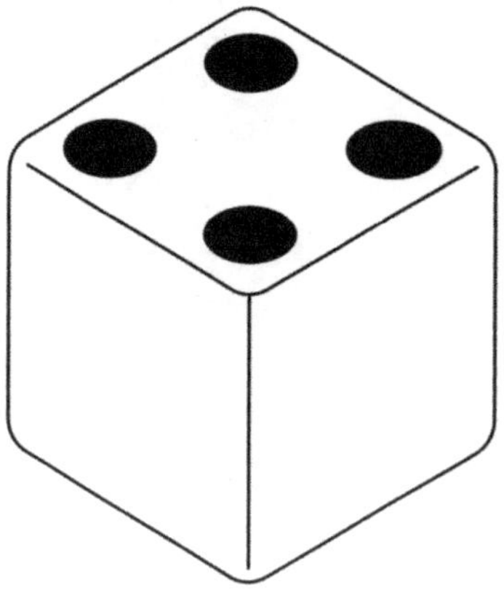

Color the groups with 4 items.

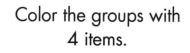

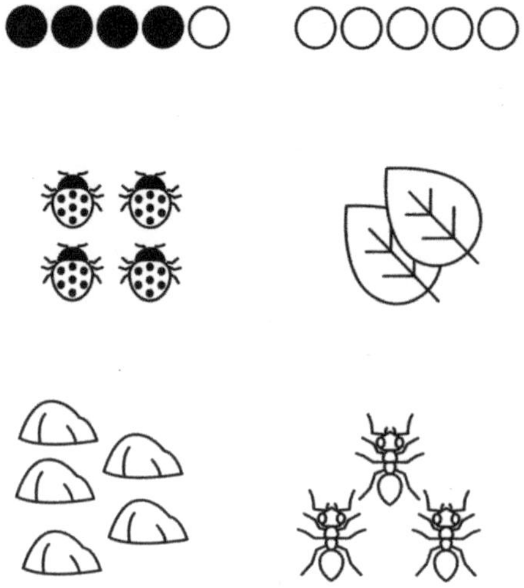

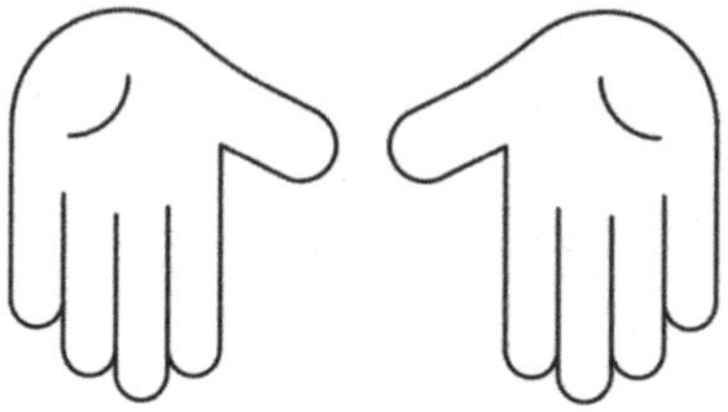

Color 4 fingers.

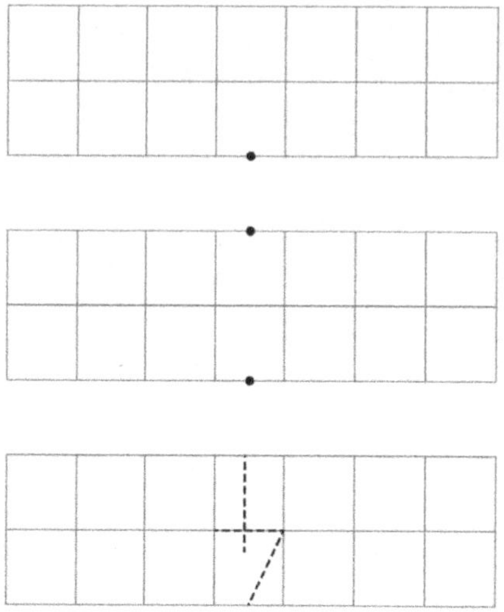

Write the number 4.

Color the number 4.

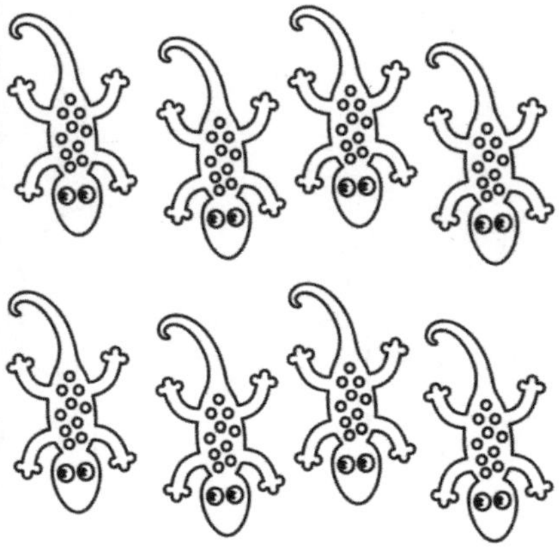

Circle groups of 4 lizards.

Draw some squares like the one below.

5 on the die.

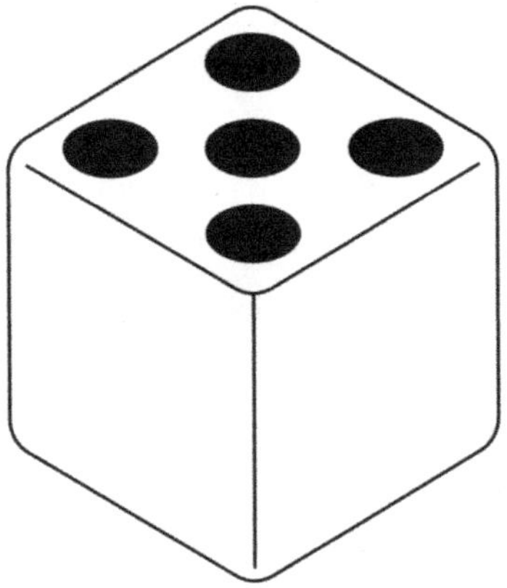

Color the groups with 5 items.

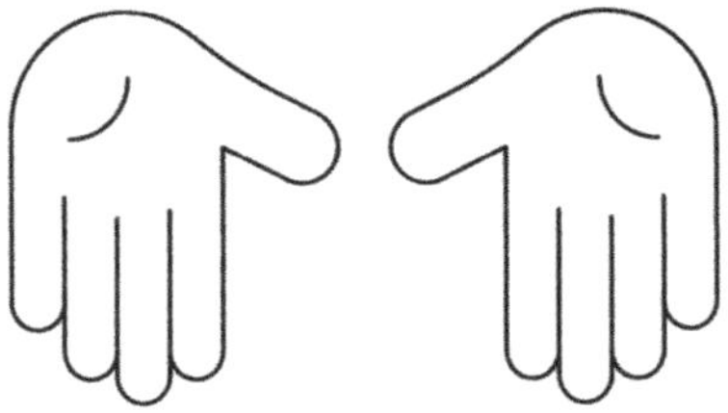

Color 5 fingers.

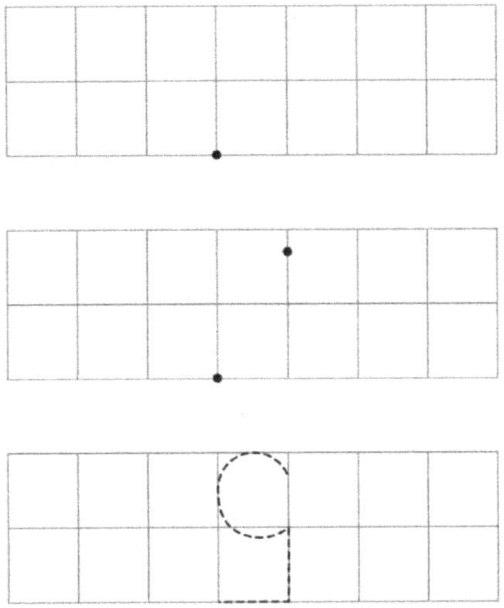

Write the number 5.

Color the number 5.

Circle groups of 5 ladybugs.

Draw some figures with 5 sides like the one below.

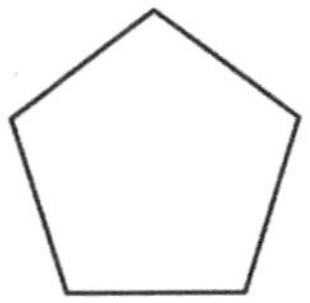

Circle groups of 6 caterpillars.

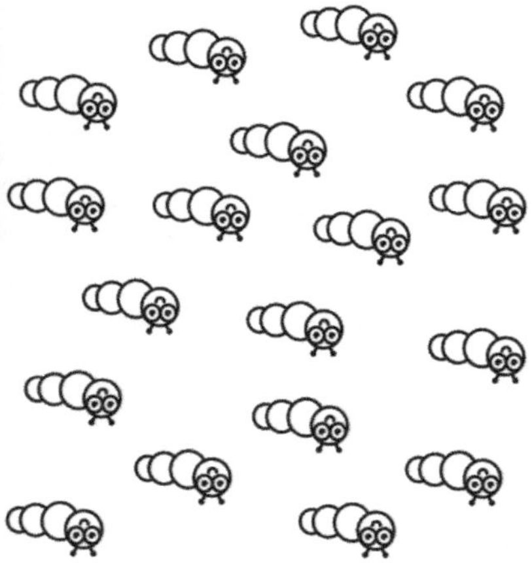

Color the number 6.

Write the number 6.

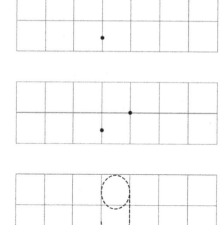

Color 6 fingers.

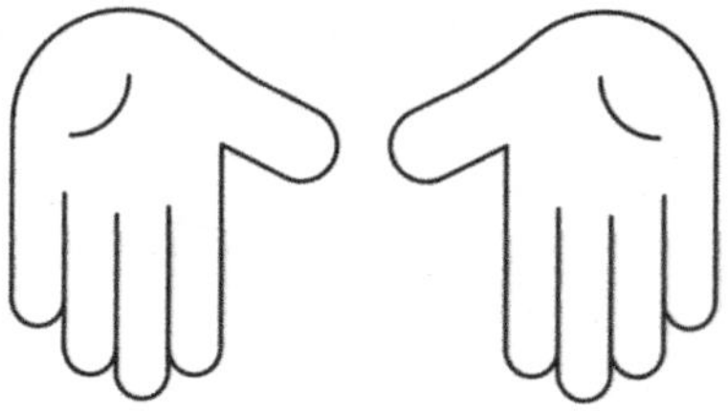

Draw some figures with 6 sides like the one below.

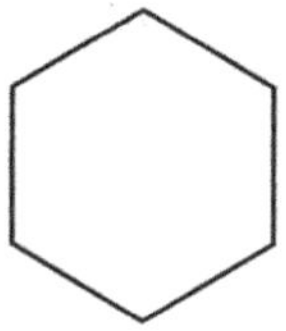

6 on the die.

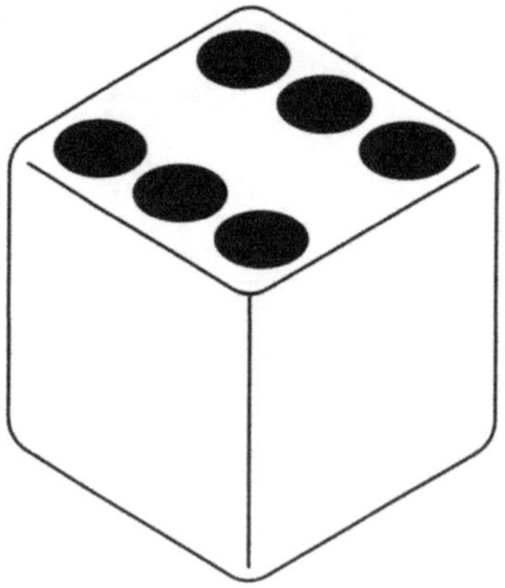

Color the groups with 6 items.

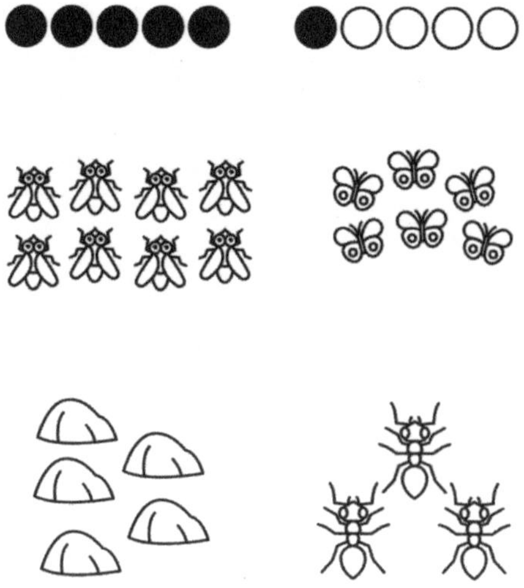

7

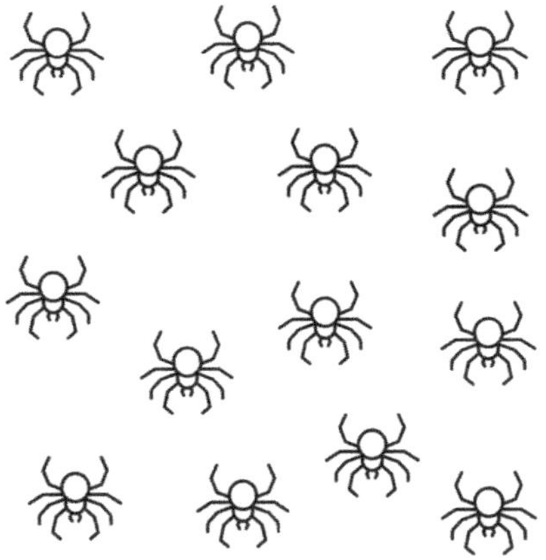

Circle groups of 7 spiders.

6

Color the number 7.

5

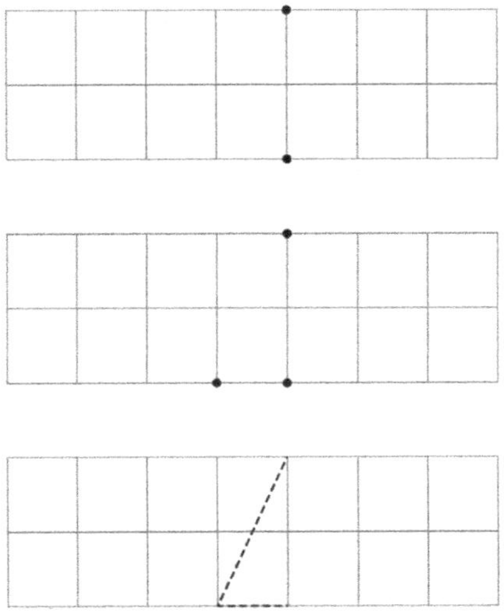

Write the number 7.

4

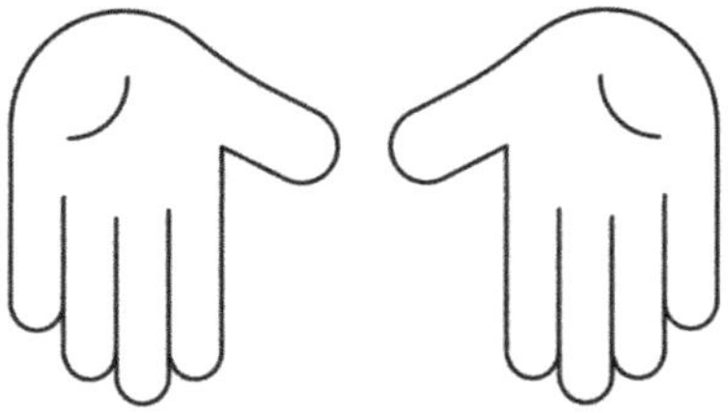

Color 7 fingers.

Review and trace these figures with 7 sides.

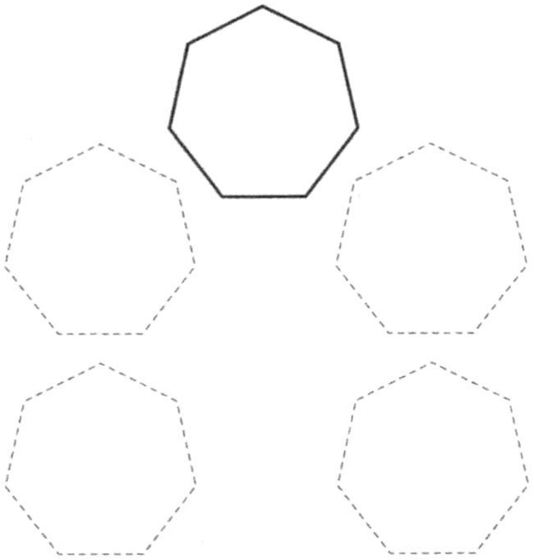

8

7 on the dice.

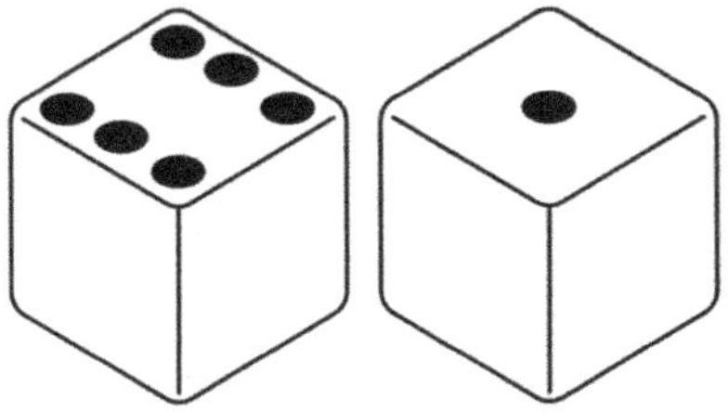

2

Color the groups with 7 items.

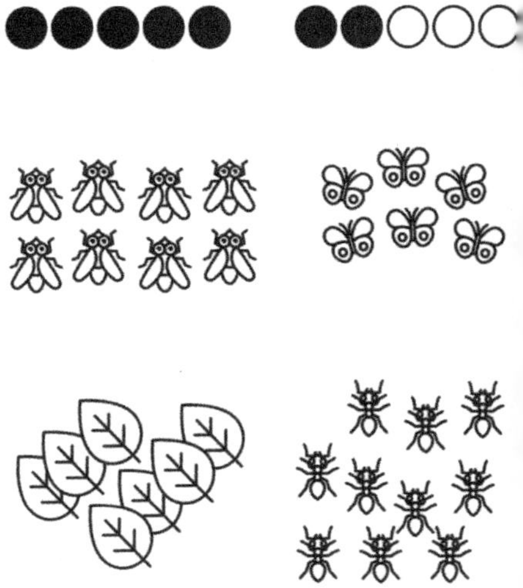

3

8 on the dice.

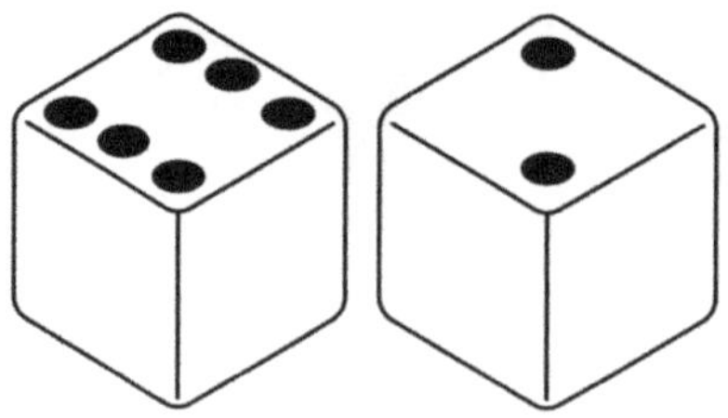

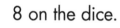

Color the groups with 8 items.

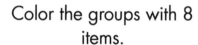

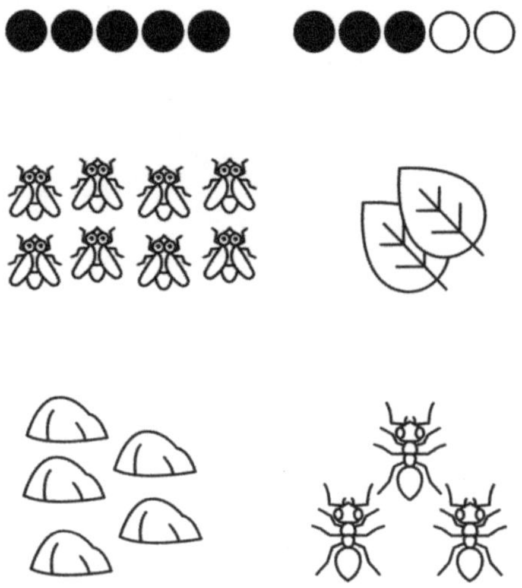

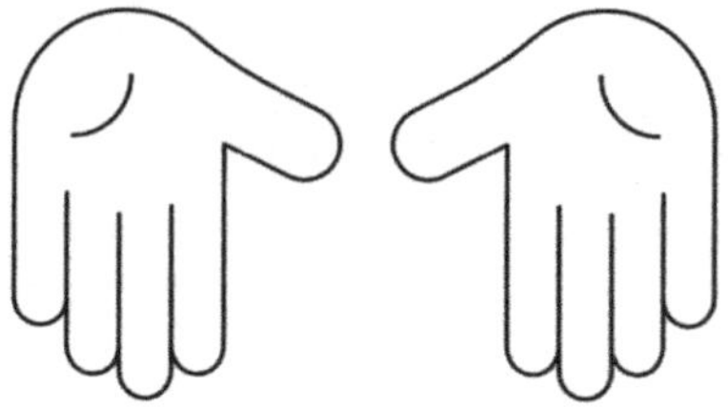

Color 8 fingers.

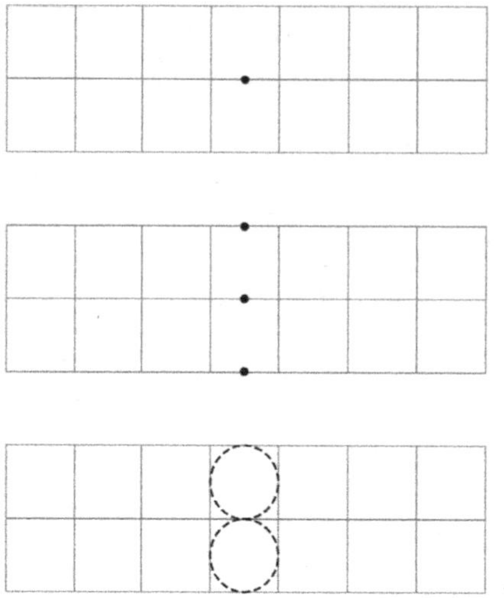

Write the number 8.

Color the number 8.

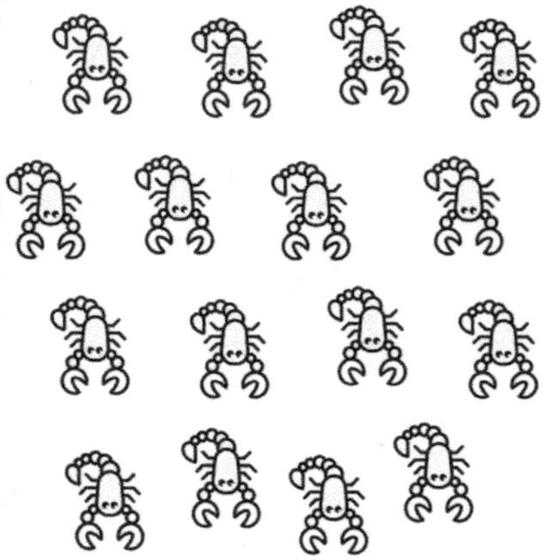

Circle groups of 8 scorpions.

Review and trace these figures with 8 sides.

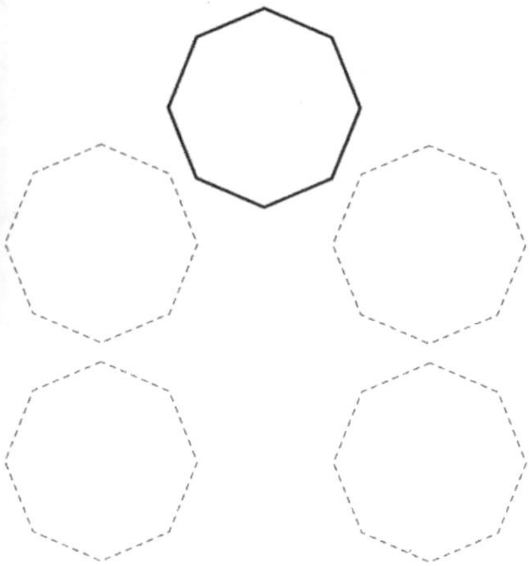

7

Circle groups of 9 chicks.

6

Color the number 9.

5

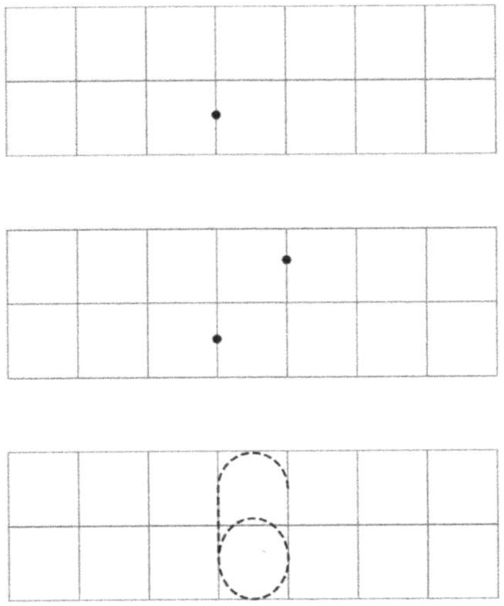

Write the number 9.

4

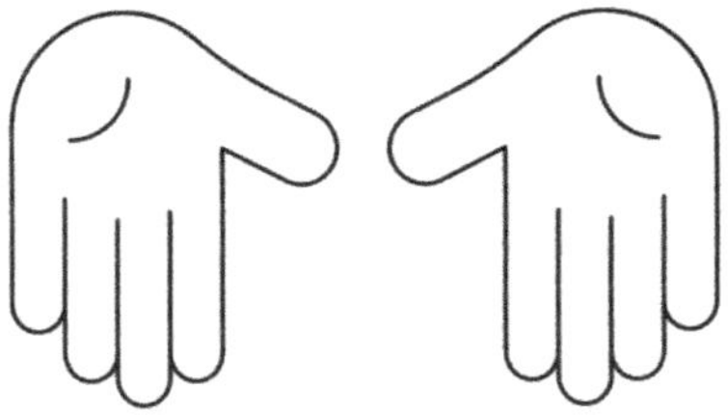

Color 9 fingers.

Review and trace these figures with 9 sides.

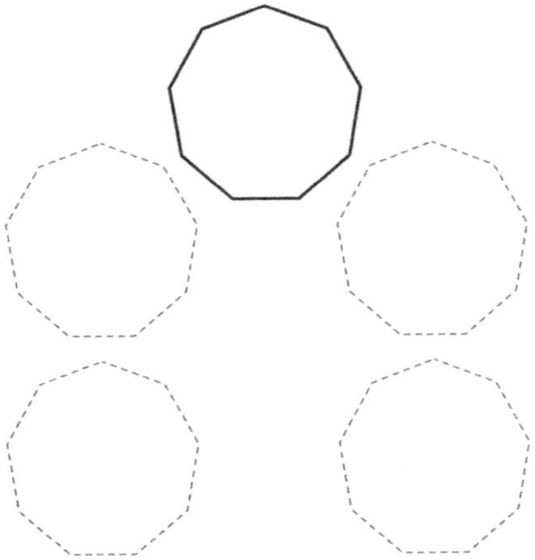

8

9 on the dice.

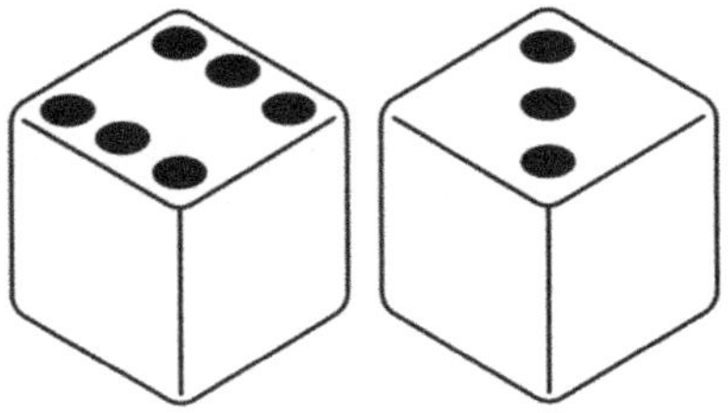

2

Color the groups with 9 items.

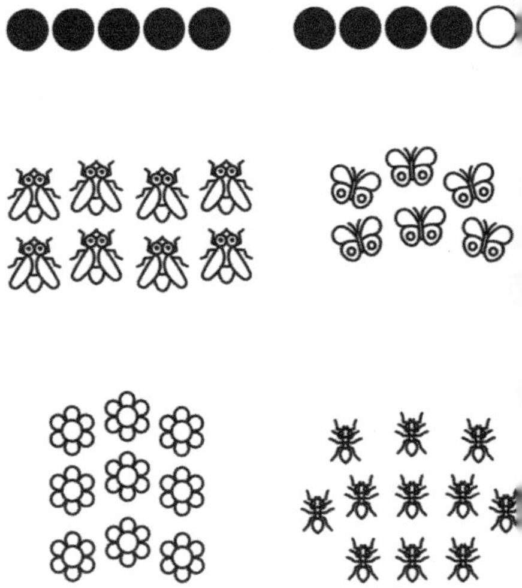

3

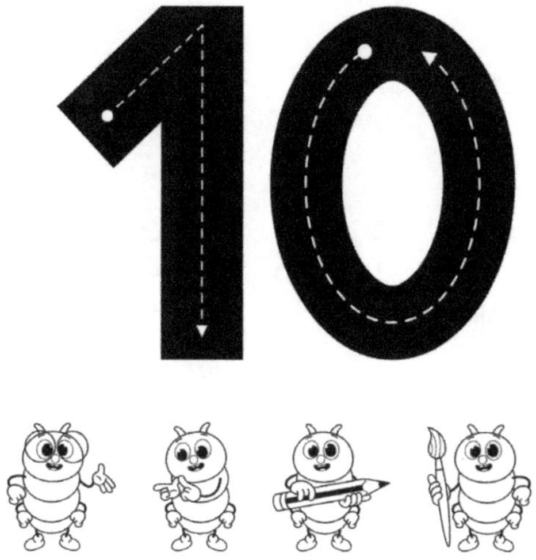

28

10 on the dice.

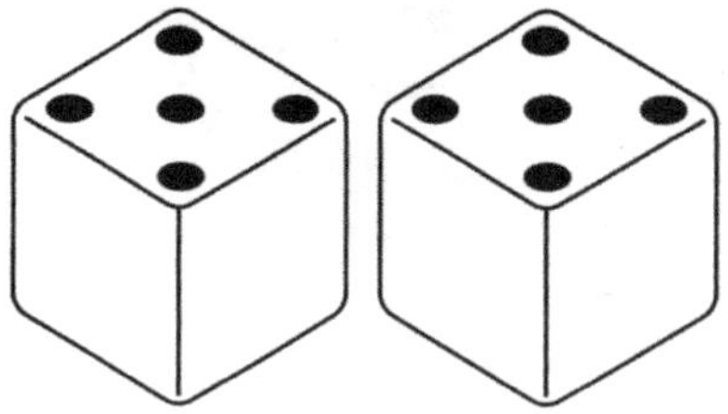

2

Color the groups with 10 items.

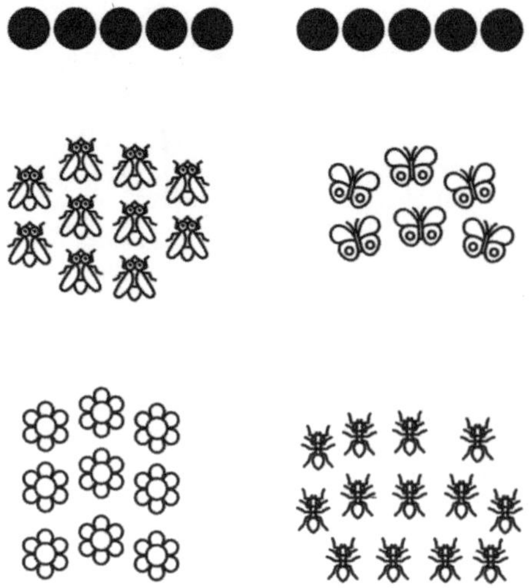

3

Color 10 fingers.

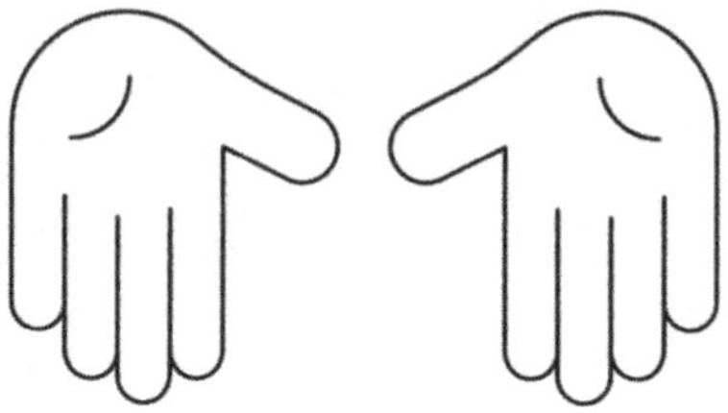

4

Write the number 10.

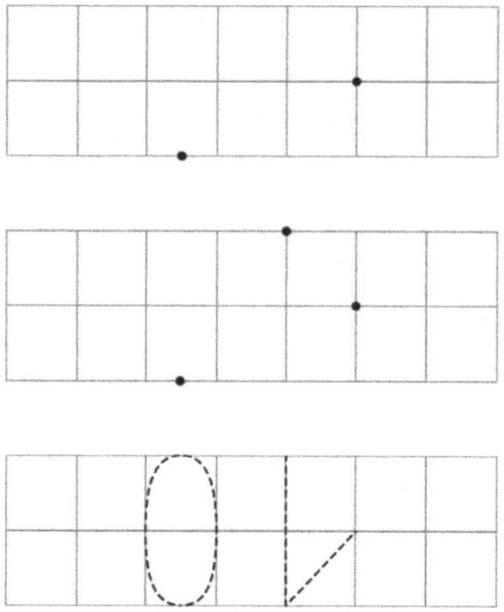

5

Color the number 10.

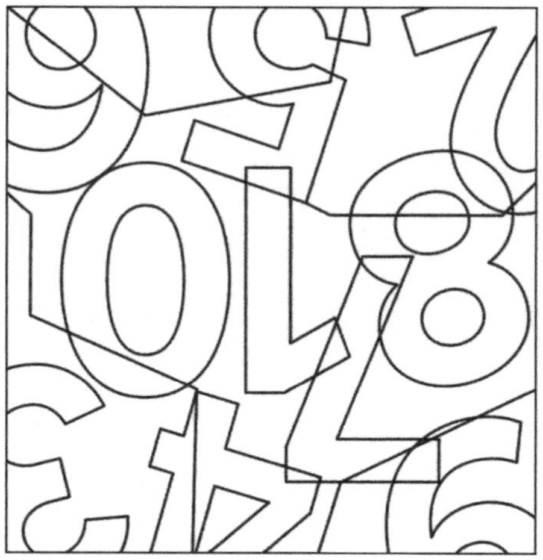

6

Circle groups of 10 worms.

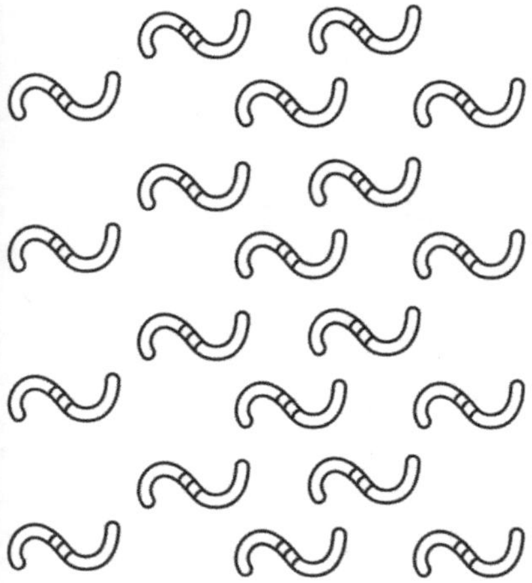

7

Review and trace these figures with 10 sides.

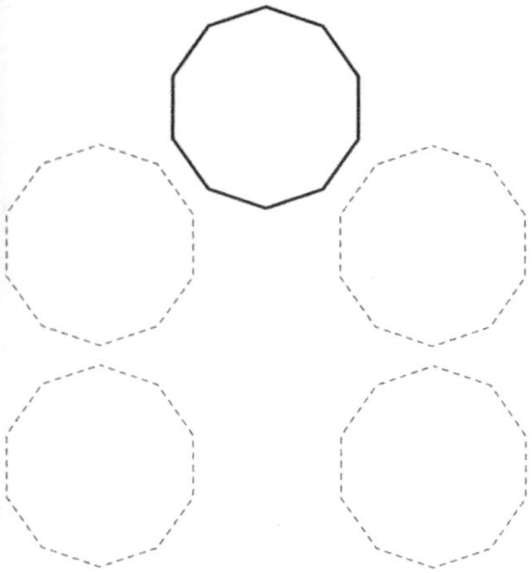

8

Color 11 items.

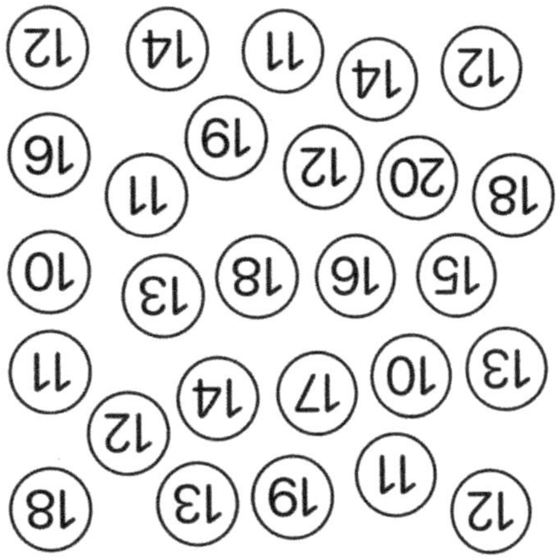

Color the number 11.

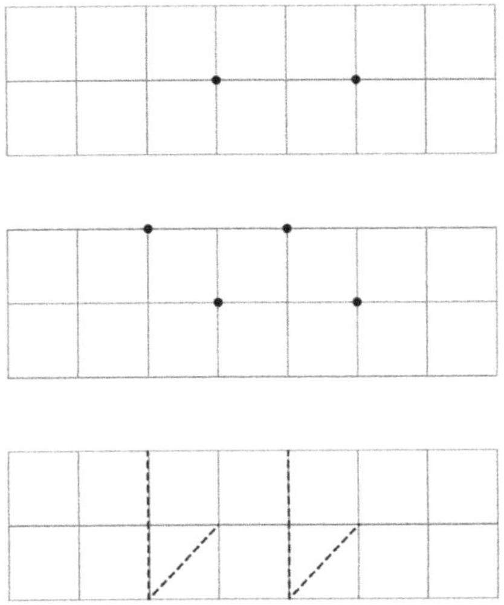

Write the number 11.

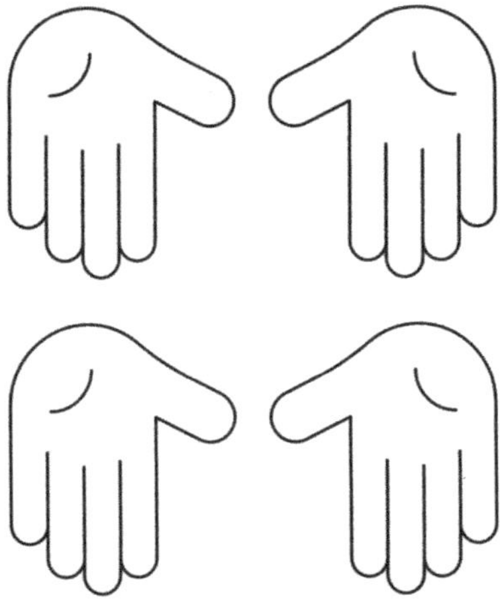

Color 11 fingers.

Draw what you like with 11 sticks.

COLOR THE AREAS WITH DOTS AND DISCOVER...

number **11.**

11 on the dice.

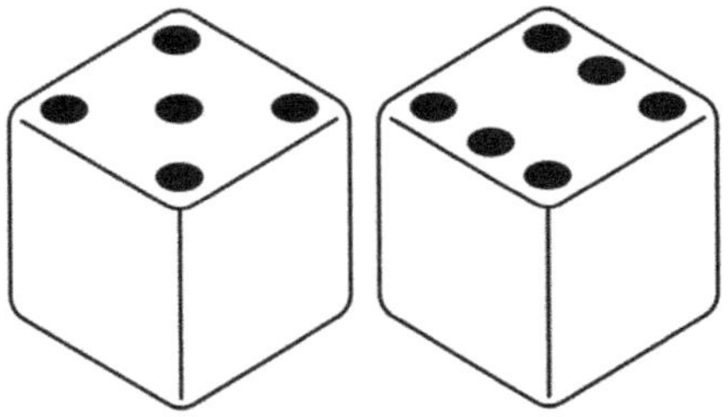

Color the groups with 11 items.

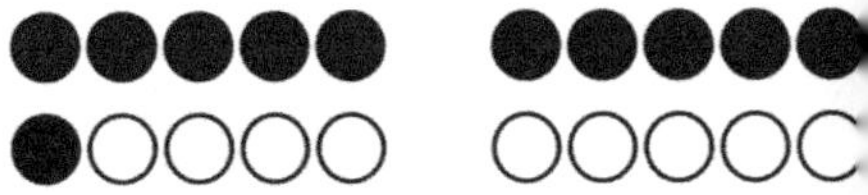

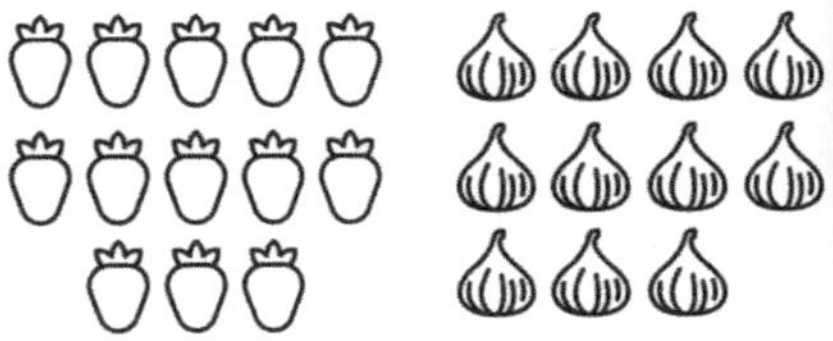

4

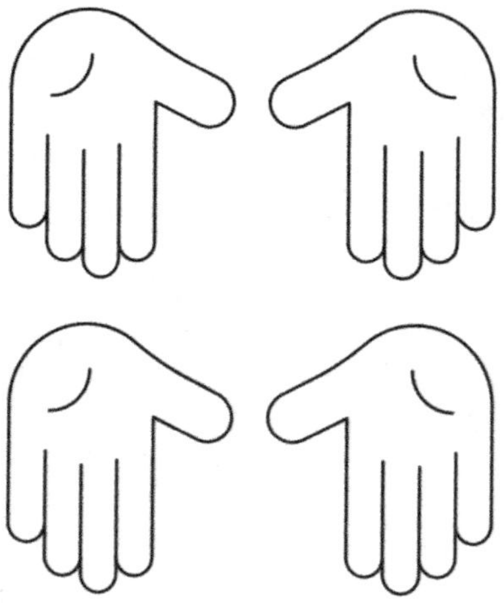

Color 12 fingers.

5

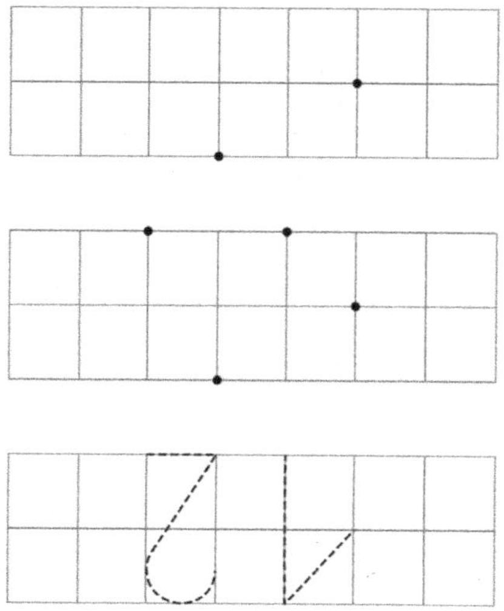

Write the number 12.

6

Color the number 12.

7

Color 12 items.

Draw what you like with 12 triangles.

8

COLOR THE AREAS WITH DOTS AND DISCOVER...

number **12**.

12 on the dice.

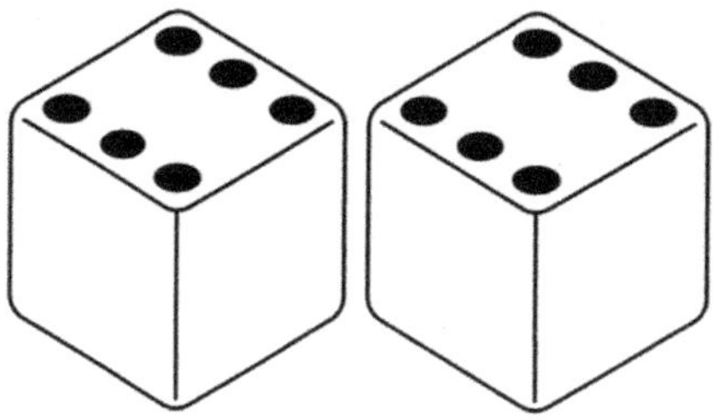

2

Color the groups with 12 items.

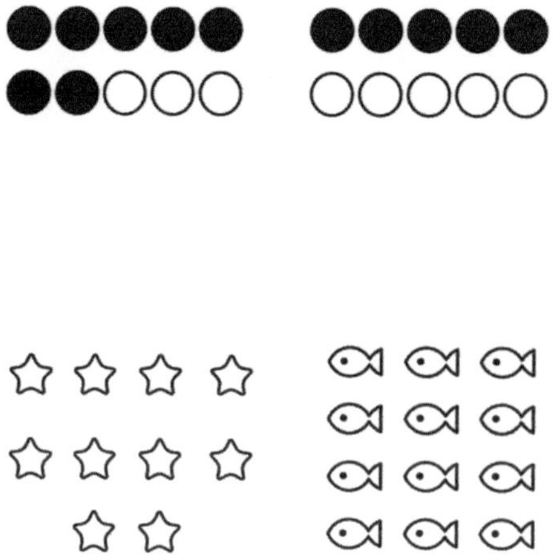

3

COLOR THE AREAS WITH DOTS AND DISCOVER...

number **13.**

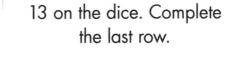

13 on the dice. Complete the last row.

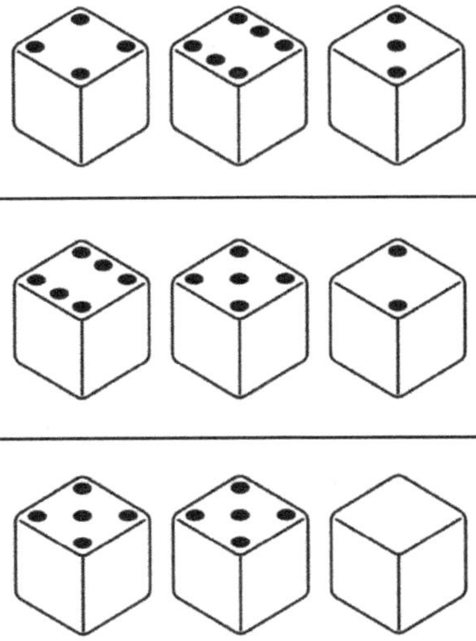

Color the groups with 13 items.

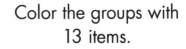

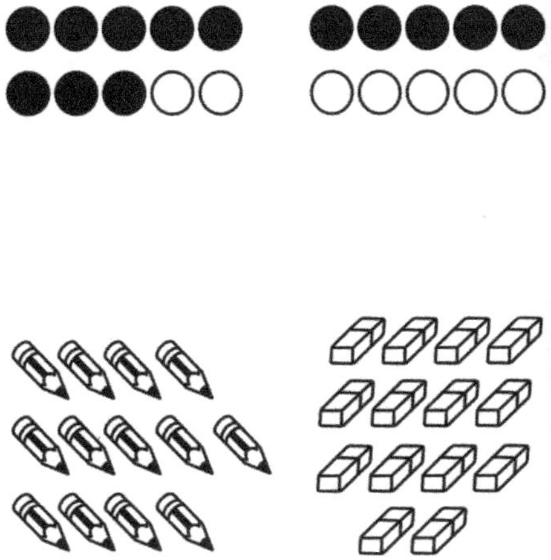

Color 13 fingers.

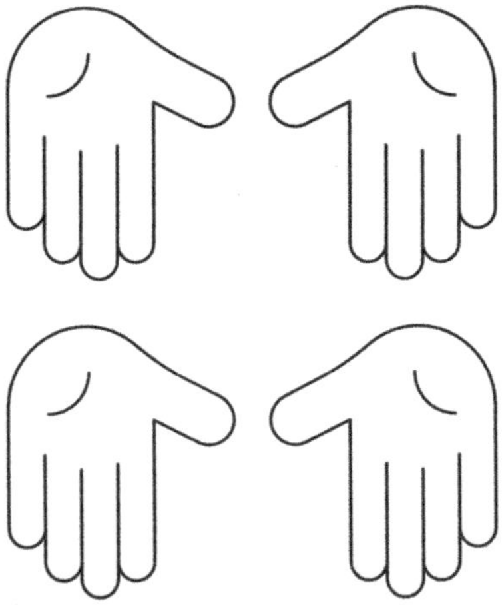

Write the number 13.

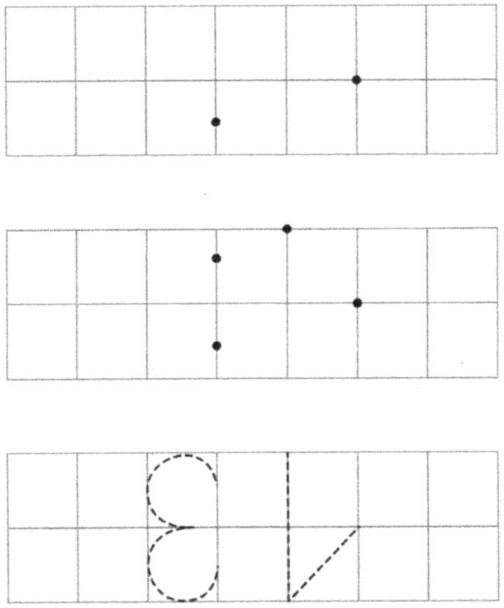

Color the number 13.

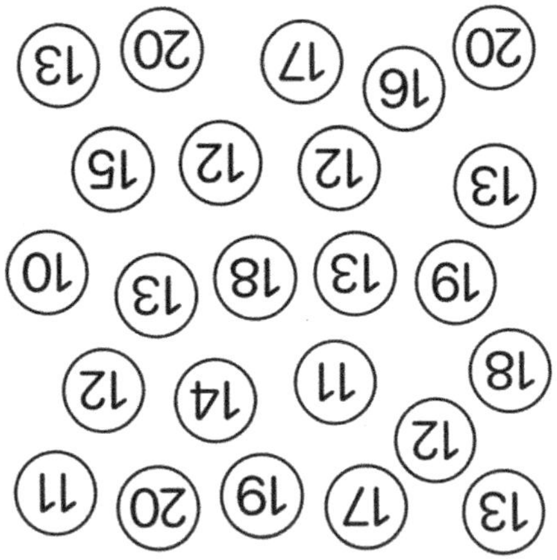

Color 13 items.

Draw what you like with 13 squares.

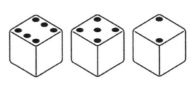

COLOR THE AREAS WITH DOTS AND DISCOVER...

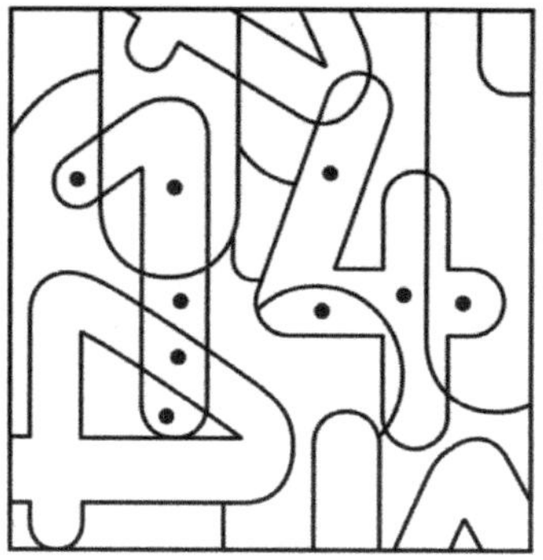

number **14.**

14 on the dice. Complete the last row.

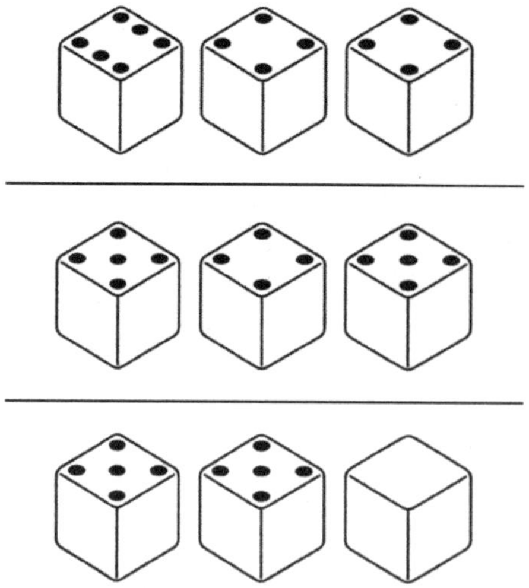

Color the groups with 14 items.

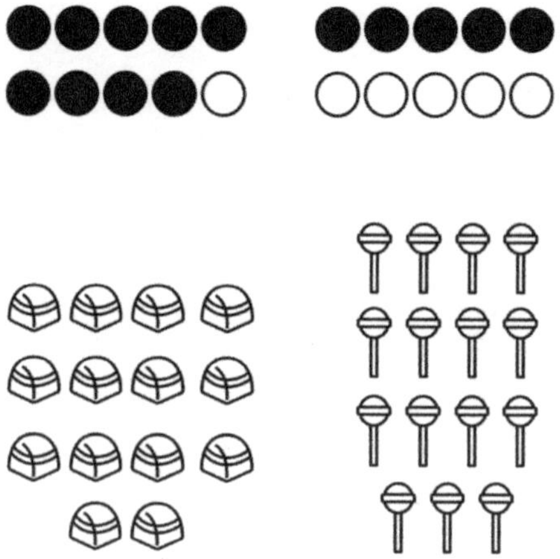

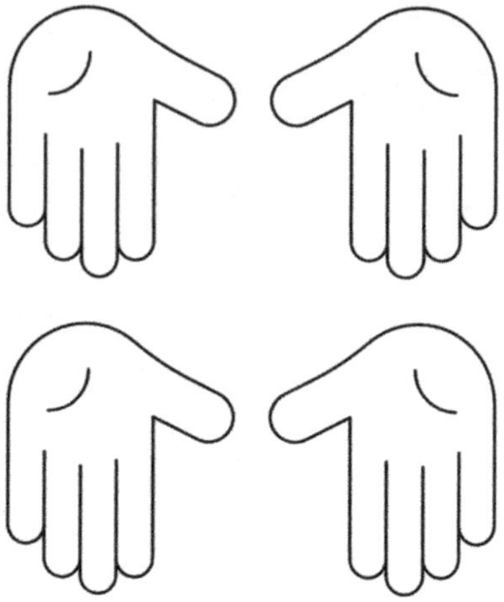

Color 14 fingers.

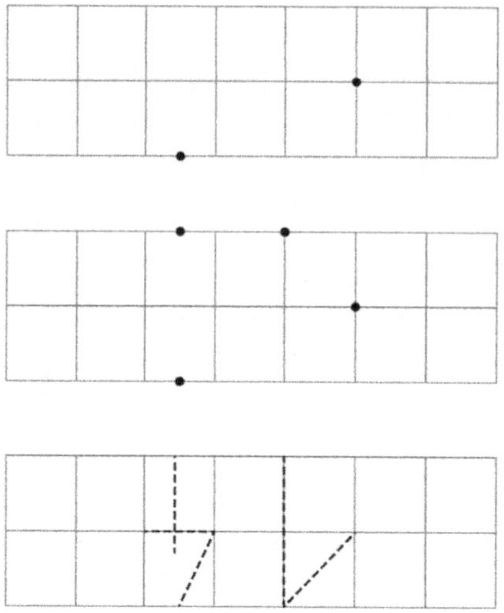

Write the number 14.

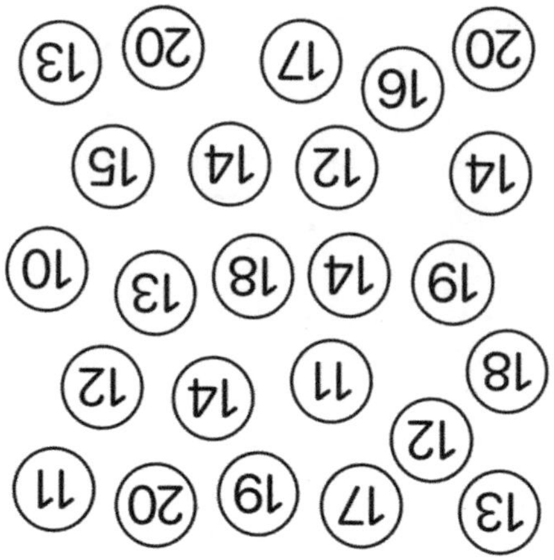

Color the number 14.

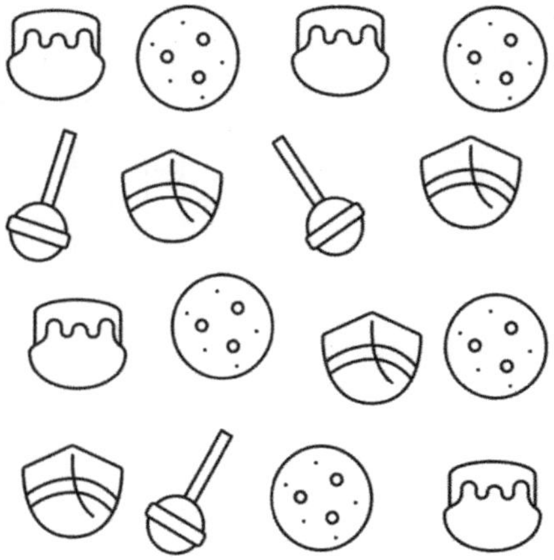

Color 14 items.

Draw what you like with 14 circles.

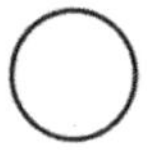

Connect the numbers from 1 to 15.

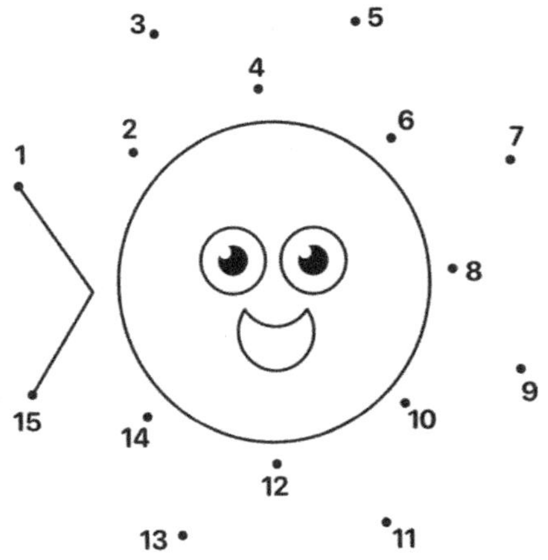

COLOR THE AREAS WITH DOTS AND DISCOVER...

number **15.**

15 on the dice. Complete the last row.

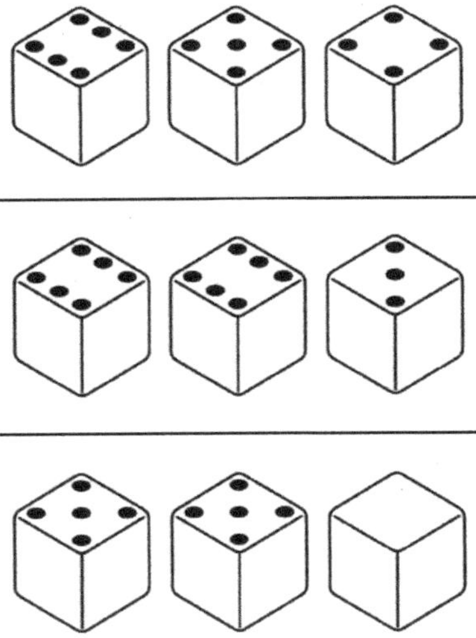

Color the groups with 15 items.

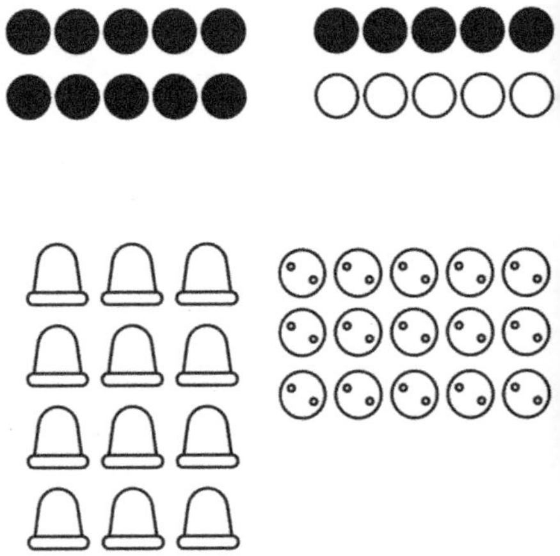

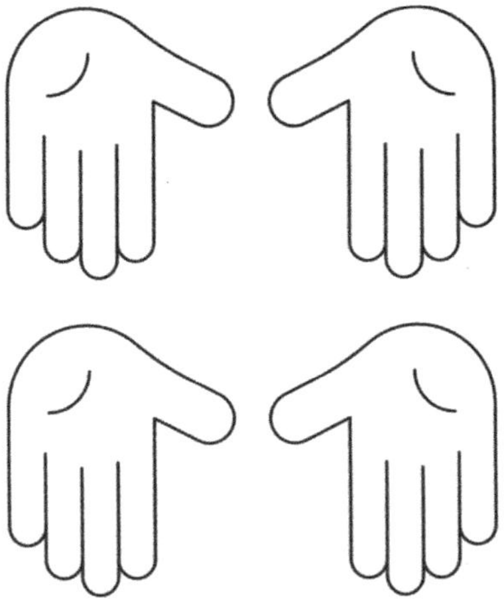

Color 15 fingers.

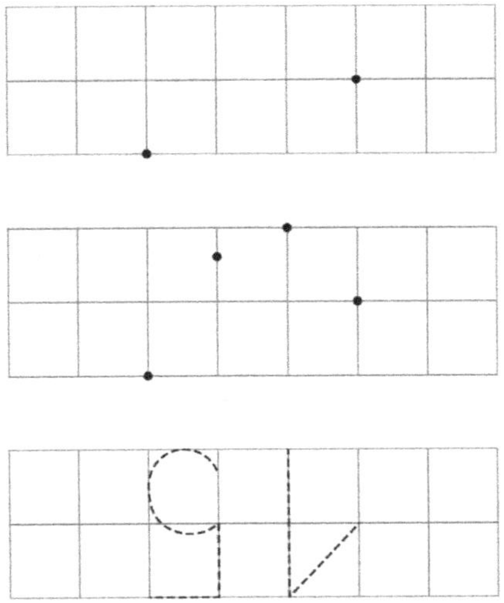

Write the number 15.

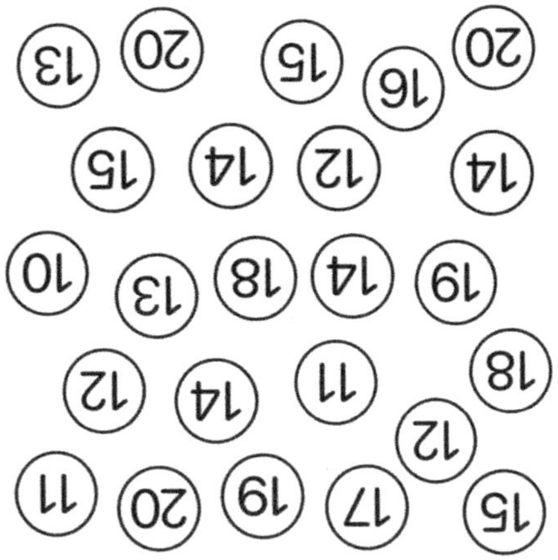

Color the number 15.

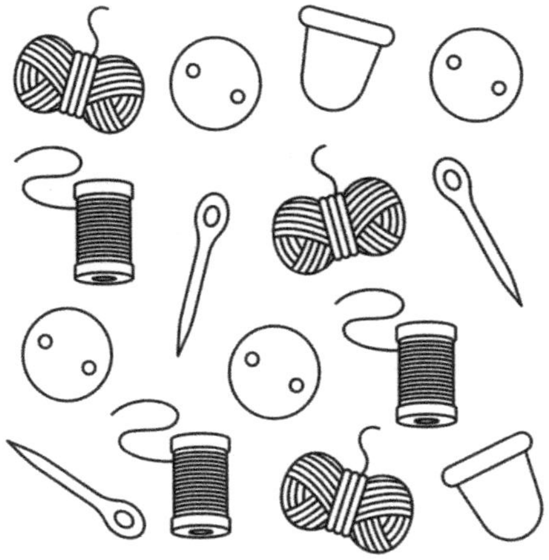

Color 15 items.

COLOR THE AREAS WITH DOTS AND DISCOVER...

number **16.**

16 on the dice. Complete the last row.

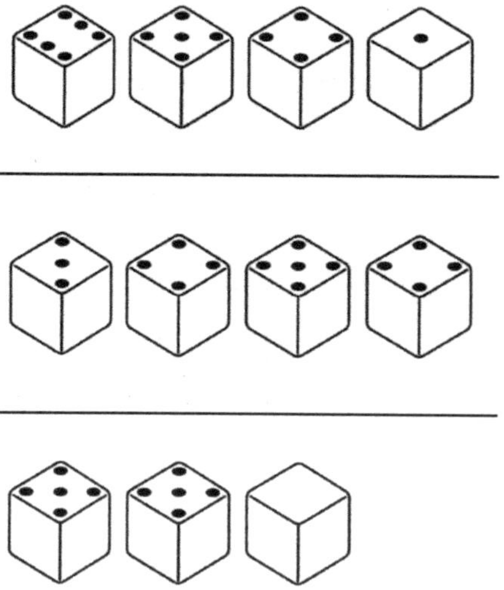

Color the groups with 16 items.

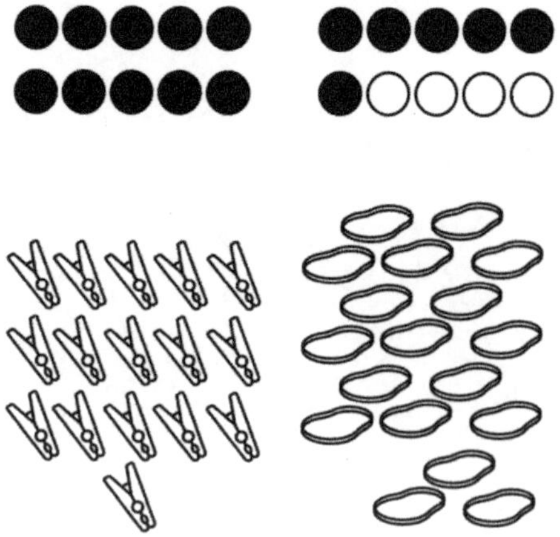

Color 16 fingers.

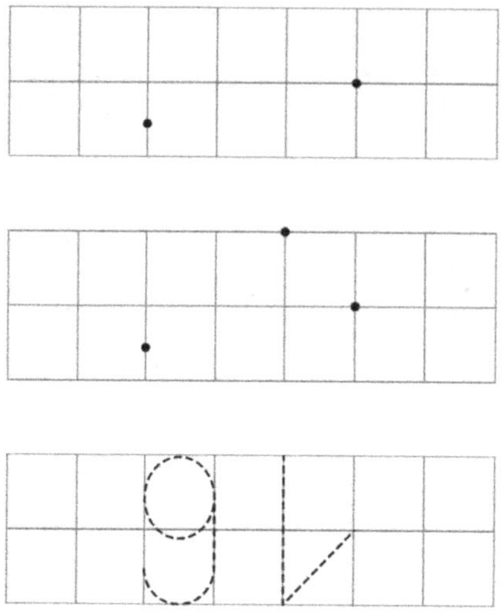

Write the number 16.

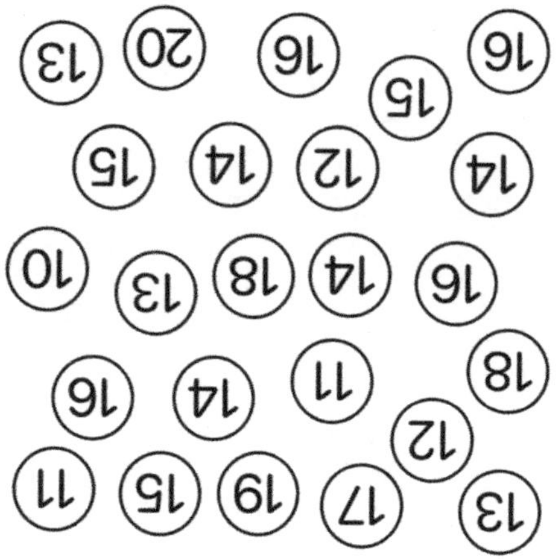

Color the number 16.

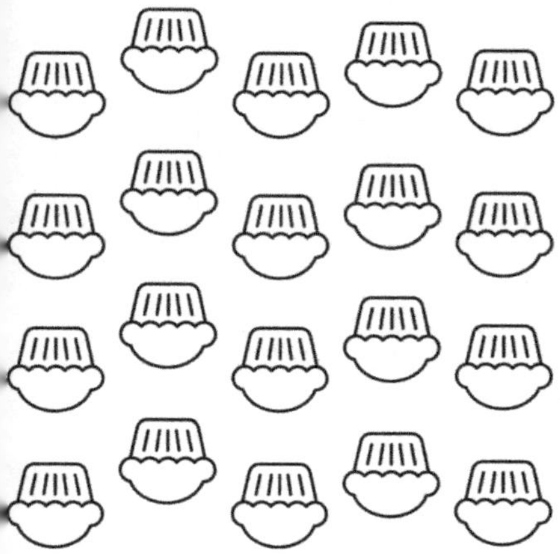

Color 16 items.

Connect the numbers from 1 to 16.

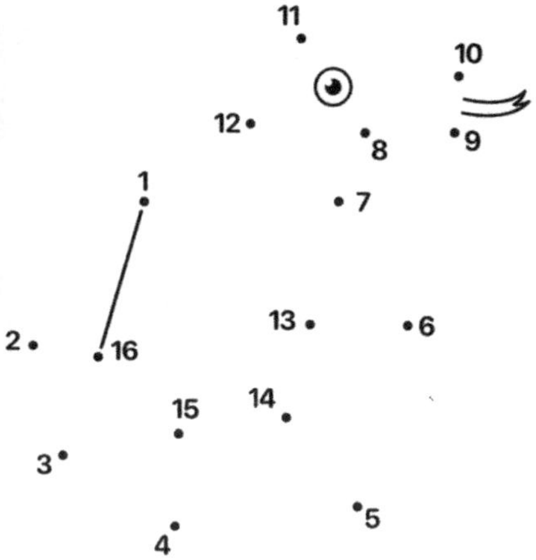

COLOR THE AREAS WITH DOTS AND DISCOVER...

number **17.**

17 on the dice. Complete the last row.

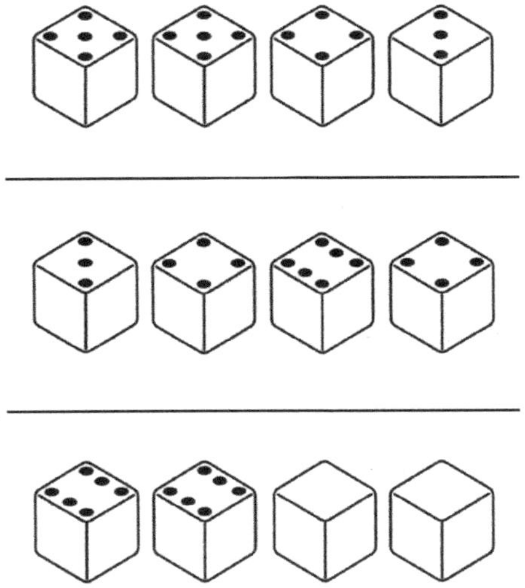

Color the groups with 17 items.

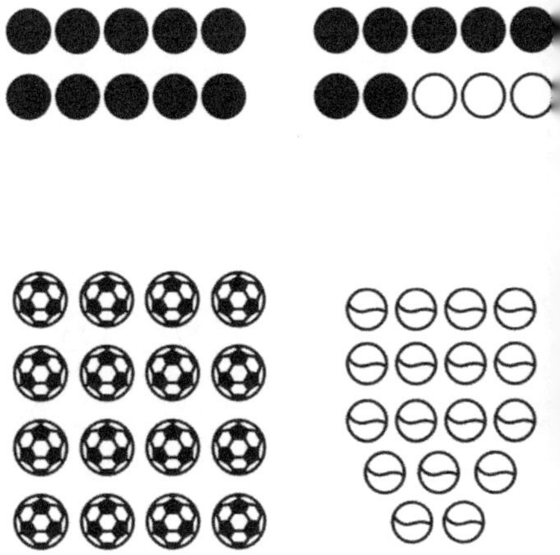

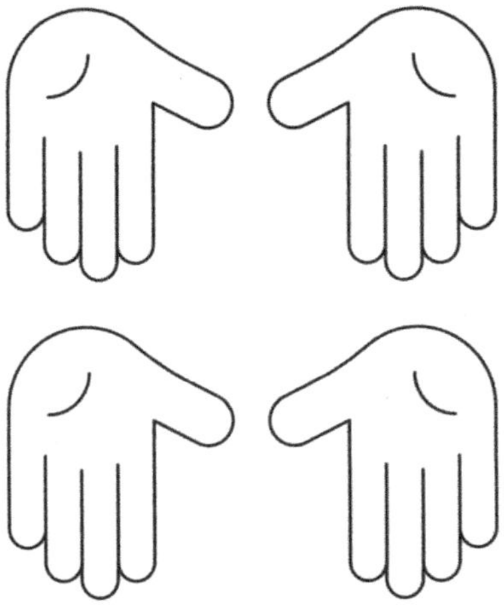

Color 17 fingers.

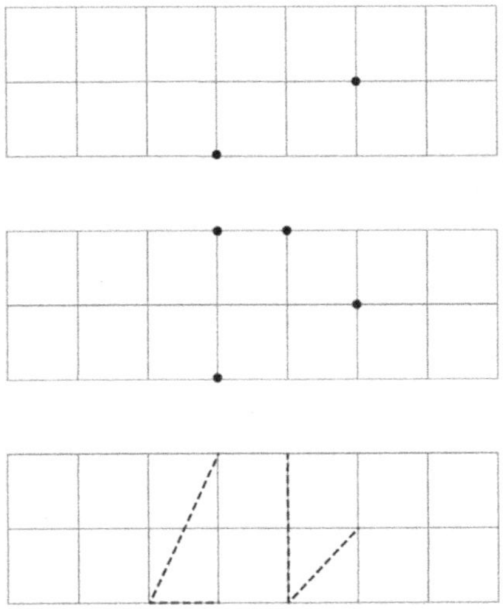

Write the number 17.

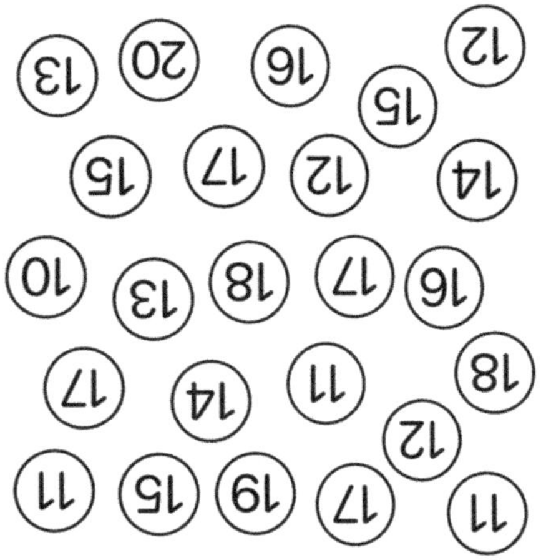

Color the number 17.

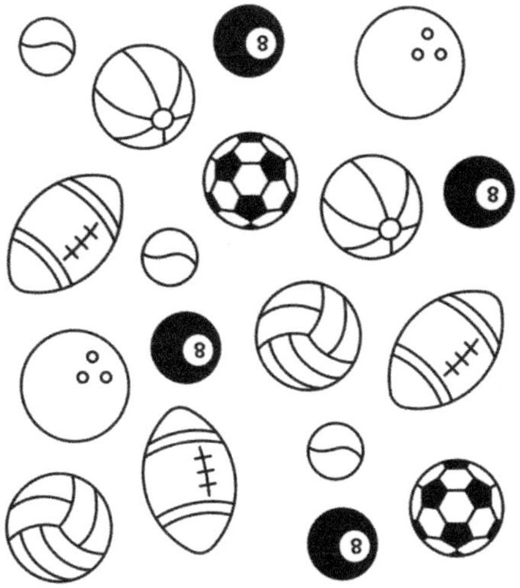

Color 17 items.

Connect the numbers from 1 to 17.

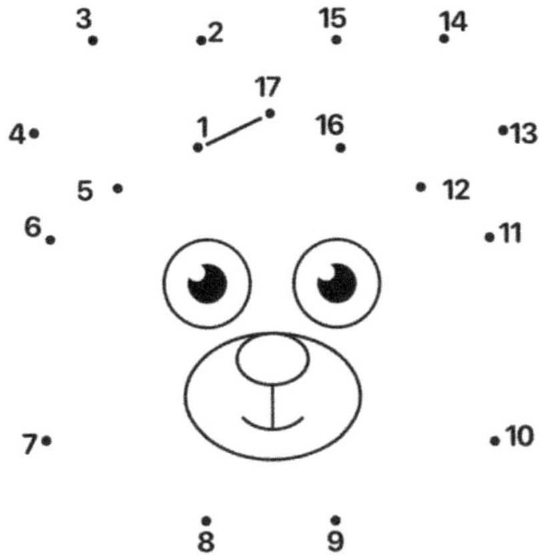

COLOR THE AREAS WITH DOTS AND DISCOVER...

number **18.**

18 on the dice. Complete the last row.

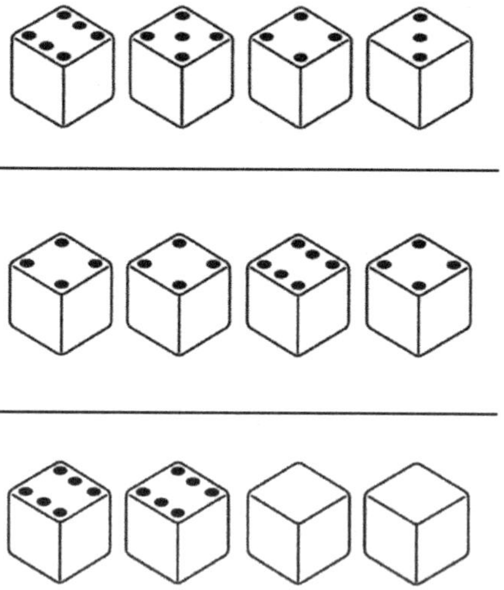

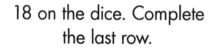

Color the groups with 18 items.

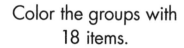

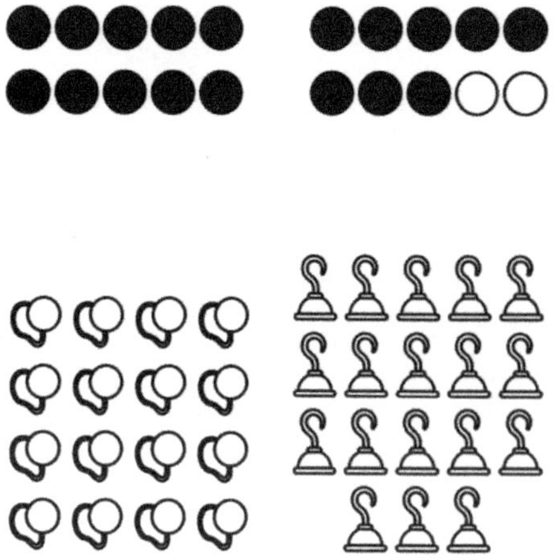

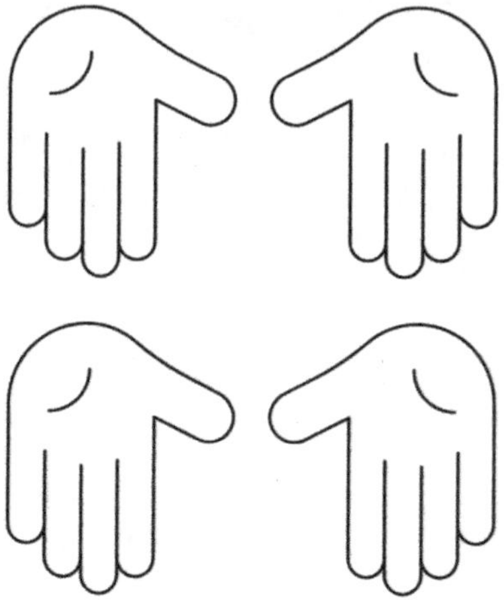

Color 18 fingers.

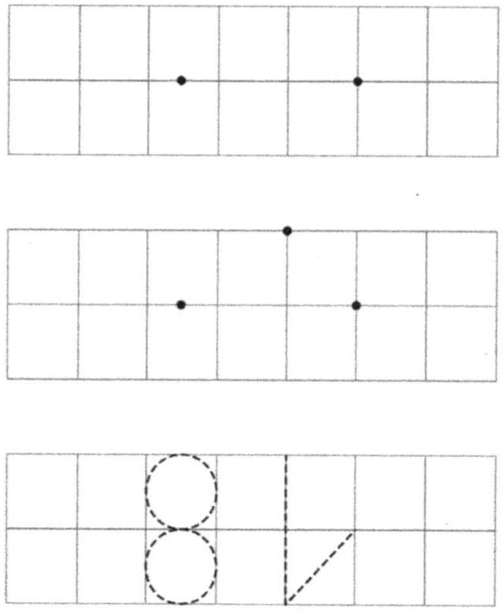

Write the number 18.

Color the number 18.

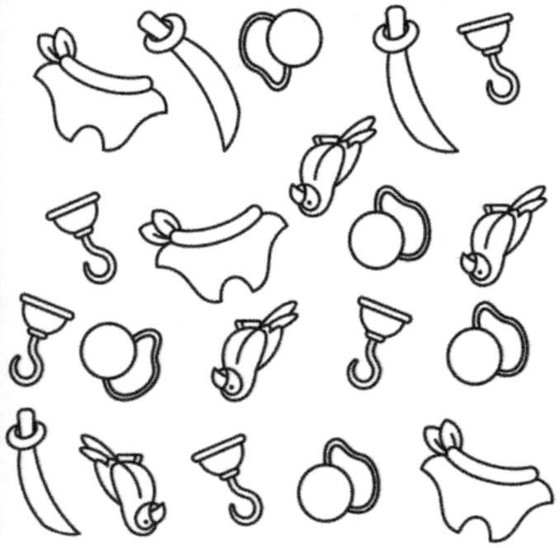

Color 18 items.

Connect the numbers from 1 to 18.

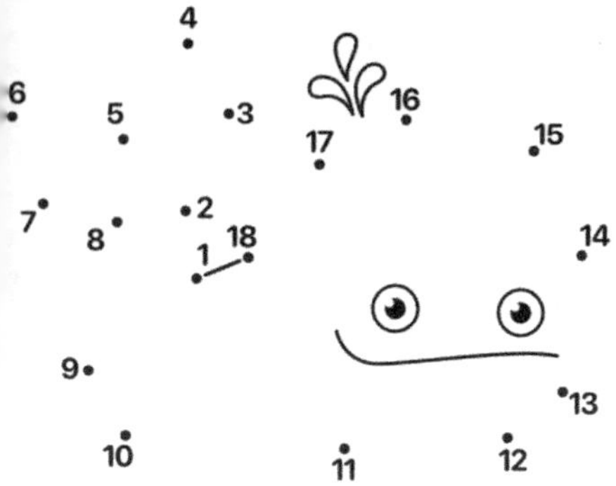

Connect the numbers from 1 to 19.

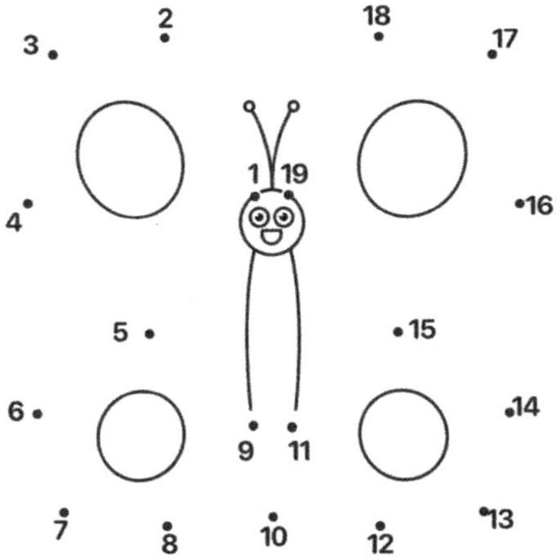

COLOR THE AREAS WITH DOTS AND DISCOVER...

number **19.**

19 on the dice. Complete the last row.

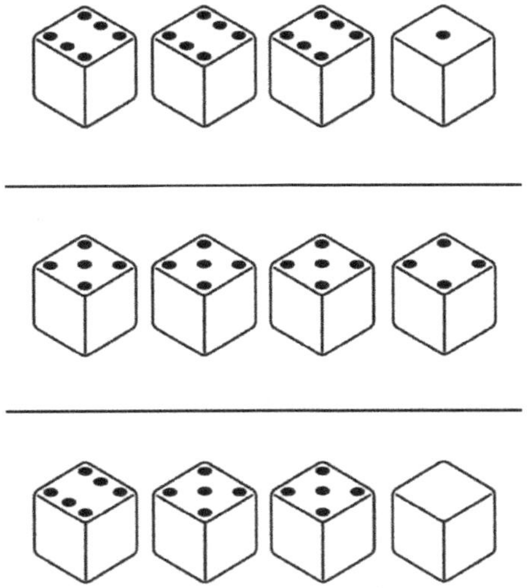

Color the groups with 19 items.

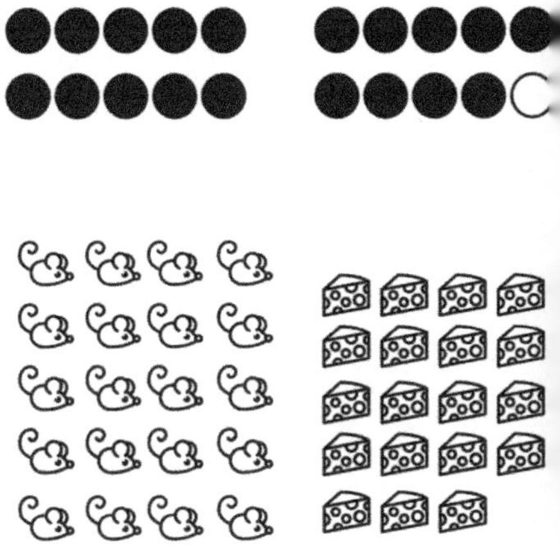

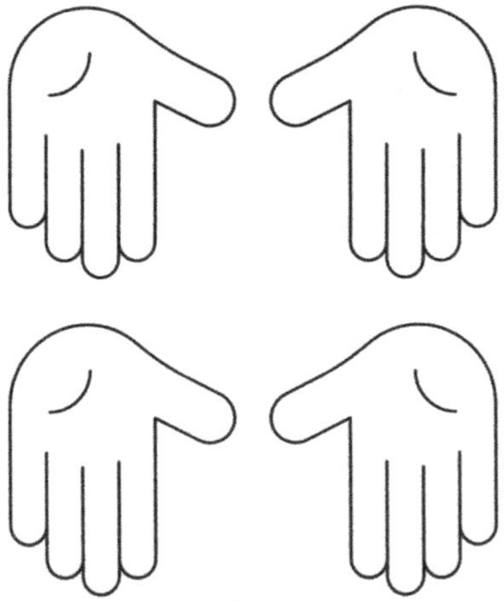

Color 19 fingers.

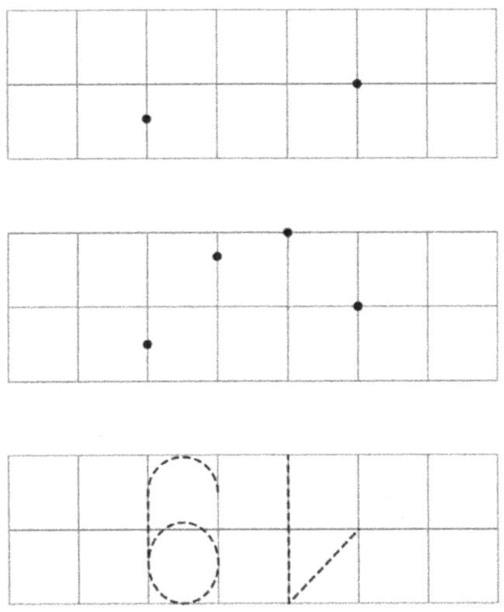

Write the number 19.

Color the number 19.

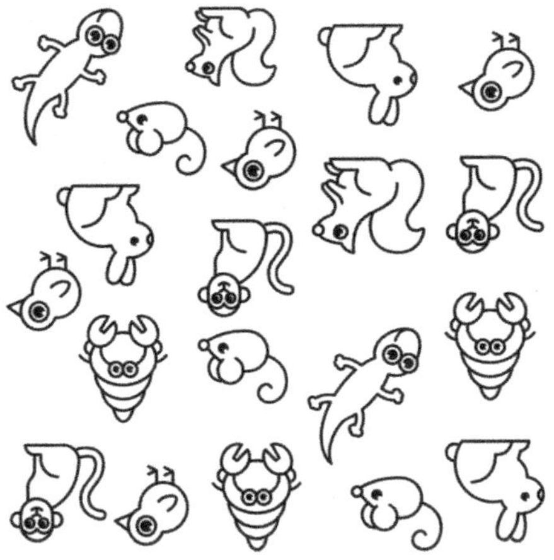

Color 19 items.

COLOR THE AREAS WITH DOTS AND DISCOVER...

number **20.**

20 on the dice. Complete the last row.

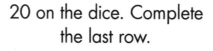

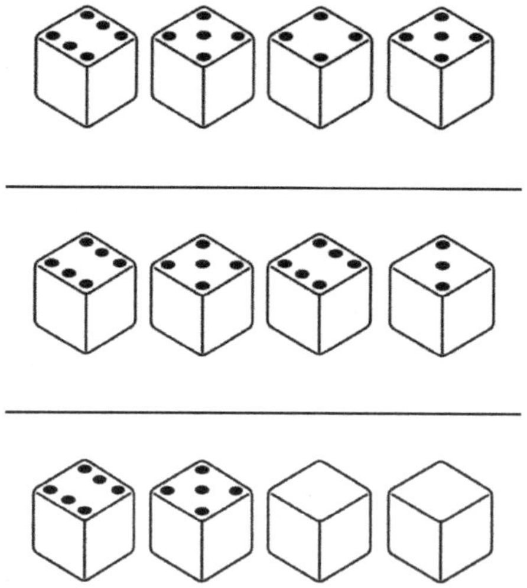

Color the groups with 20 items.

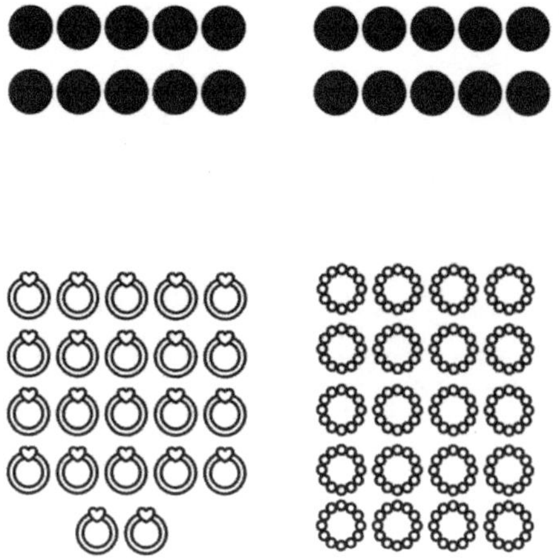

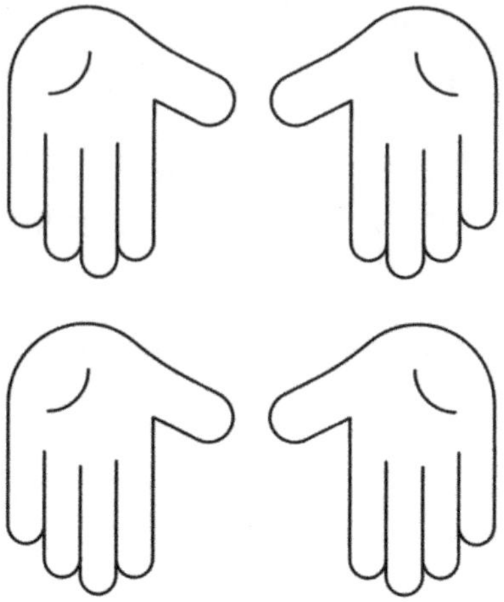

Color 20 fingers.

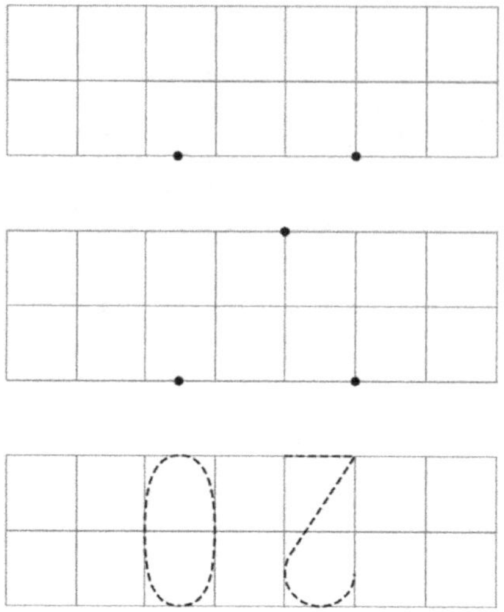

Write the number 20.

Color the number 20.

Color 20 items.

Connect the numbers from 1 to 20.

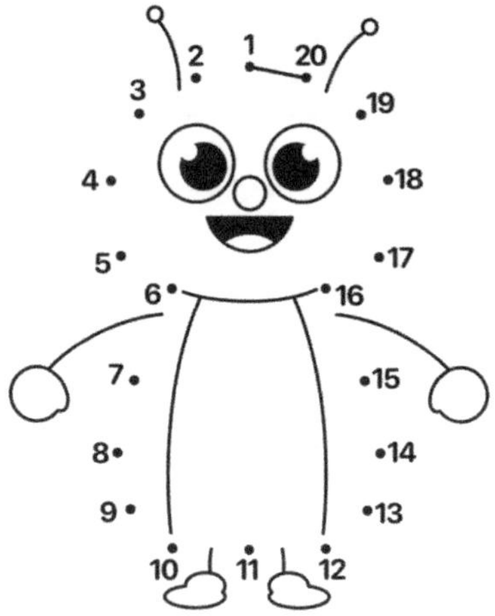

COUNT THE INSECTS

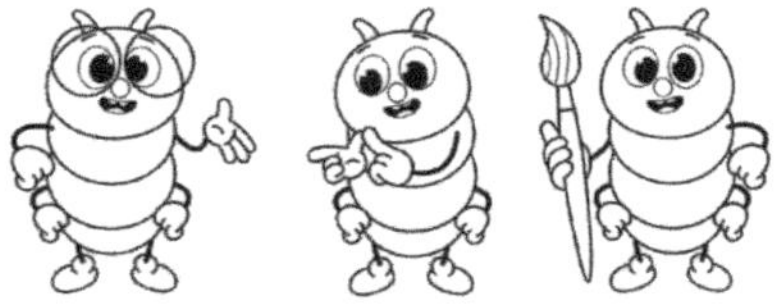

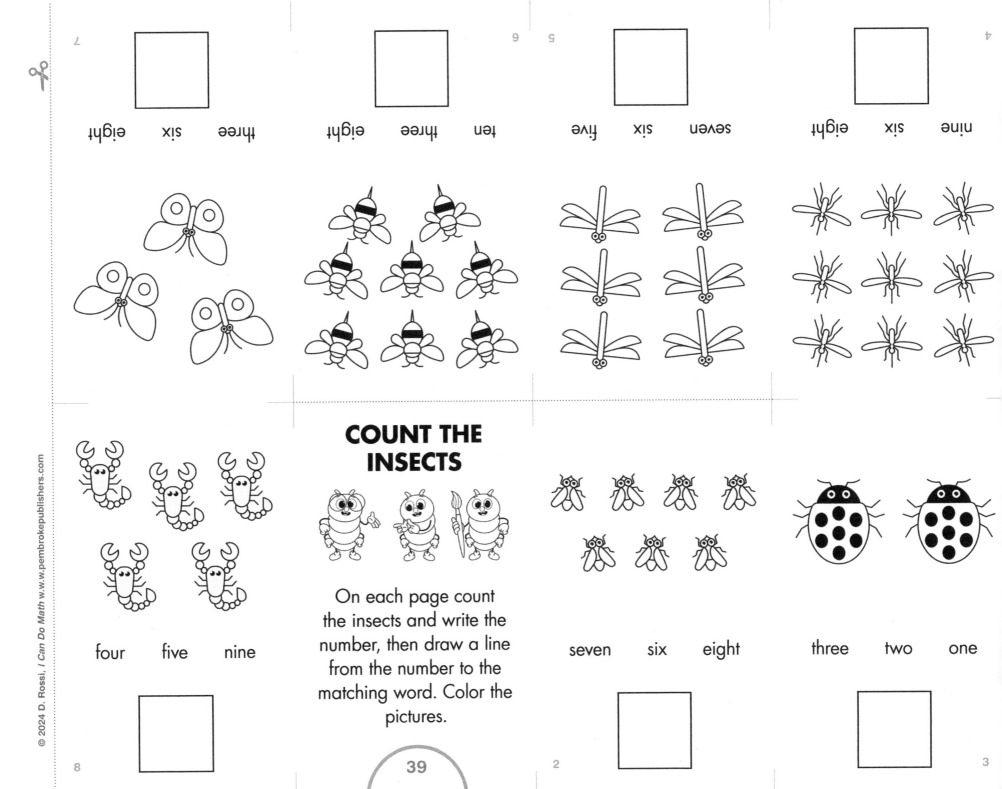

On each page count the insects and write the number, then draw a line from the number to the matching word. Color the pictures.

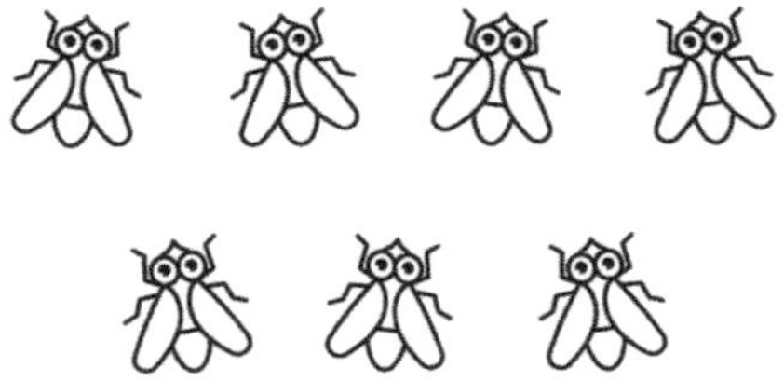

seven six eight

2

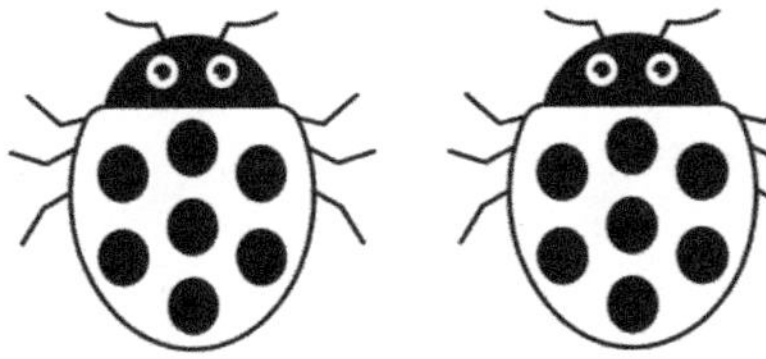

three two one

3

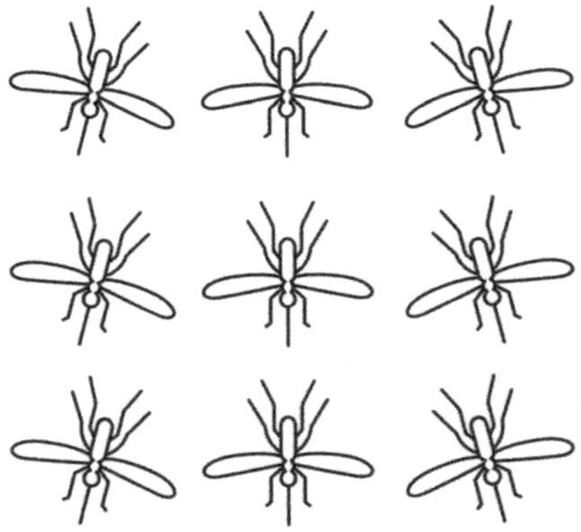

nine six eight

4

seven six five

5

ten three eight

6

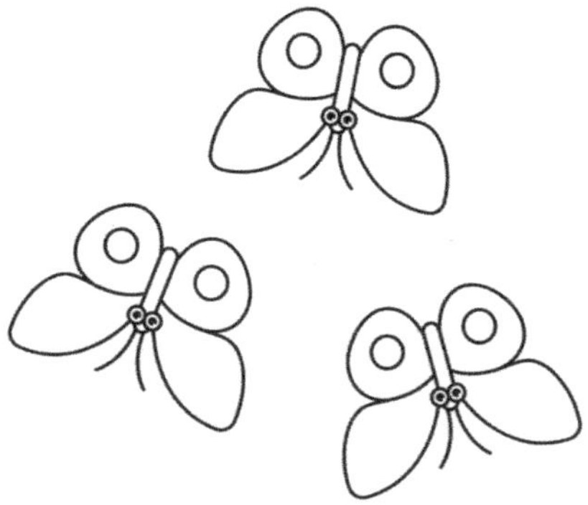

three six eight

7

four five nine

8

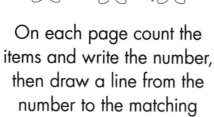

COUNTING AT THE BOTTOM OF THE SEA

On each page count the items and write the number, then draw a line from the number to the matching word. Color the pictures.

2

thirteen ten three

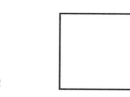

3

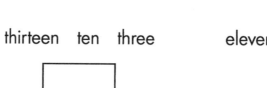

eleven one ten

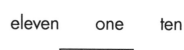

4

six sixteen nineteen

5

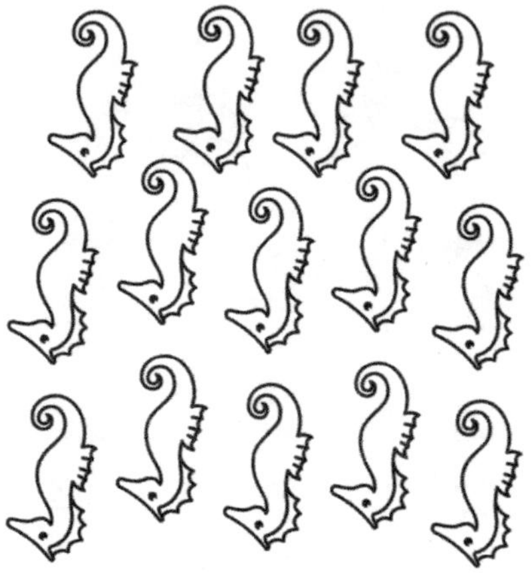

four fourteen fifteen

6

nine nineteen ten

7

twelve fourteen two

8

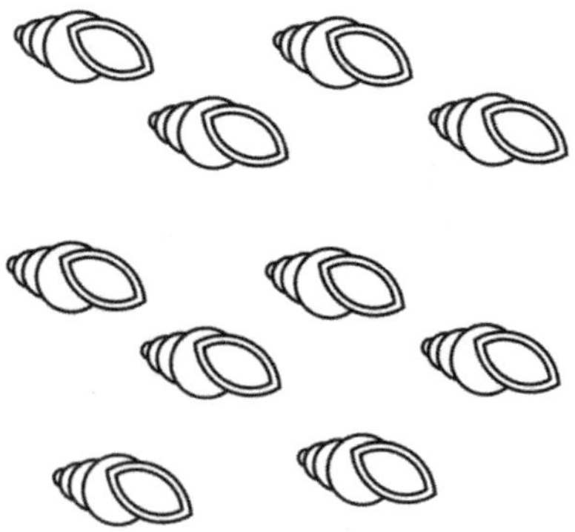

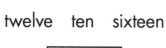

twelve ten sixteen

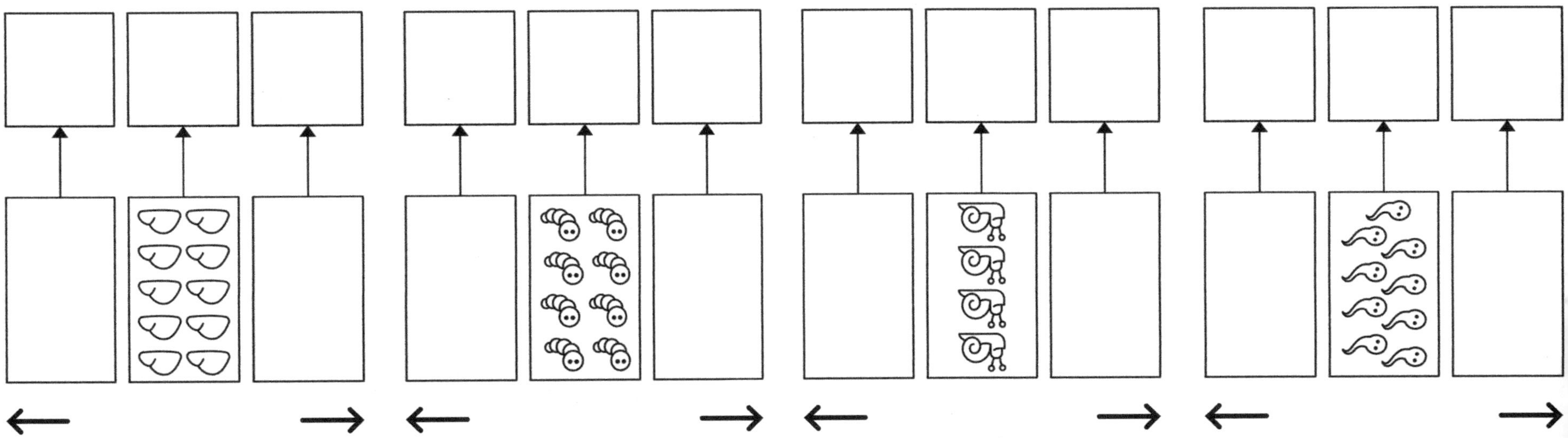

BEFORE AND AFTER

On each page count the items and write the number below, then write the number that comes before it and the number that comes after it. Draw the same number of items.

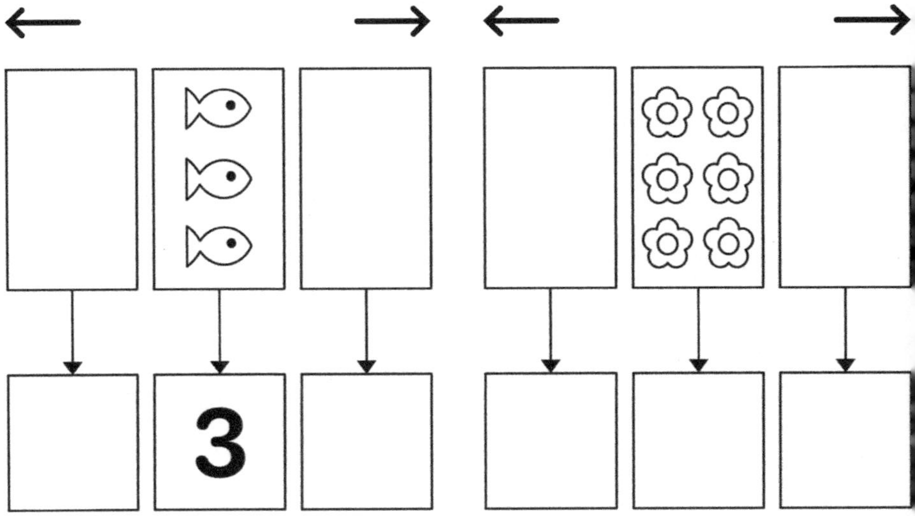

THE BARREL JUMP

On each page write the missing numbers before or after on the barrels.

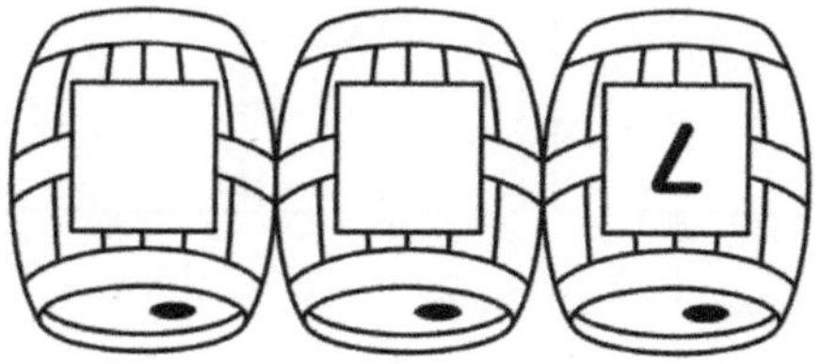

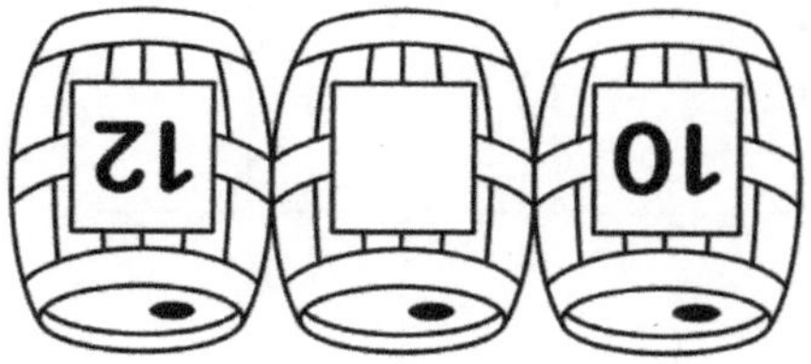

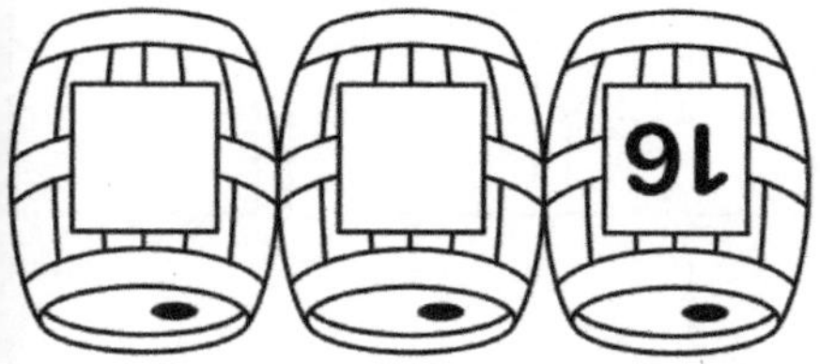

Complete the last tile.

NUMBER TILES

Each tile represents two numbers. Pictures represent the number that is one less than the digit on the right.

Write the missing number.

Complete with the missing picture.

Complete as on the previous page.

Complete as on the previous page.

Complete as on the previous page.

Complete as on the previous page.

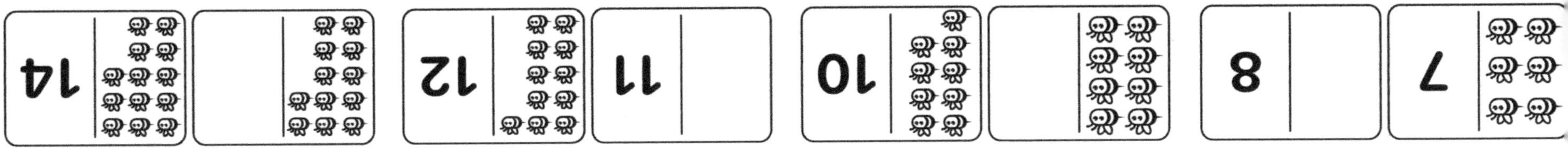

> GREATER THAN

Frog has his mouth open towards the greatest number of insects.

Go over the frog's mouth with a red crayon.

5 > 3

Go over the frog's mouth with a red crayon.

8 > 4

Draw the matching number of insects in the empty space.

3 > 2

Complete as on the previous page.

4 > 3

Complete as on the previous page.

6 > 5

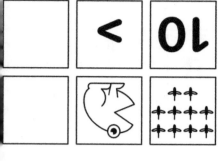

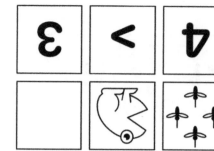

Draw mosquitoes and write the matching number in the blank spaces.

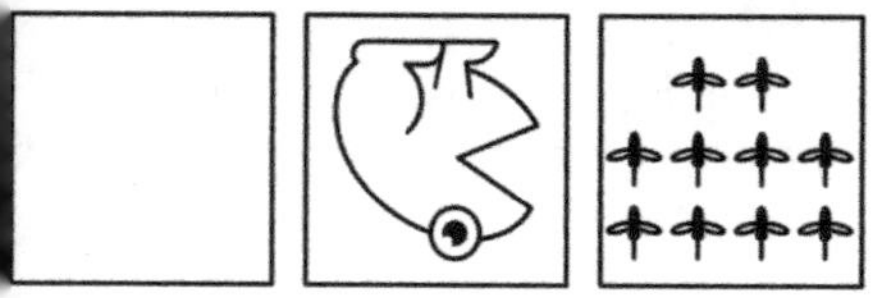

10 >

Write numbers and draw mosquitoes in the blank spaces.

>

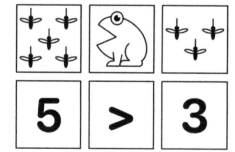

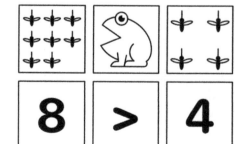

< LESS THAN

Frog has his mouth open towards the largest group of insects.

Go over the frog's mouth with a red crayon.

7	<	10

Go over the frog's mouth with a red crayon.

7	<	8

Draw ladybugs in the empty space to match the number below.

2	<	4

Draw insects in the empty space to match the number below.

3	<	6

Draw ladybugs in the blank spaces to match the numbers below.

4	<	5

Draw ladybugs and write the matching number in the blank spaces.

10	<	

Draw ladybugs and write matching numbers in the blank spaces.

	<	

= EQUAL

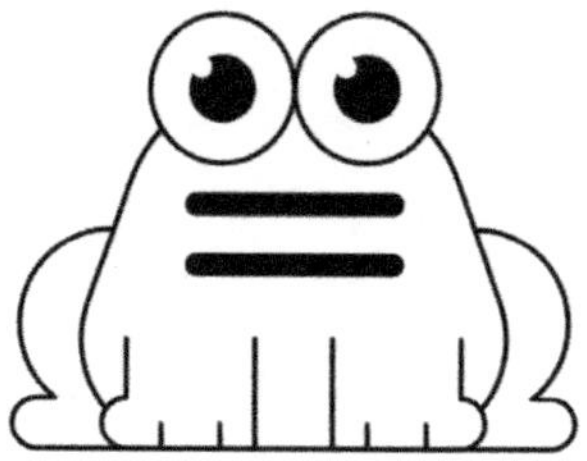

Frog doesn't know which way to turn because the number of worms is the same.

Go over the frog's mouth with a red crayon.

12 = 12

Go over the frog's mouth with a red crayon.

7 = 7

Complete the page: write the number and draw the worms.

1 =

Complete as on the previous page.

3 =

Complete the page: write the numbers and draw the worms.

=

Complete the page: write the numbers and draw the worms.

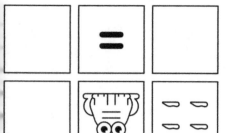

=

Write the numbers and draw the worms in the blank spaces.

=

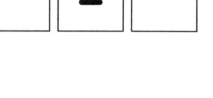

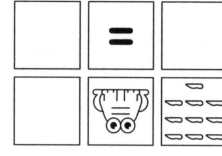

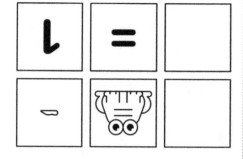

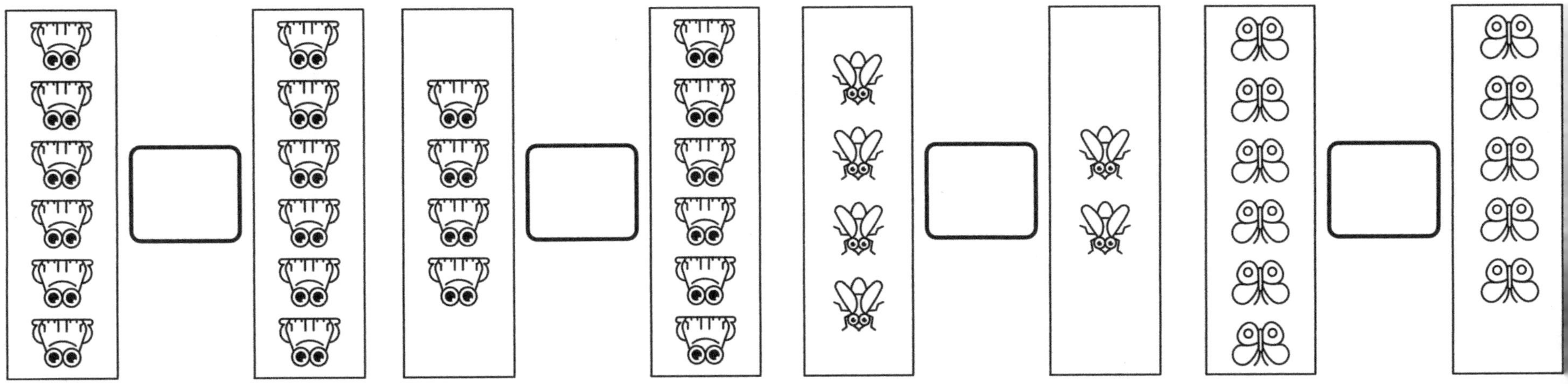

Color the bigger number in each pair.

10	6
2	5
20	17
13	12
1	10
9	6
2	12
17	19
18	17
8	18

COMPARING

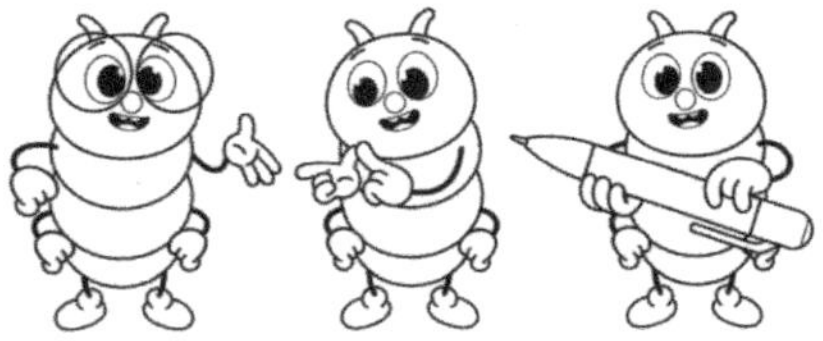

Compare the two columns and write the correct symbol between them:
<, >, or =

Count and write the greater than, less than, or equal symbol.

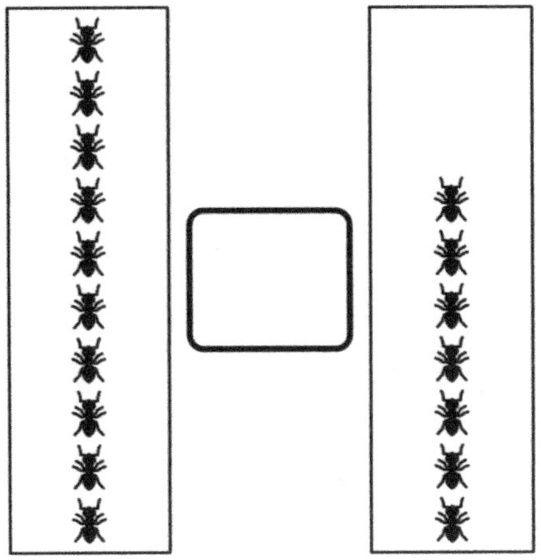

Complete as on the previous page.

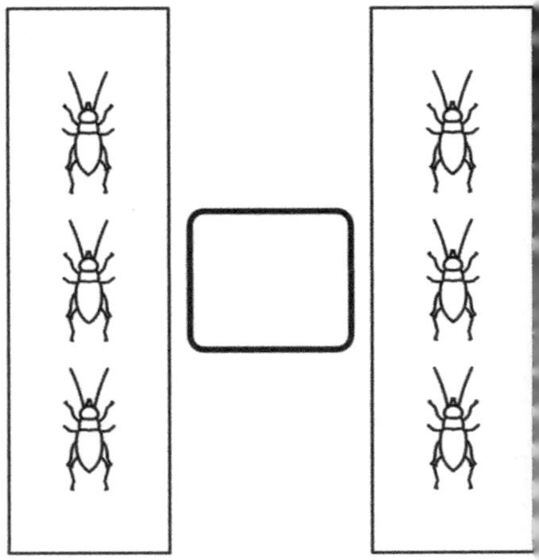

NUMBERS IN A JAR

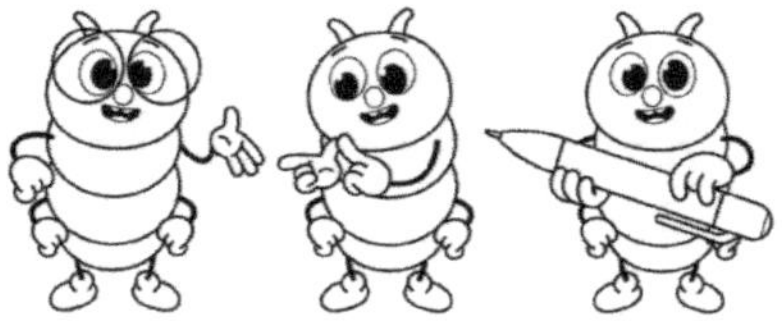

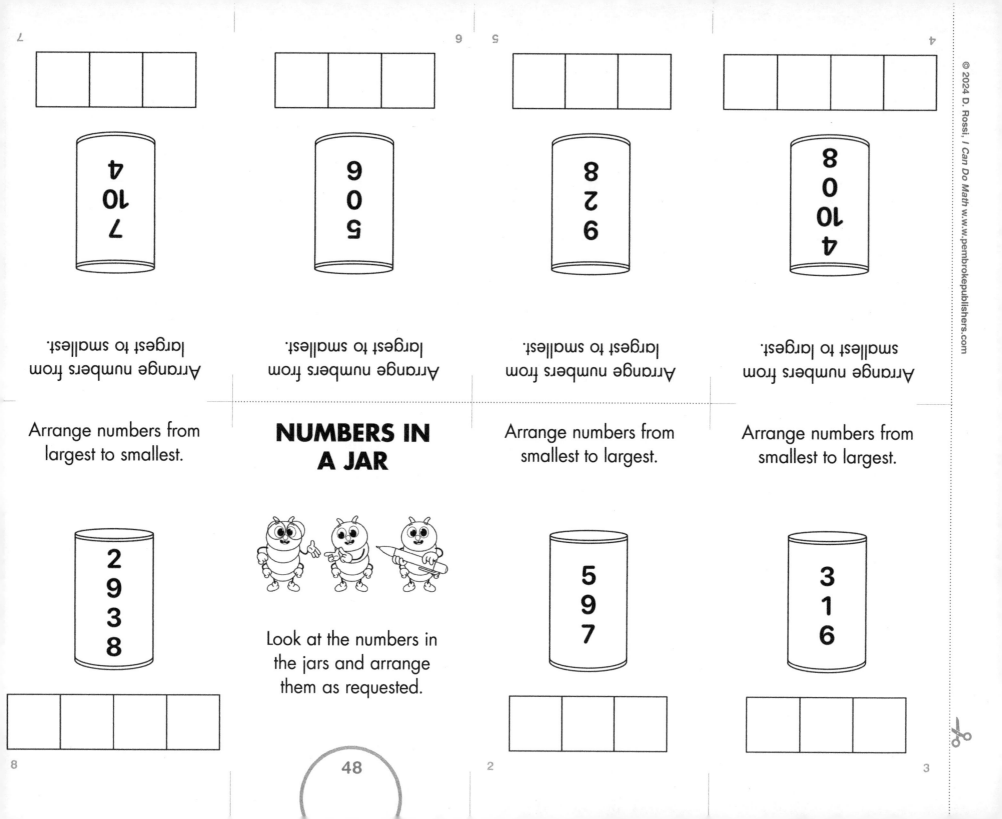

Look at the numbers in the jars and arrange them as requested.

Arrange numbers from smallest to largest.

5
9
7

2

Arrange numbers from smallest to largest.

3
1
6

3

Arrange numbers from smallest to largest.

4
10
0
8

4

Arrange numbers from largest to smallest.

6
2
8

5

Arrange numbers from largest to smallest.

5
0
6

6

Arrange numbers from largest to smallest.

7
10
4

7

Arrange numbers from largest to smallest.

2
9
3
8

8

ORDERING

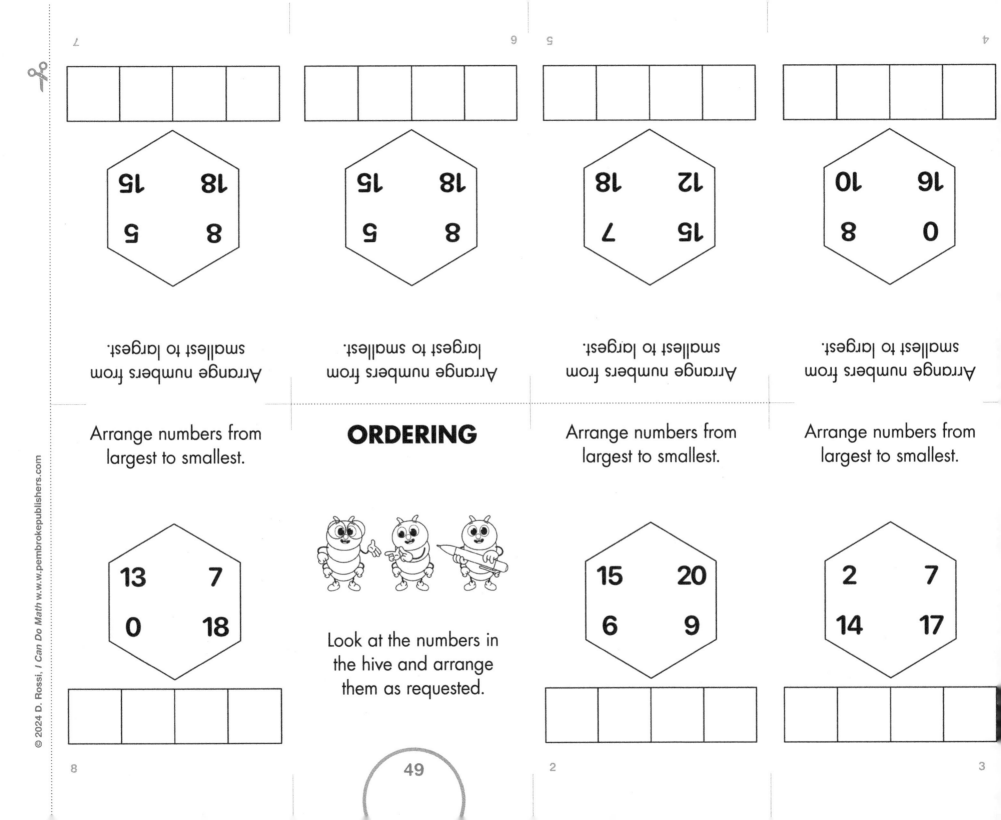

Look at the numbers in the hive and arrange them as requested.

Arrange numbers from largest to smallest.

15	20
6	9

2

Arrange numbers from largest to smallest.

2	7
14	17

3

Arrange numbers from smallest to largest.

0	8
16	10

4

Arrange numbers from smallest to largest.

15	7
12	18

5

Arrange numbers from largest to smallest.

8	5
18	15

6

Arrange numbers from smallest to largest.

8	5
18	15

7

Arrange numbers from largest to smallest.

13	7
0	18

8

	TEN 10
	ONE 1

	TEN 10
	ONE 1

	TEN 10
	ONE 1

	TEN 10
	ONE 1

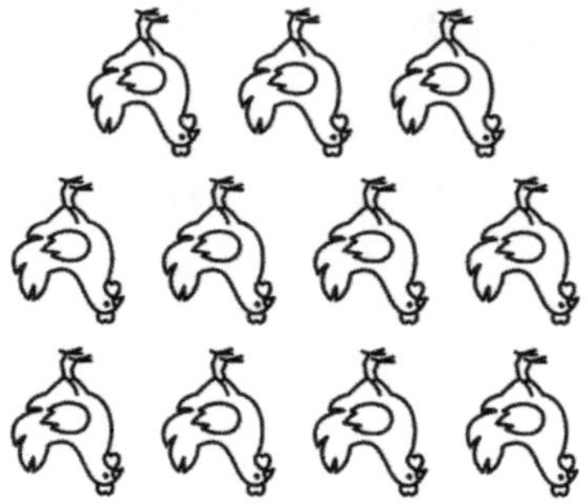

How did it go? Compare your work with a classmate's to see if everything is correct. How did you feel?

GROUP BY 10

Make a group of 10 with 10 1s.

50

Group by 10 and then write how many 1s are left.

1	TEN 10
	ONE 1

Group by 10 and then write how many 1s are left.

1	TEN 10
	ONE 1

10s AND 1s

Group the pictures by 10s and 1s and then color the label that matches the number.

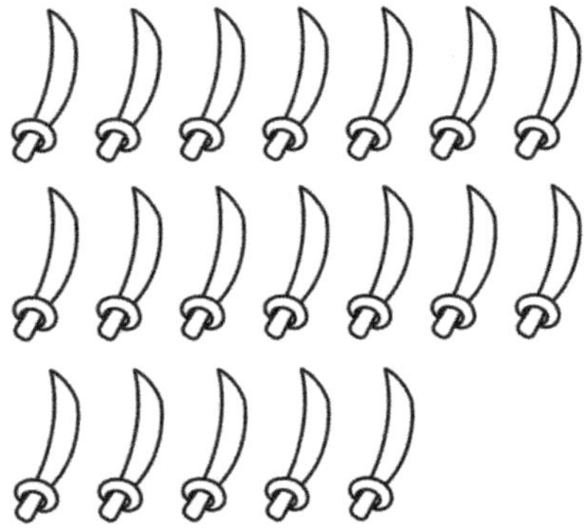

1 10 8 1s	1 10 0 1s
1 10 6 1s	1 10 9 1s

2

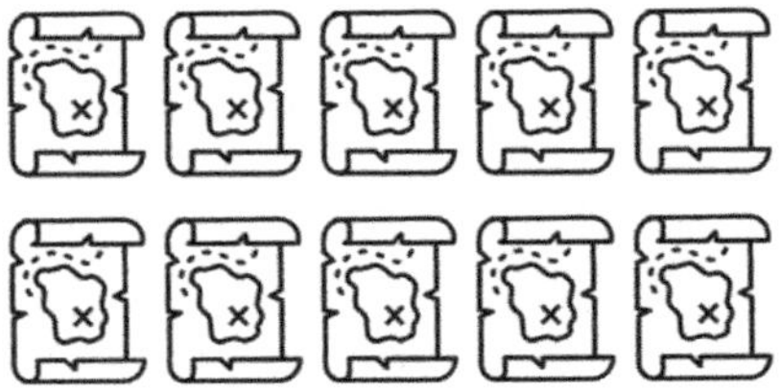

1 10 8 1s	1 10 0 1s
1 10 1 1s	9 1s

3

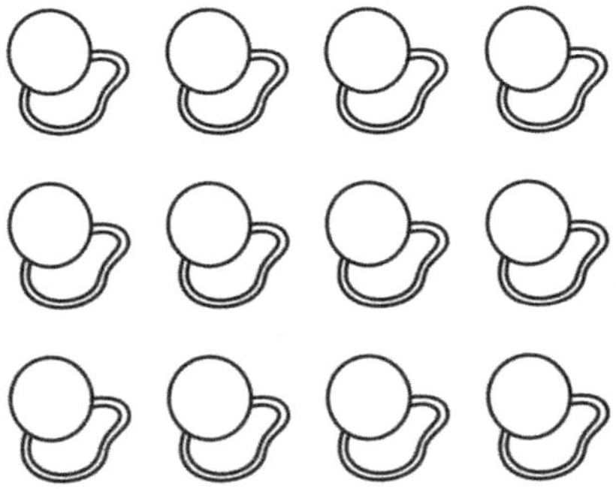

1 10 3 1s	1 10 2 1s
1 10 6 1s	1 10 9 u1s

4

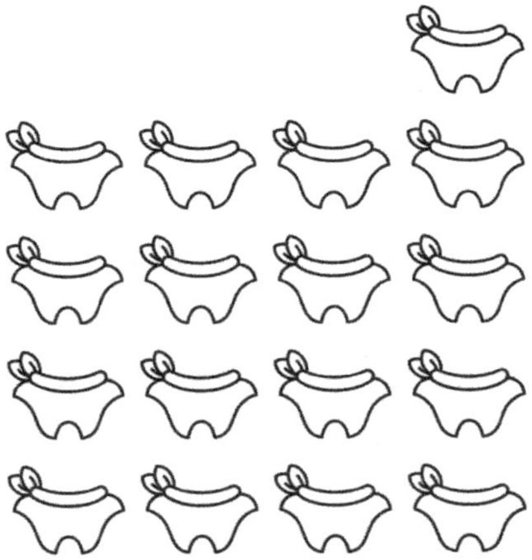

7 1s	1 10 7 1s
1 10 6 1s	1 10 9 1s

5

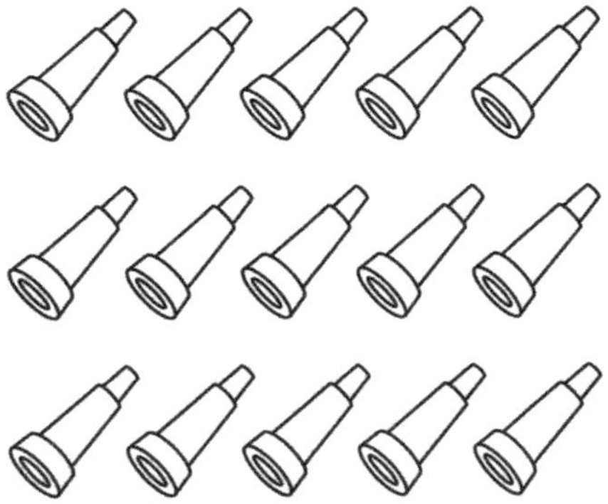

1 10 3 1s	1 10 4 1s
1 10 5 1s	2 10 0 1s

6

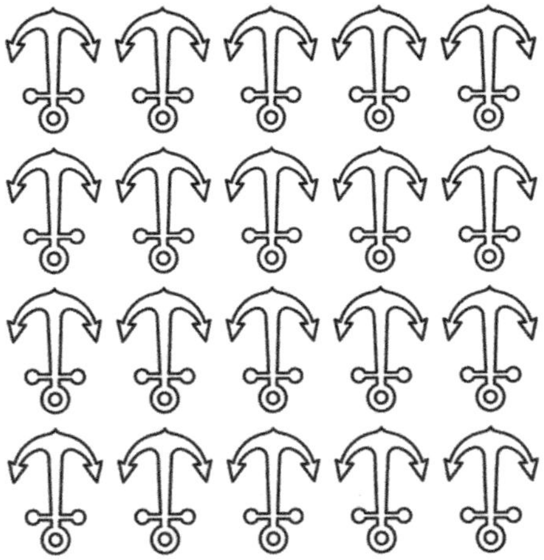

2 10s 0 1s	0 10s 2 1s
1 10 6 1s	1 10 9 1s

7

How did it go? Compare your work with a classmate's to see if everything is correct. How did you feel?

8

Necklaces of 10s and 1s

10s **1s**

52

Print how many 10s and how many 1s there are.

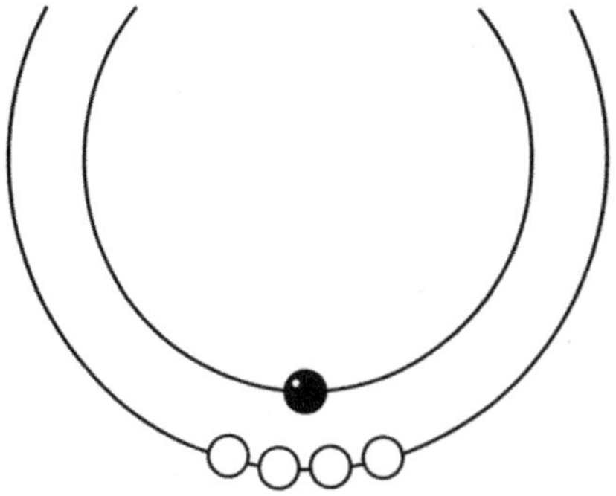

____ **10s**

____ **1s**

Do as on the previous page.

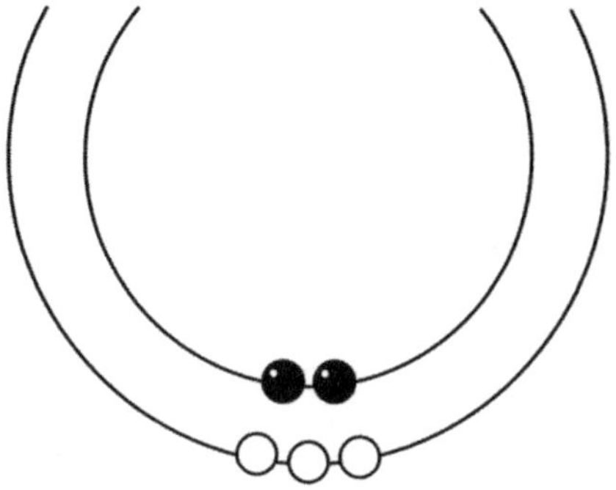

____ **10s**

____ **1s**

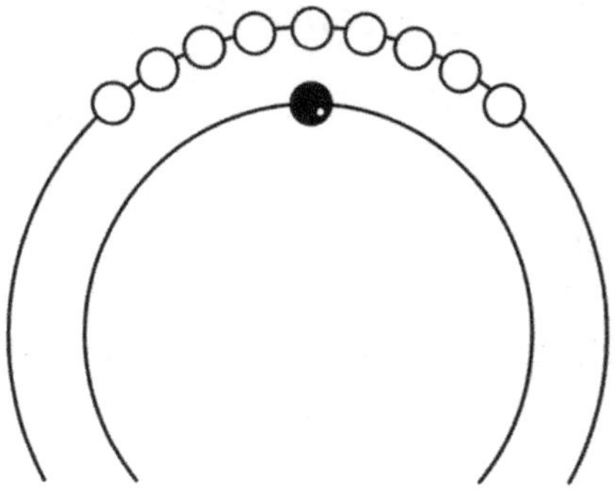

10s ____

1s ____

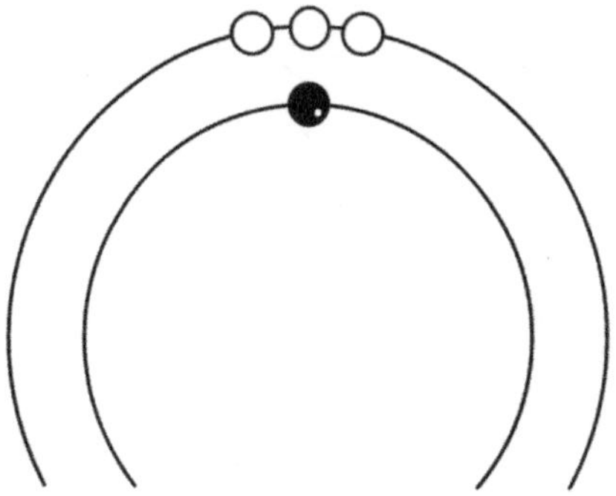

10s ____

1s ____

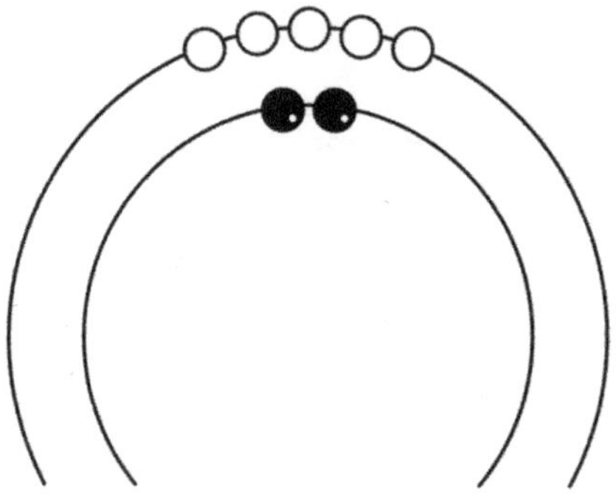

10s ____

1s ____

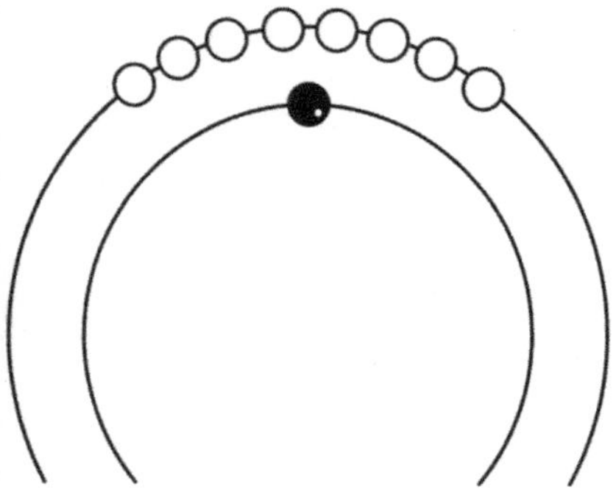

10s ____

1s ____

How did it go? Compare with a classmate to see if everything is correct. How did you feel?

FILL THE BASKET TO GET 10 APPLES

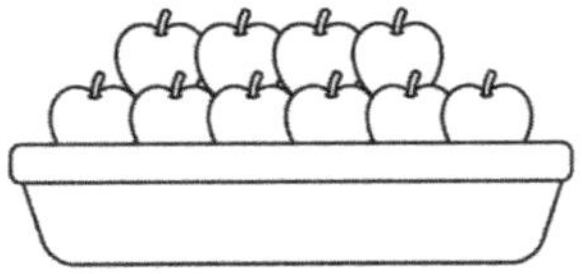

Look at the basket, draw the apples you need to get to 10, and complete the page.

You can use the shaded and non-shaded circles to solve the problem.

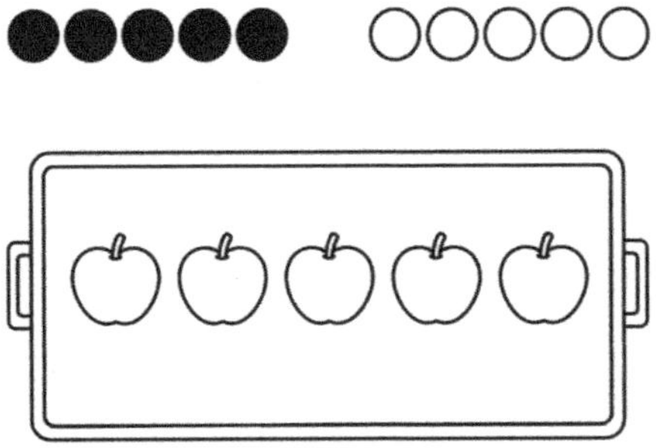

Apples in the basket

Apples

2

Complete as before.

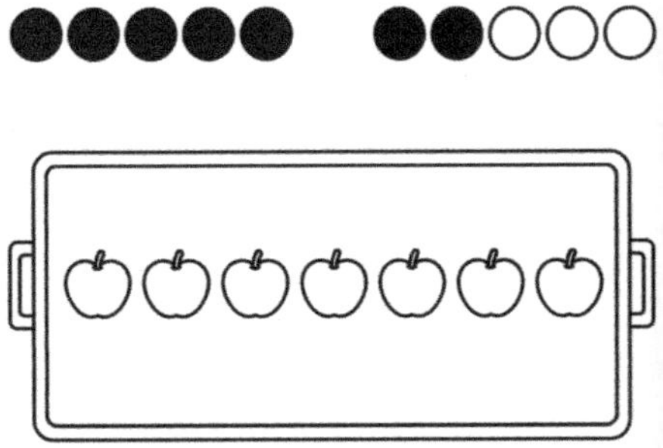

Apples in the basket

Apples

3

Complete as before.

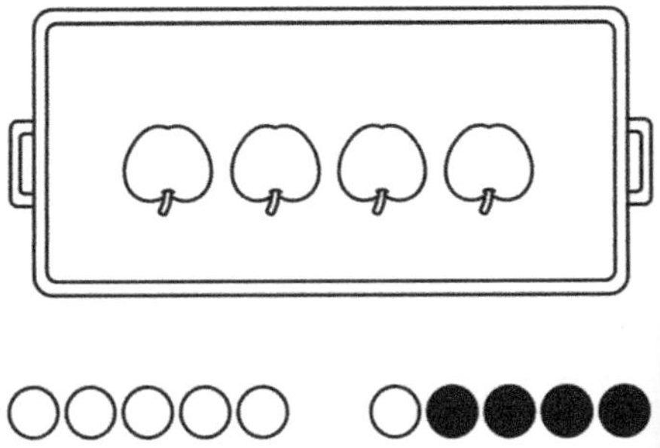

Apples in the basket

Apples

4

Complete as before.

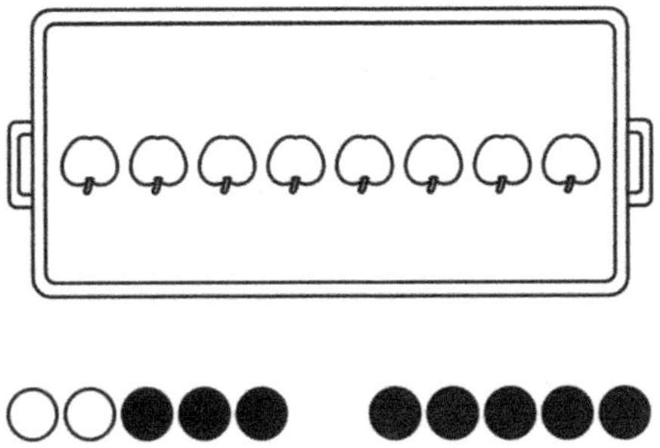

Apples in the basket

Apples

5

Complete as before.

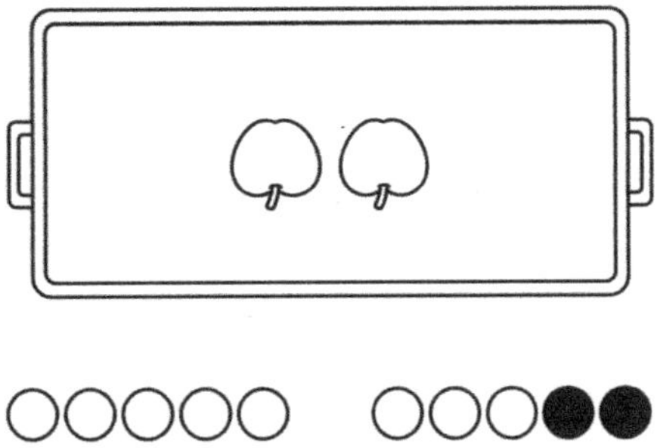

Apples in the basket

Apples

6

Complete as before.

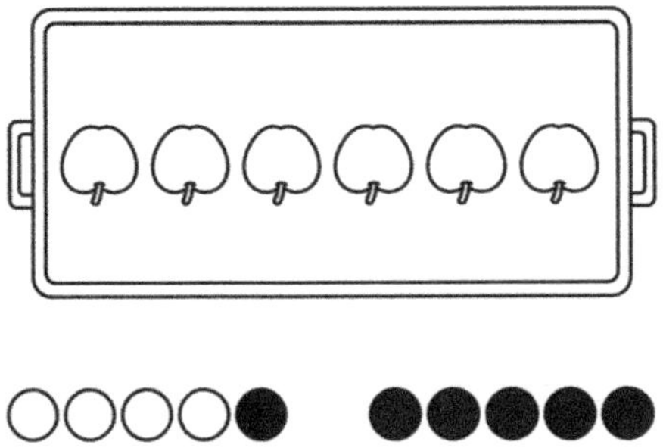

Apples in the basket

Apples

7

Complete as before.

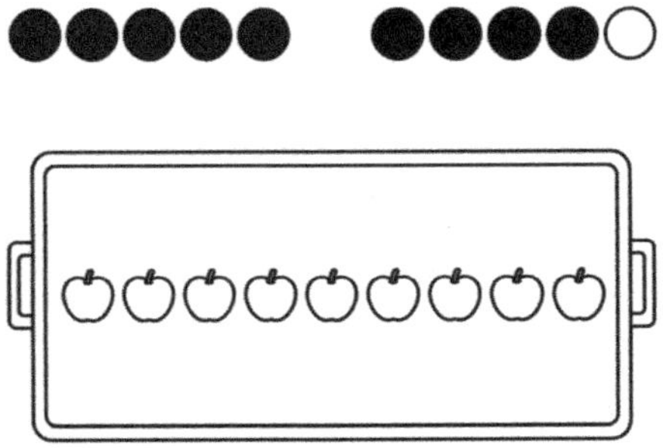

Apples in the basket

Apples

8

CARDS OF 10

Color the numbers that together make 10 (friends of 10) with the same color.

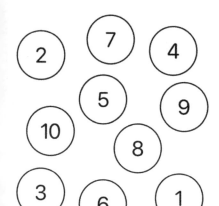

2 7 4 5 9 10 8 3 6 1

5 5

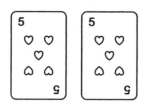

Fill in the blank card to get to 10 and write the number below.

1st Card	2nd Card	1st Card	2nd Card
6		3	
6	___	3	___

1st Card	2nd Card	1st Card	2nd Card
9		8	
9	___	8	___

1st Card	2nd Card	1st Card	2nd Card
9			
9	___	___	___

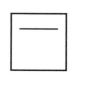

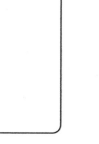

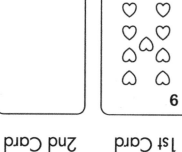

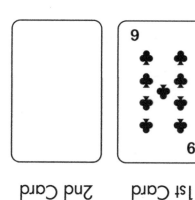

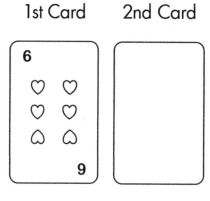

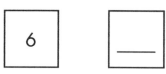

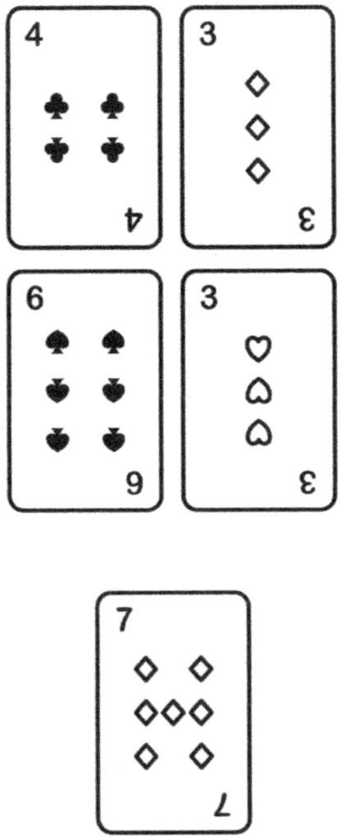

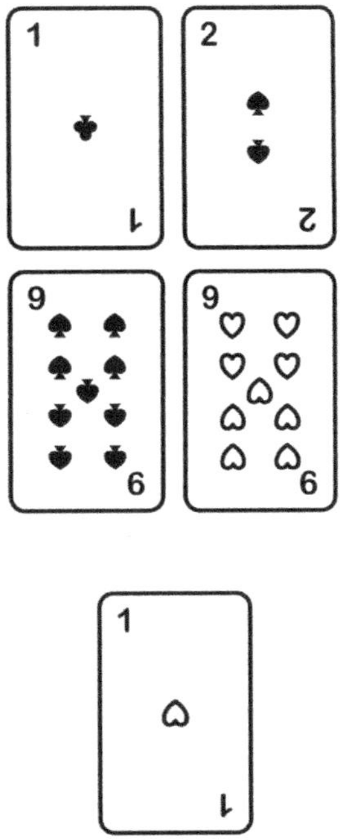

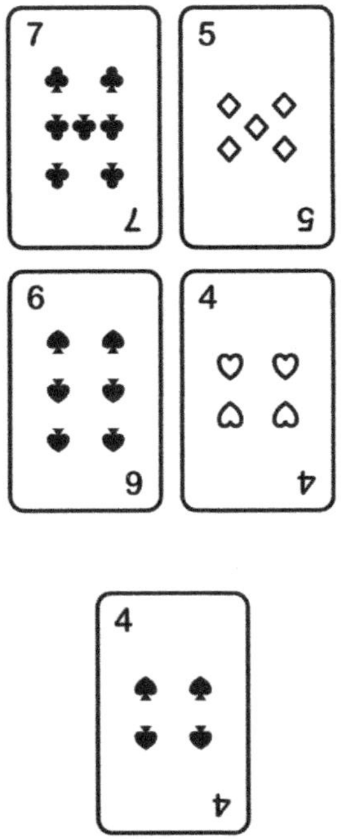

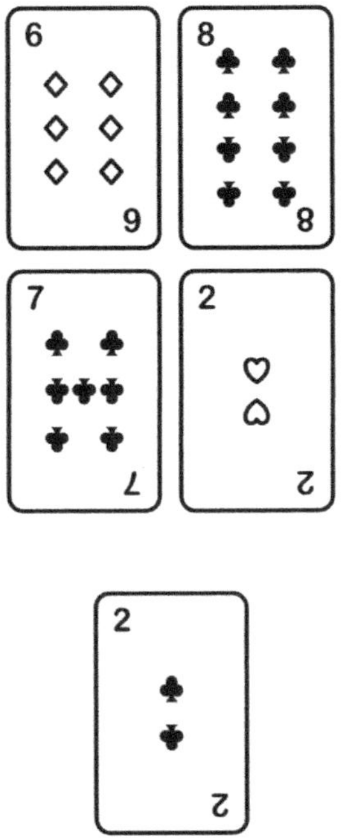

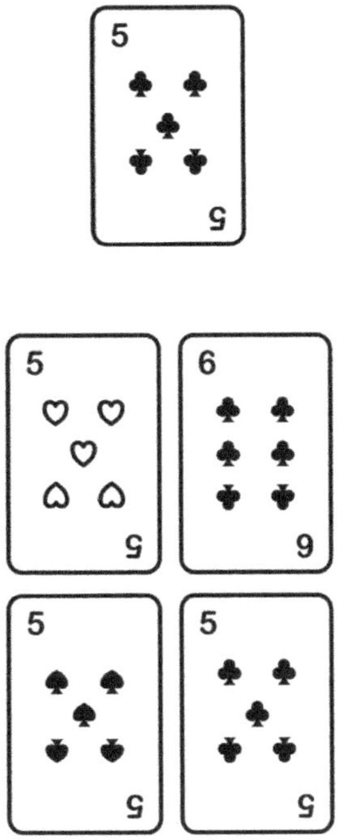

FRIENDS OF 10

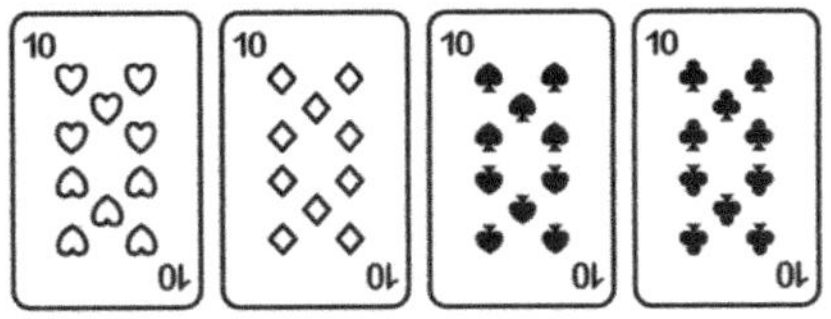

Look at the top card and match it with a card of the same symbol (suit) to make 10.

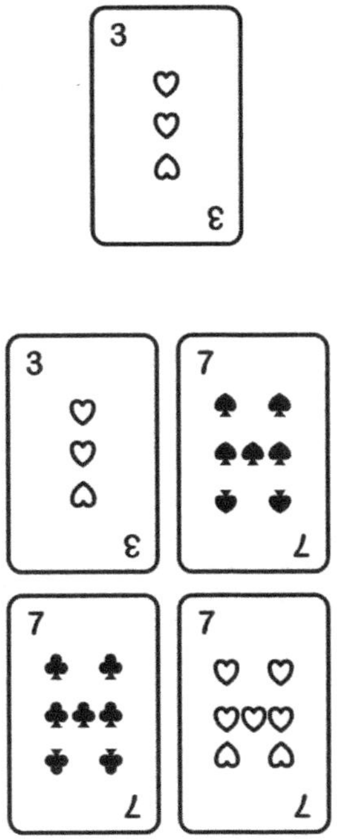

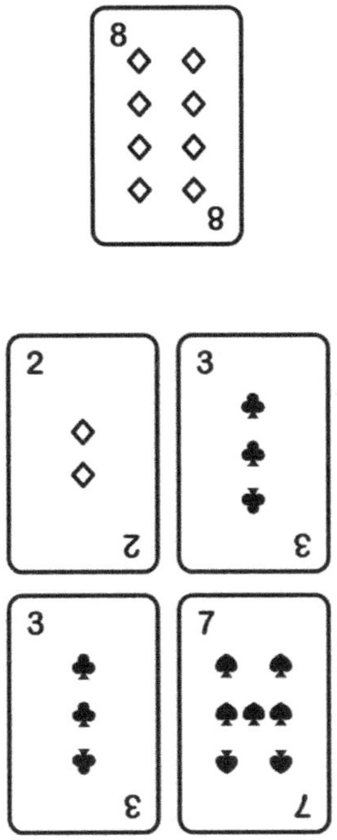

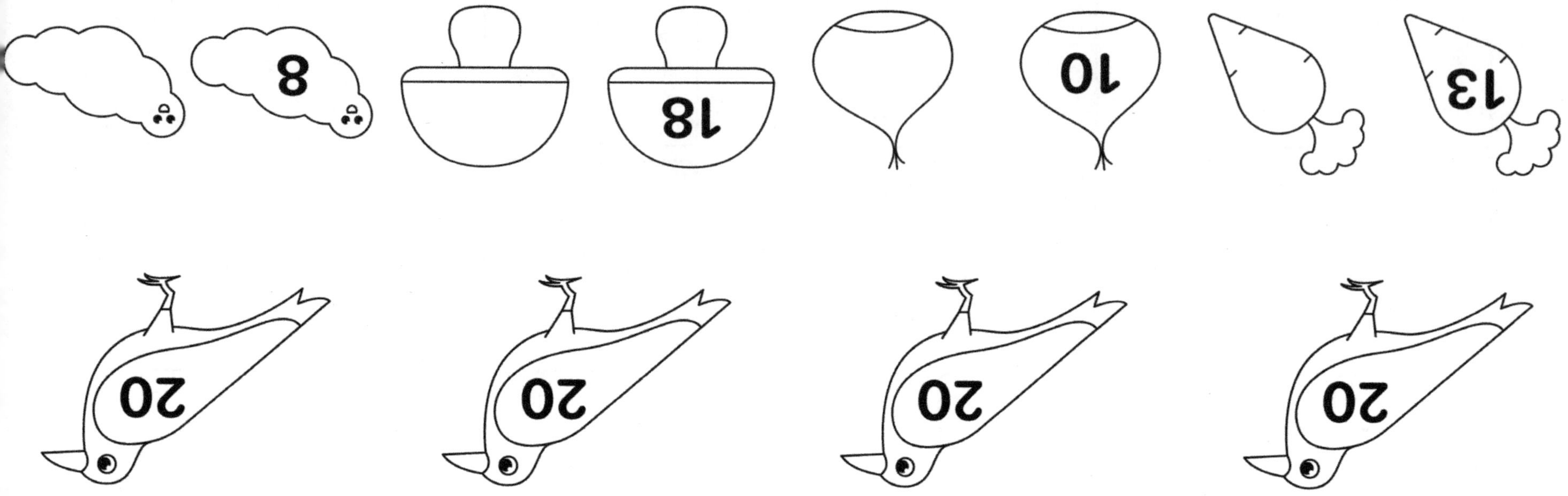

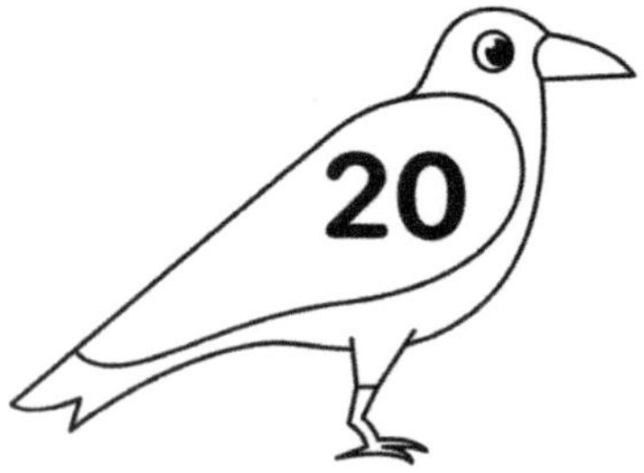

THE BIRD EATS 20

On each page look at the number and write what number is needed to get to 20.

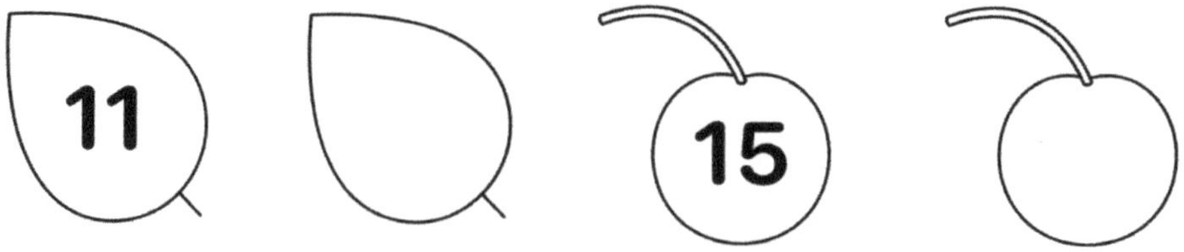

7 6 5 4

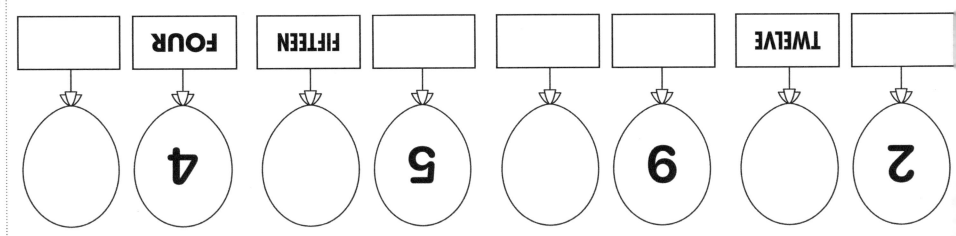

	FOUR	FIFTEEN				TWELVE	
	4		5		9		2

10 MORE

Look at the given number and write the number that is 10 more. Write the number as a digit in the balloon, and using letters in the label below.

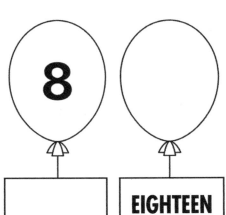

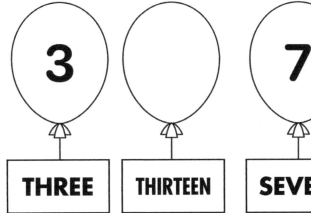

8		3		7	
	EIGHTEEN	THREE	THIRTEEN	SEVEN	

Addition & Subtraction to 20

STUDENT	ADDITION & SUBTRACTION TO 20			
	Addition (Sum to 10)	Addition (Sum to 20)	Subtraction (Difference to 10)	Subtraction (Difference to 20)

ADDITION AND SUBTRACTION TO 20

Addition and Subtraction to 20

When children begin counting, they often use concrete supports such as fingers or objects and may do oral counting. They use similar supports when they begin to add and subtract. As students become more confident with addition and subtraction, they begin to use more efficient strategies. Siegler and Mitchell (in Lucangeli et al., 2003) highlight that the confidence level of children plays a significant role in the decisions they make when carrying out addition and subtraction. Eventually children abandon concrete supports and strategies for more traditional visuals and symbols.

Students are introduced to new and more efficient strategies as their learning develops. While students initially count their fingers for each number being added, they eventually learn to count on from the largest addend, requiring less effort. Students are also introduced to new vocabulary associated with addition and subtraction symbols, developing their understanding of these concepts. Traditionally addition is accompanied by words such as "put together," "all together," "combine," and "add"; and subtraction uses words such as "remove," "take away," "difference," and "left over." However, it must be noted that such words (as listed in the previous sentence) does not mean that it is an addition or subtraction problem. When working with children, the teacher should reinforce that they shouldn't rely on a key word to determine the operation. It is the meaning of the problem that signifies the operation to select.

As children develop their number sense, their understanding of concepts involving numbers will become more automatic (such as "make ten") and will become strategies they use to understand and support more complex concepts. This automaticity will build a bank of known math facts that students recall quickly and ably. Research shows that fact recall is an indicator of mathematical achievement.

NOTES FROM THE CLASSROOM

Addition and subtraction are introduced in Kindergarten through Grade 2 and are continued in subsequent grades. Students' conceptual understanding of addition and subtraction in primary grades forms the foundation for operational fluency.

The workshops and minibooks presented in this section provide students with opportunities to practice addition and subtraction.

Students will have opportunities to engage with addition and subtraction both in and out of the context of the classroom. These opportunities allow students to have intentional practice of concepts that they will continue to engage with over their years in school.

Addition and subtraction is often emphasized as a mathematical area that requires additional support to aid students. Addition and subtraction to 20 lays the groundwork for students to work with whole numbers, and decimal numbers in later grades. As support, you'll find a tracking form (pg 90) that highlights the key learning areas within addition and subtraction to 20: addition to 10; addition to 20; subtraction to 10; and subtraction to 20. Teachers can use this form to monitor student learning within the key learning areas and can use the information gathered to guide instruction.

Bibliography

Lucangeli D., Poli S. and Molin A. (2003), *L'intelligenza numerica – Volume 1*, Trento, Erickson.

AT THE NURSERY

Goal

Introduce the concept of sum as a combination of quantities through a real-world task.

Materials and Resources

- Sheets, pencils, colors, price tags, black permanent marker
- Small section of school garden or large box/pot with soil to create a mini school garden

Directions

Discuss how you and the class will be designing a small school garden, and that part of this experience involves deciding which seeds, plants, and/or bulbs will be purchased. Provide the class with a budget for the garden ($20 or less).

Brainstorm with the children what will be possible to buy and what is worth buying for their garden based on the allocated budget. Visit a website or look through flyers to determine the prices of various seeds, plants, and/or bulbs (be mindful to round prices to the nearest dollar). Ask the children to record the numbers of the products of interest on a sheet of paper and add them one at a time to your "shopping basket." Check that the total does not exceed the starting budget.

Once children decide on what to purchase, encourage them to design and draw their garden (either virtually or paper/pencil/crayon). Students can then share their design with school administration.

THROWING CANS

Goal

Start the concept of subtraction as a reduction of a quantity, starting from a basic quantity (10 in a first phase, 20 in an advanced phase). avanzata).

Materials and Resources

- Recycled or clean tin cans
- Two tennis balls
- Paper and pen for recording scores (set per team)

Directions

Ask children to bring empty tin cans to school.
Divide the class into two groups. In front of each group, place ten cans on a desk. Arrange the cans in a pyramid formation, one on top of the other. This will be the target for the throw.
Members of each group take turns throwing a tennis ball at the tin can pyramid target. Their goal will be to knock down as many cans as possible. Record the starting point as 10. Each can knocked over by a throw is recorded as minus 1 (-1). Each player's team records how many cans were knocked down by the throw and write it as a subtraction sentence. Each member gets a chance to throw the ball. The team that scores the smallest answer most often wins.
After students do well with this challenge, gradually add more cans until you are creating pyramids of 20 cans.

7

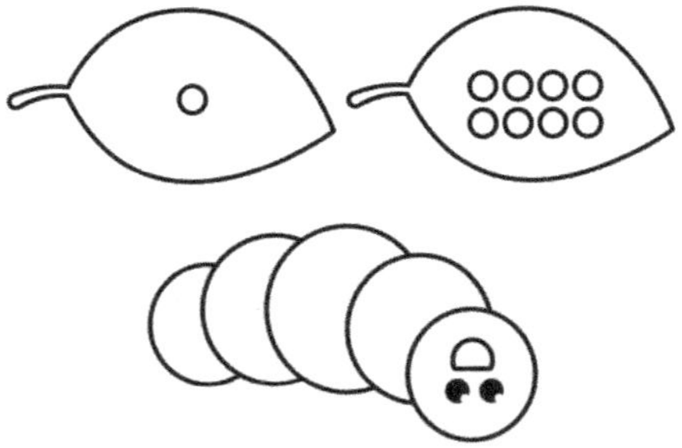

8 + 1 = ____

6

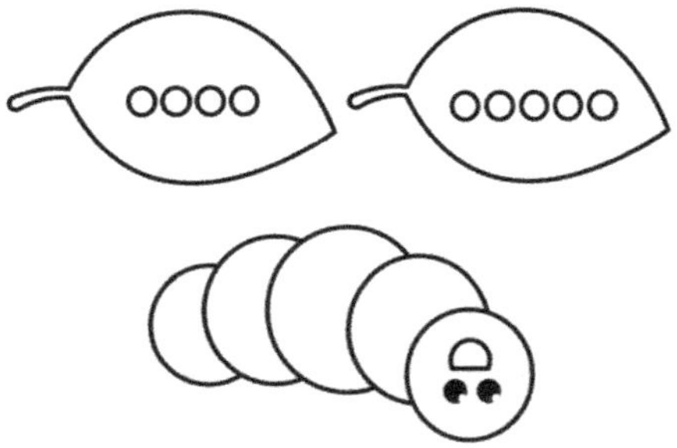

5 + 4 = ____

5

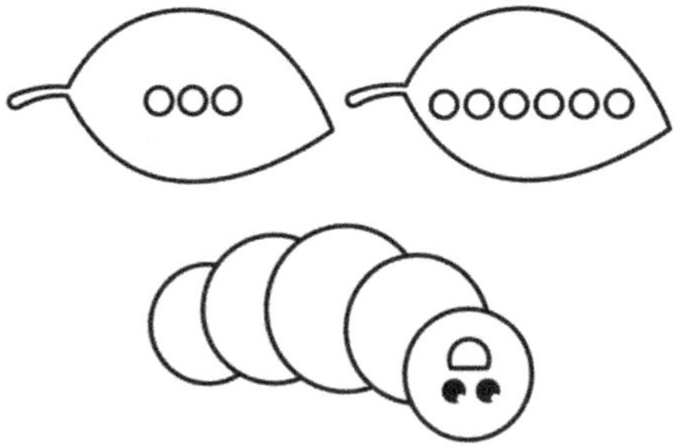

6 + 3 = ____

4

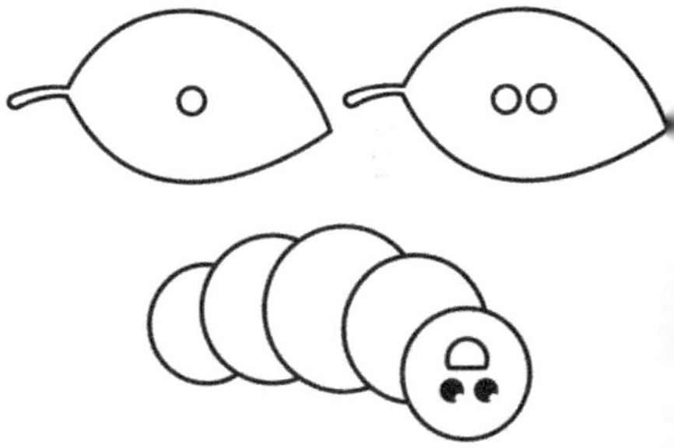

2 + 1 = ____

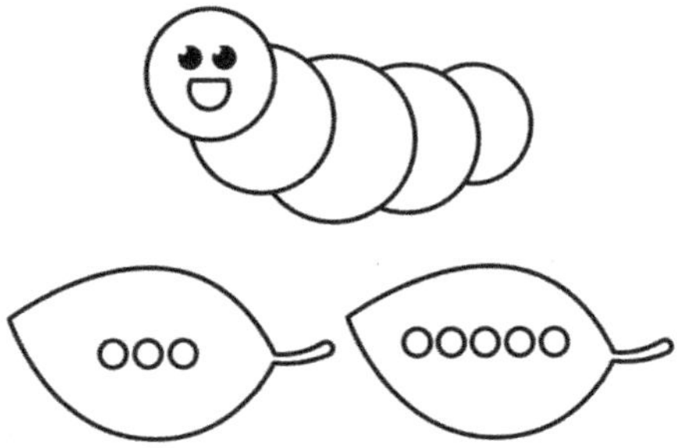

3 + 5 = ____

8

EGGS ON A LEAF

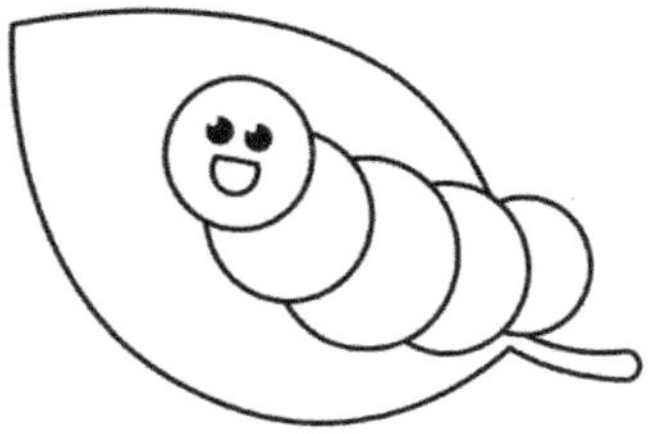

Count the eggs on the leaves and add them together. Write the sum.

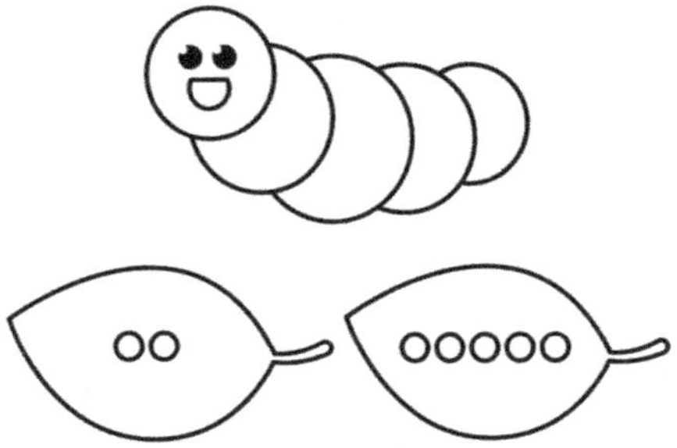

2 + 5 = ____

2

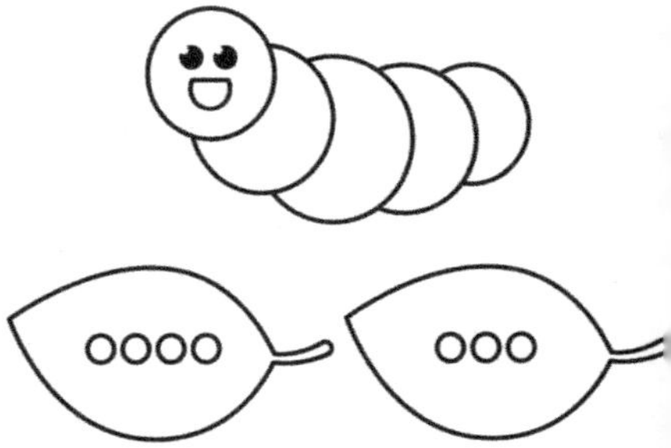

4 + 3 = ____

3

ADDING WITH DOUBLES

1 + 1 = ____

Find the sum. Color the drawings.

2 + 2 = ____

2

3 + 3 = ____

3

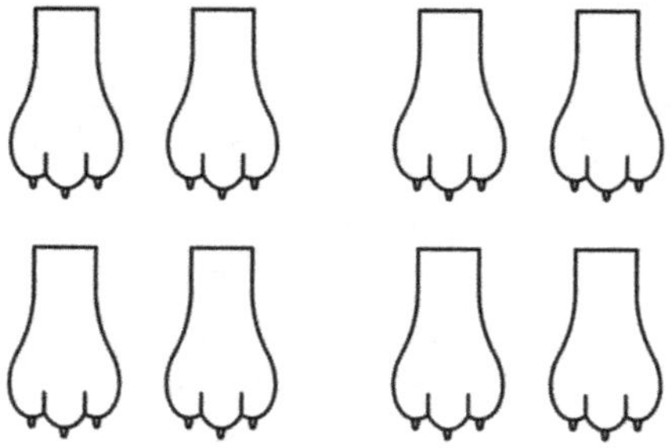

4 + 4 = ____

4

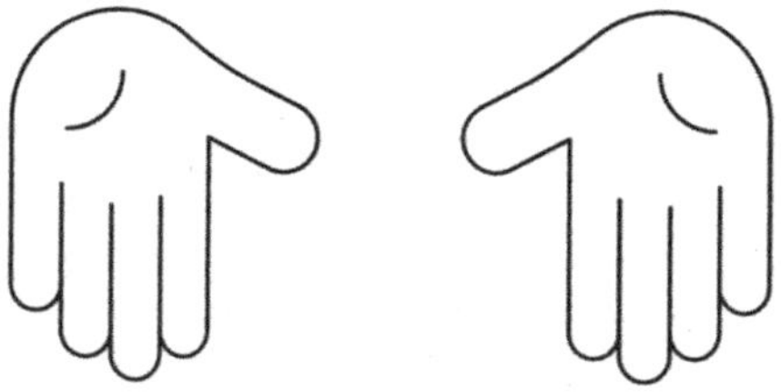

5 + 5 = ____

5

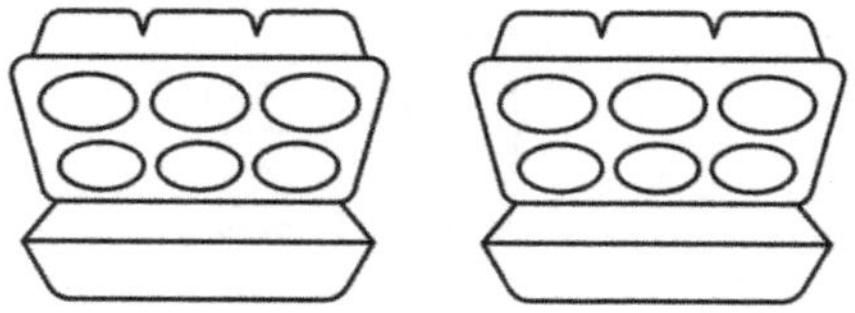

6 + 6 = ____

6

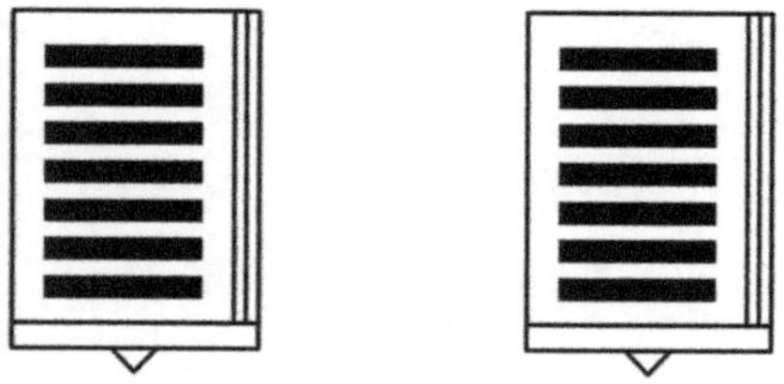

7 + 7 = ____

7

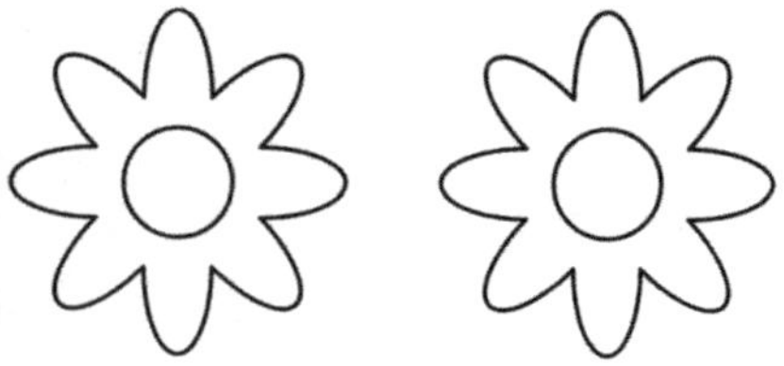

8 + 8 = ____

8

LEAPING FROG

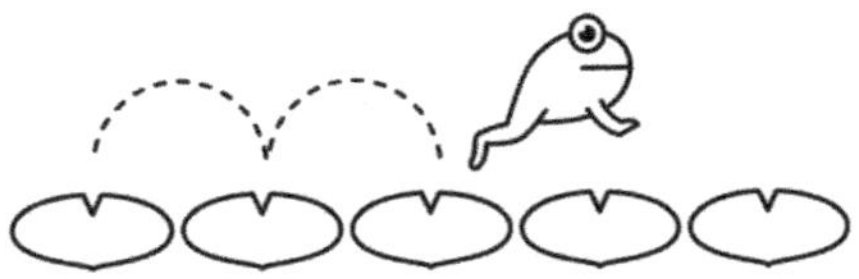

Look at where the frog starts and how many leaves forward it jumps. Record the end point. Find the sum.

2

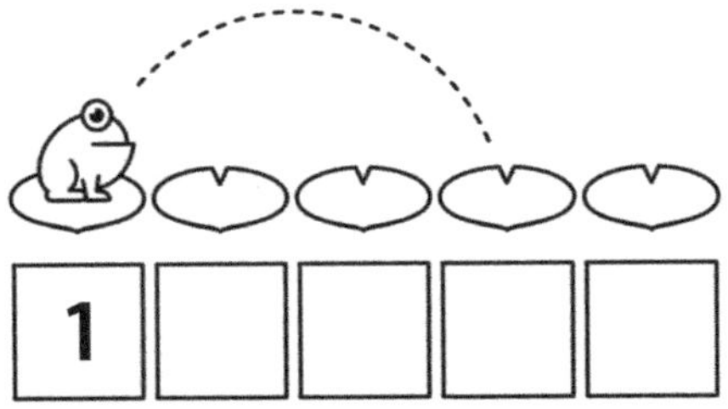

1 + 3 = ____

3

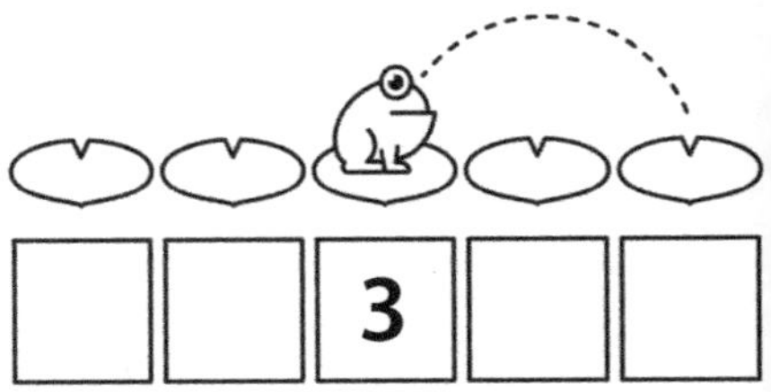

3 + 2 = ____

4

4 + 3 = ____

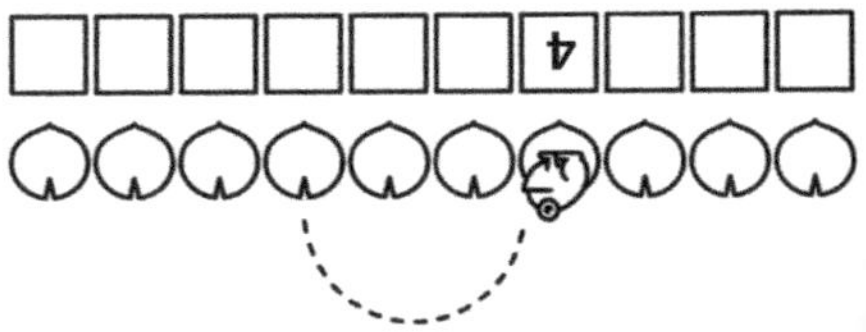

5

2 + 7 = ____

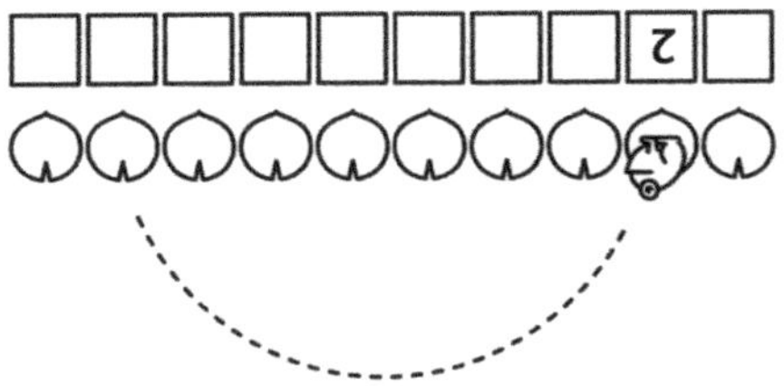

6

5 + 4 = ____

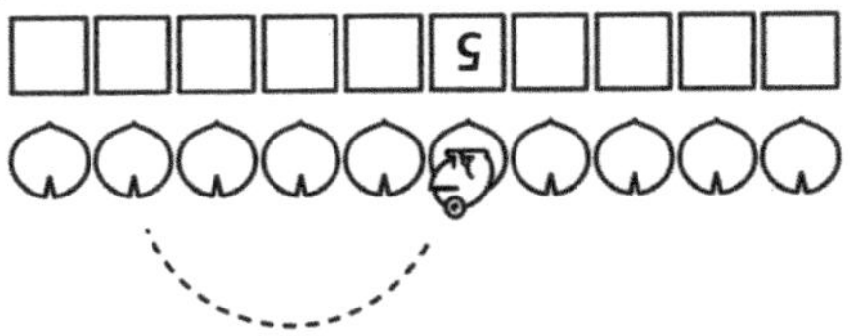

7

3 + 7 = ____

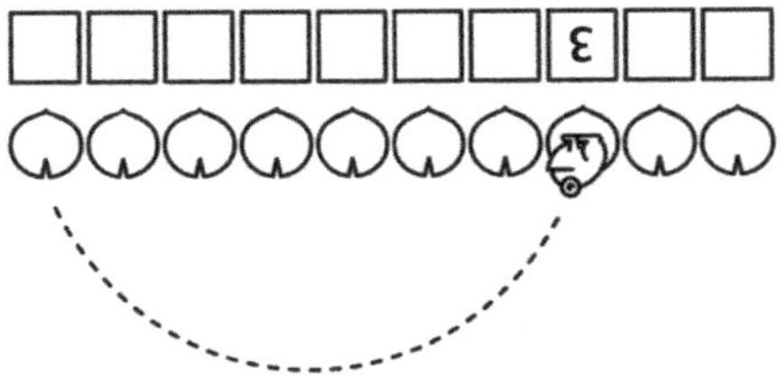

8

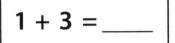

6 + 4 = ____

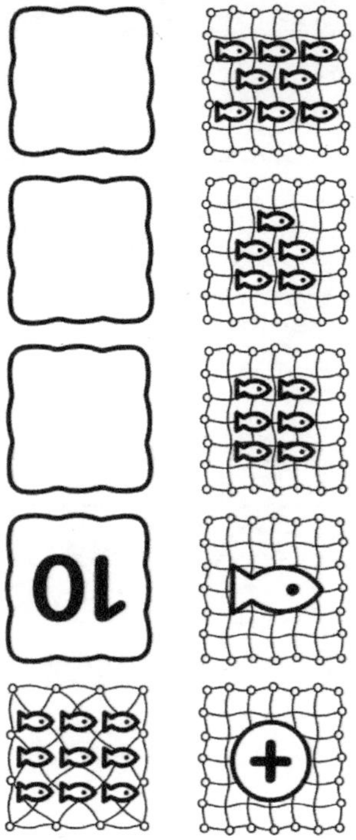

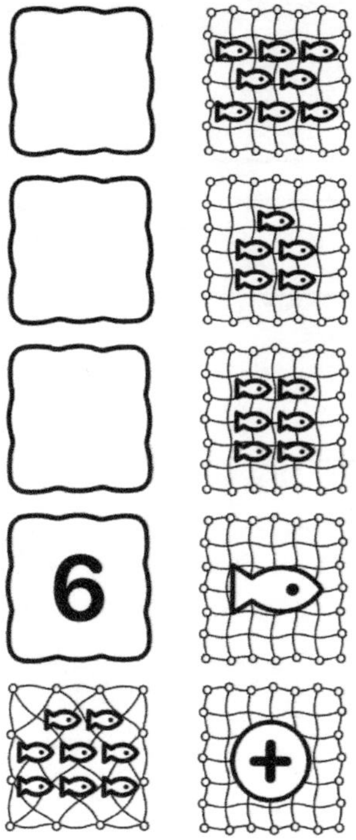

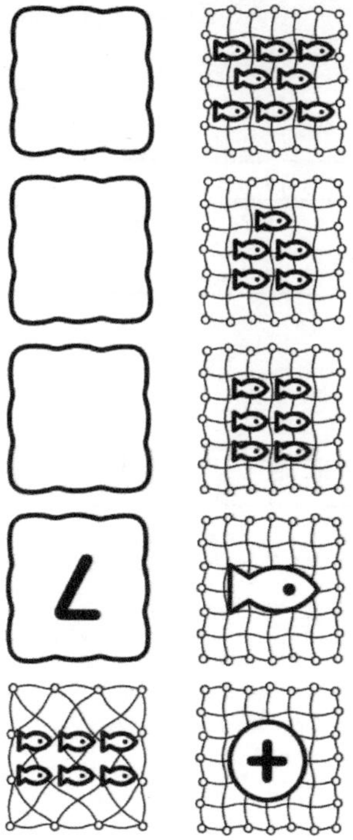

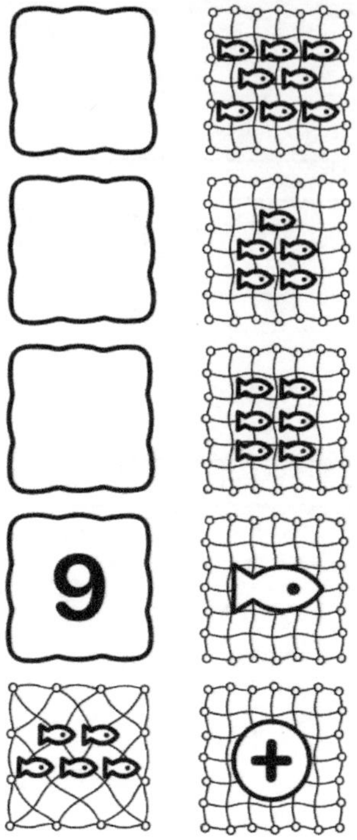

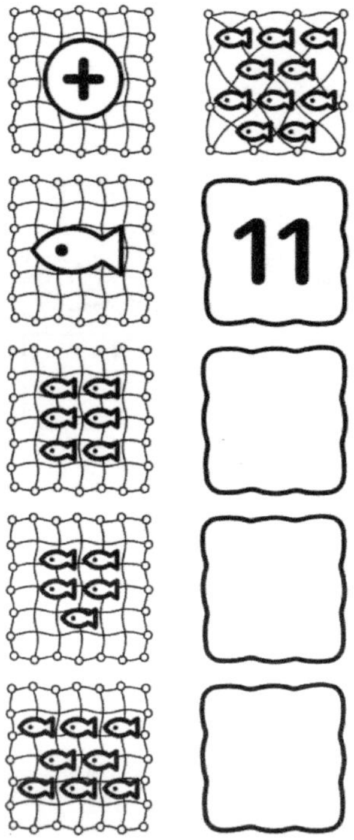

FISH IN THE NET

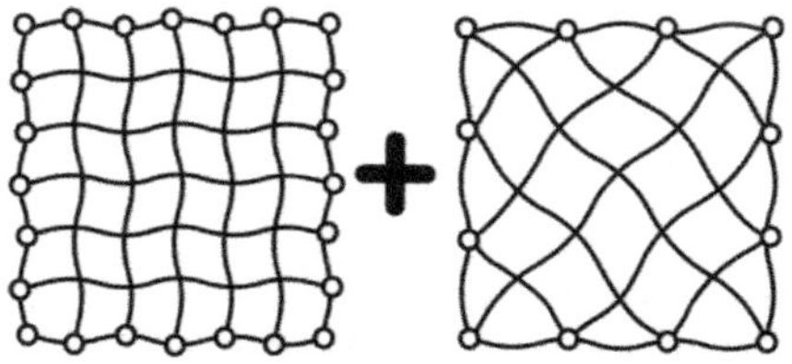

Complete the table. Add the fish in the first column to the fish at the top of the second column. The first sum is done for you as an example.

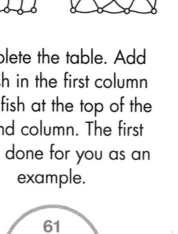

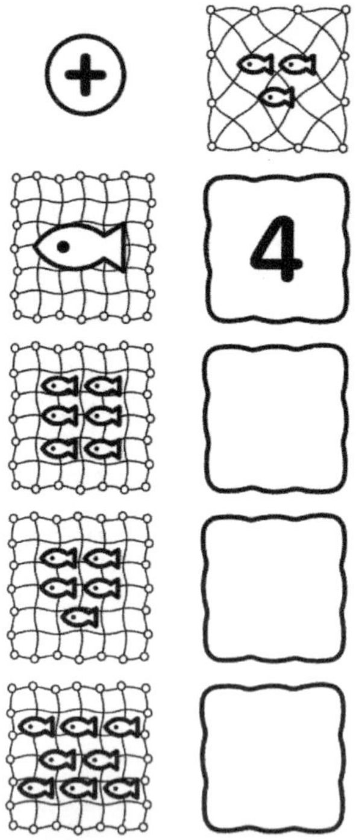

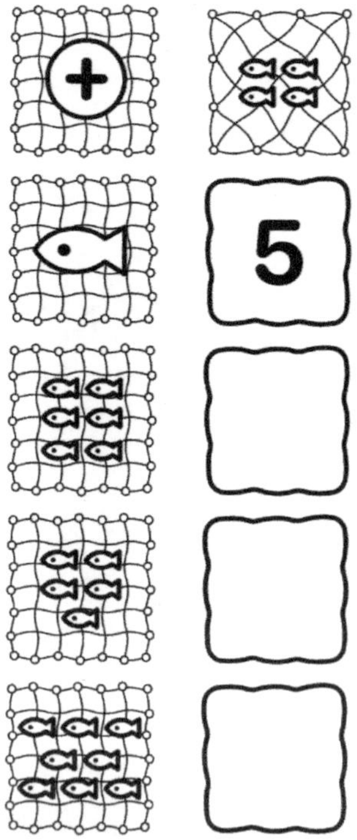

UNDERGROUND ADDITIONS

Complete the diagram with the missing number.

Complete with the missing number: the horizontal sum must equal the vertical sum.

Complete as on the previous page.

Complete as on the previous page.

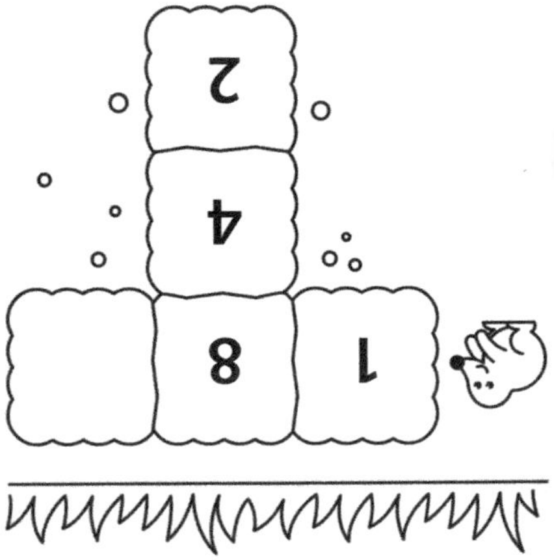

Complete as on the previous page.

Complete with the missing number: the vertical sum must be equal to the horizontal sum.

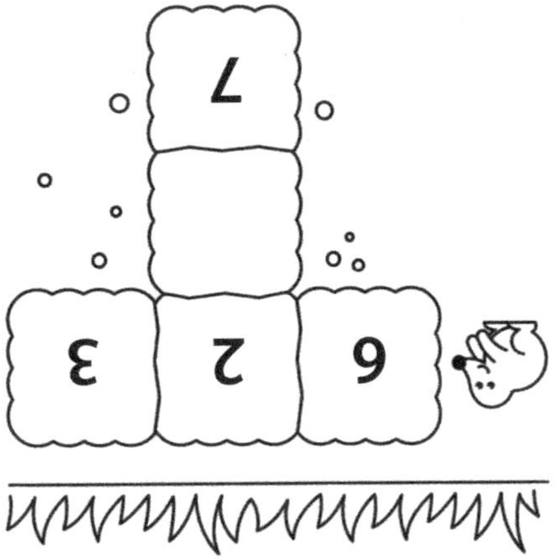

Complete as on the previous page.

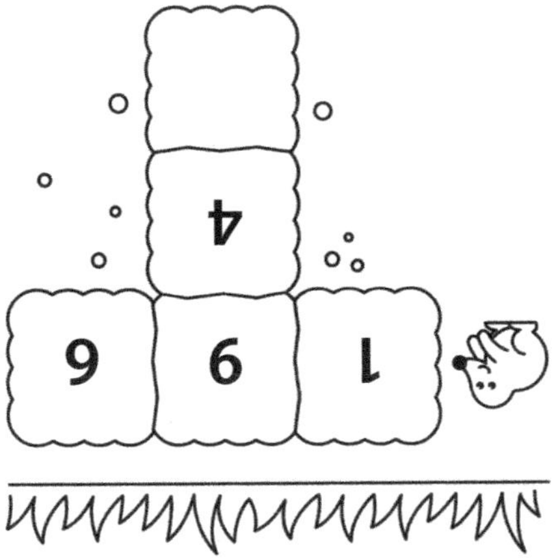

Come up with your own numbers, remembering that the vertical sum must be the same as the horizontal sum.

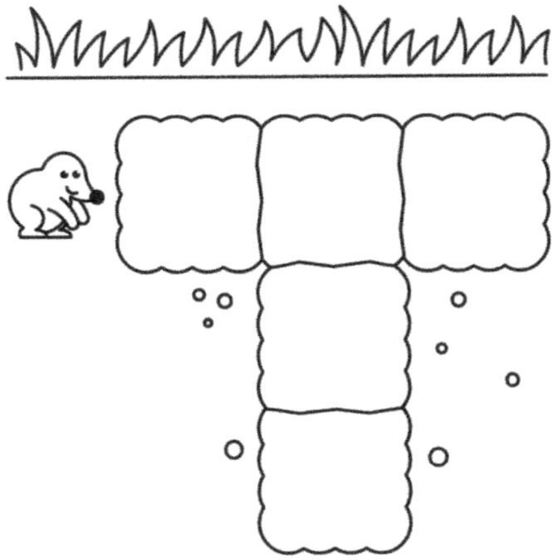

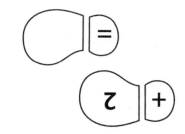

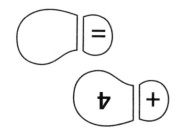

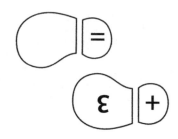

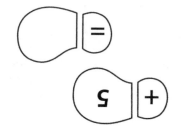

ADD AND FOLLOW THE FOOTPRINTS

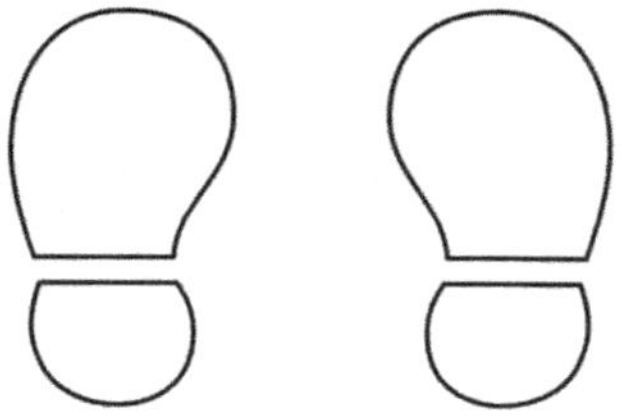

Add the numbers contained in the footprints and get to the treasure.

The sum continues from page to page.

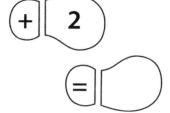

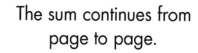

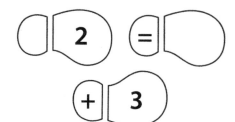

2 + 3 =

+ 2 =

+ 3 =

+ 5 =

+ 2 =

+ 4 =

+ 6 =

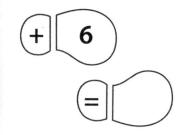

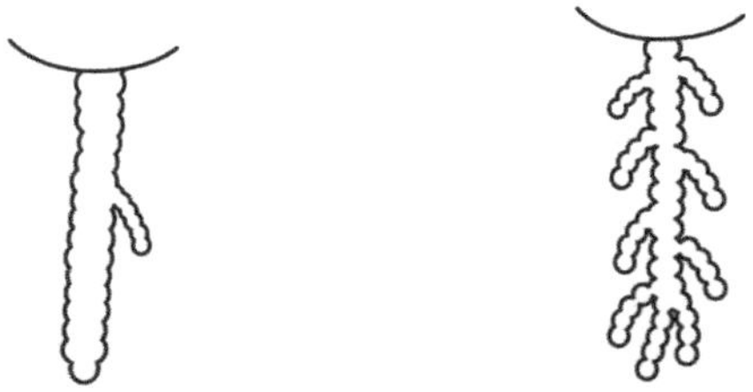

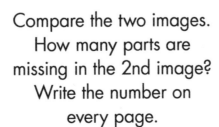

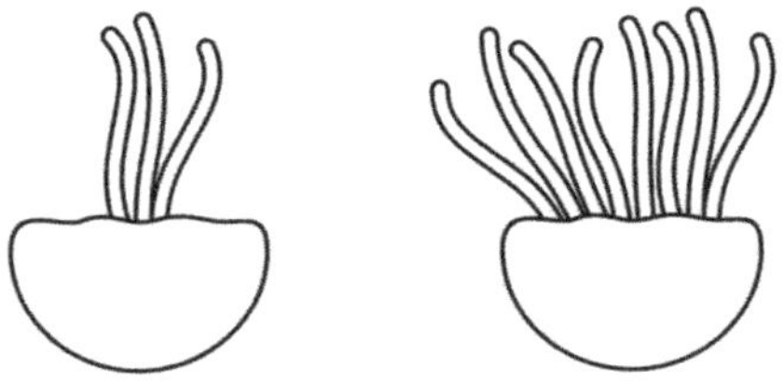

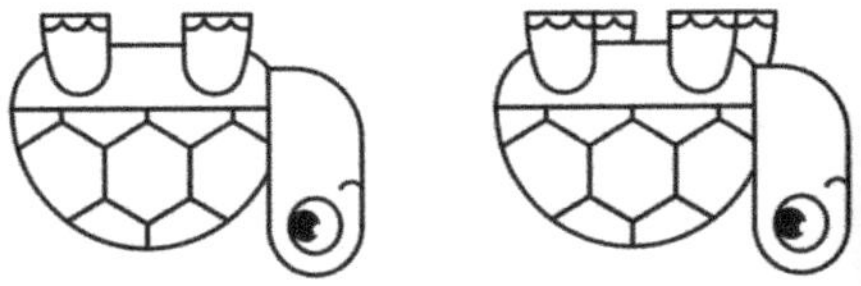

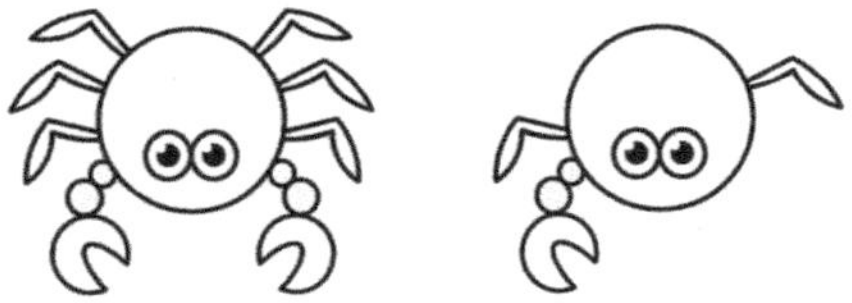

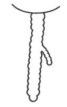

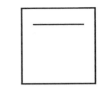

MISSING PARTS

Compare the two images.
How many parts are
missing in the 2nd image?
Write the number on
every page.

SUBTRACTION ON FINGERS

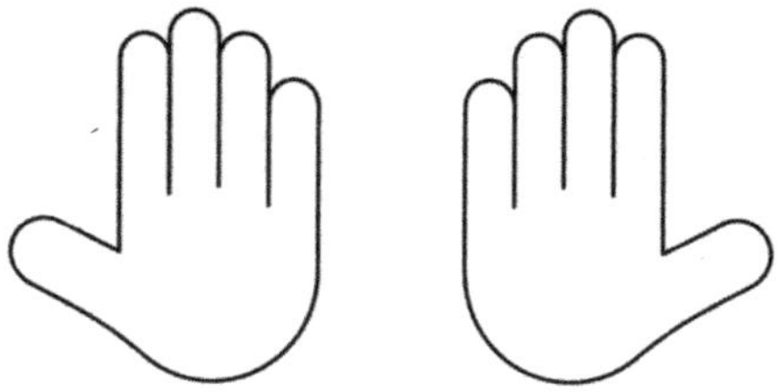

Look at the drawing and color the matching subtraction.

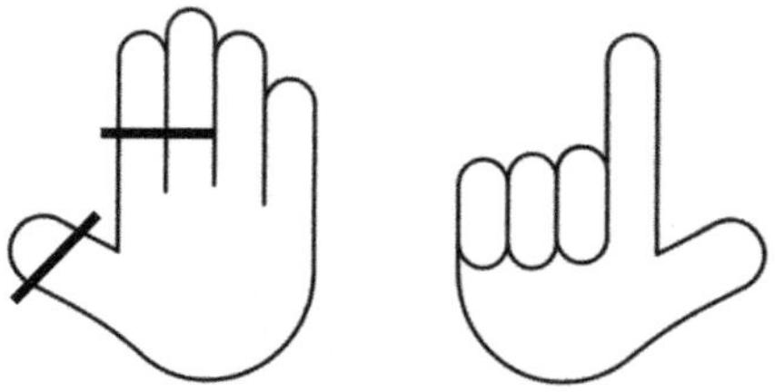

5 – 2 = 3
7 – 3 = 4

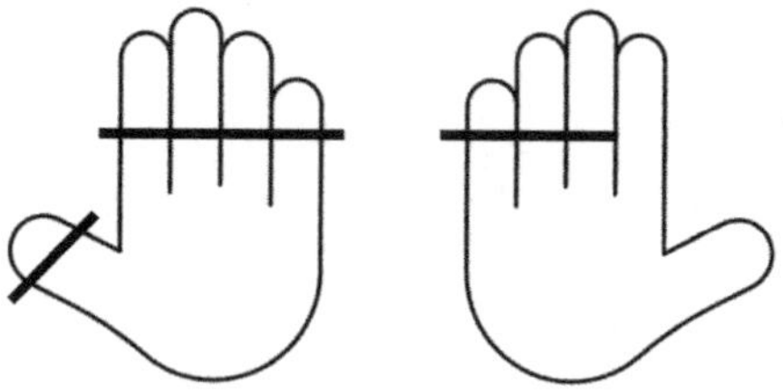

10 – 8 = 2
8 – 6 = 2

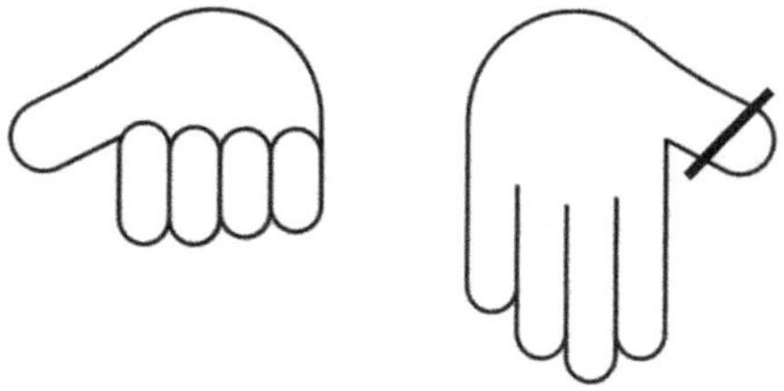

10 – 5 = 5
6 – 1 = 5

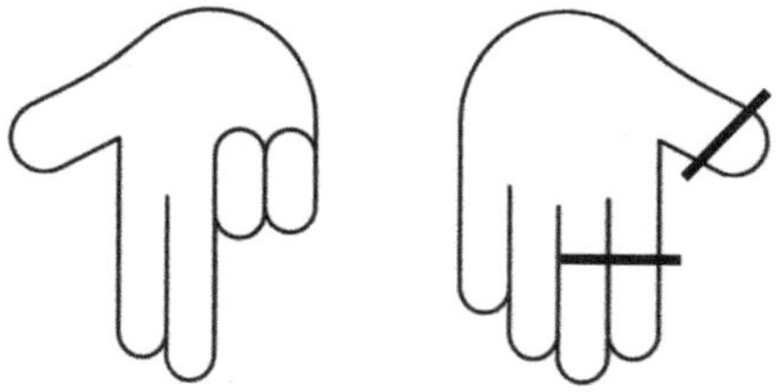

8 – 3 = 5
8 – 5 = 3

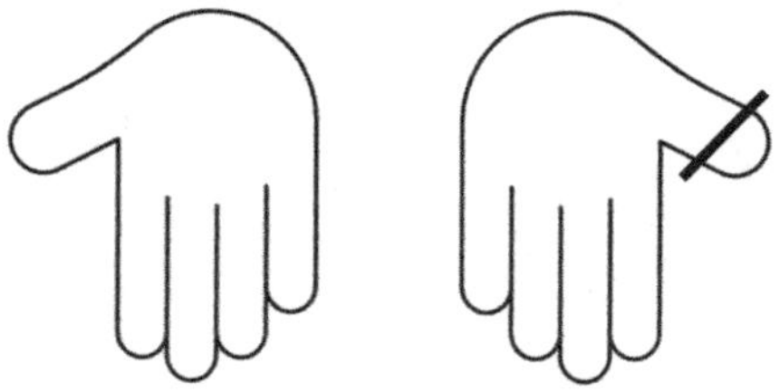

10 – 1 = 9
6 – 1 = 5

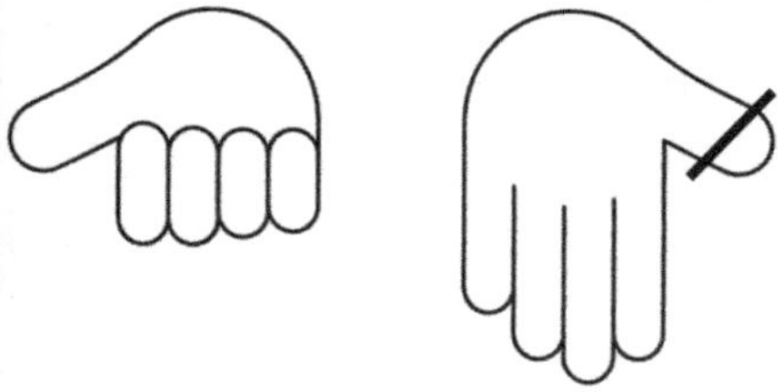

10 – 5 = 5
6 – 1 = 5

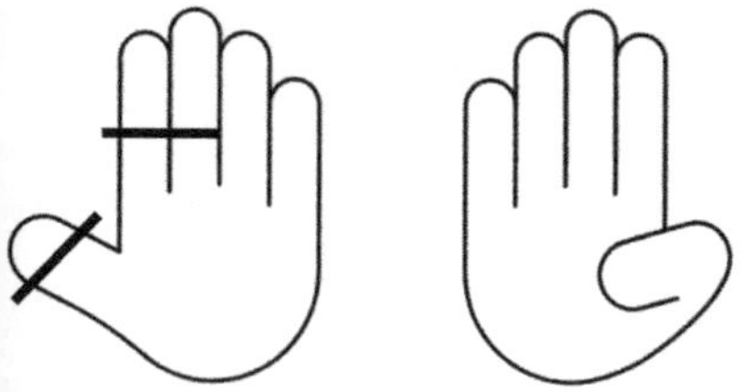

9 – 3 = 6
8 – 2 = 6

CRICKET JUMPS BACK

Look where the cricket is on the number line. Go back as many steps as indicated by the dice. What number does the cricket land on?

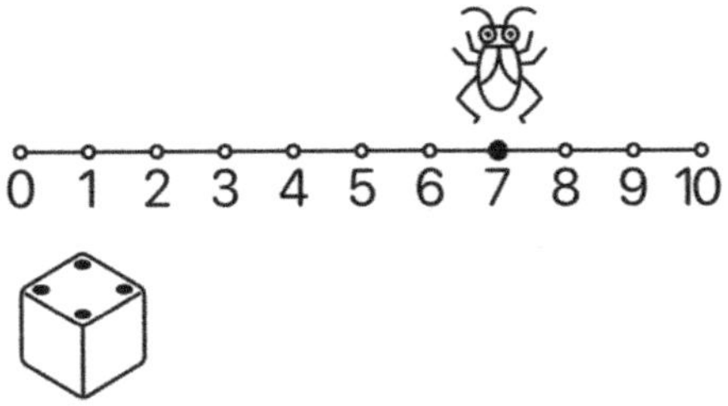

7 – 4 = ____

2

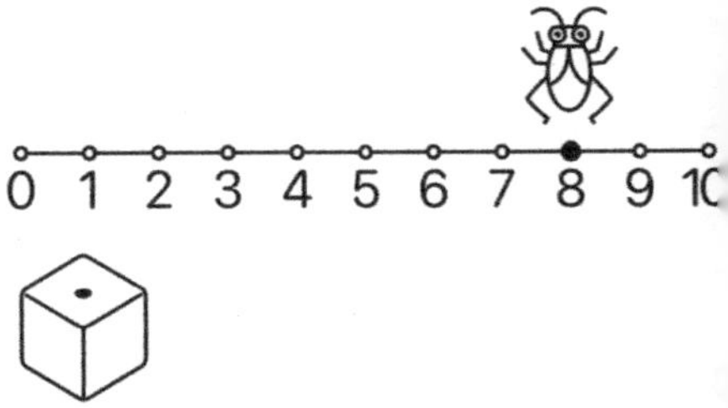

8 – 1 = ____

3

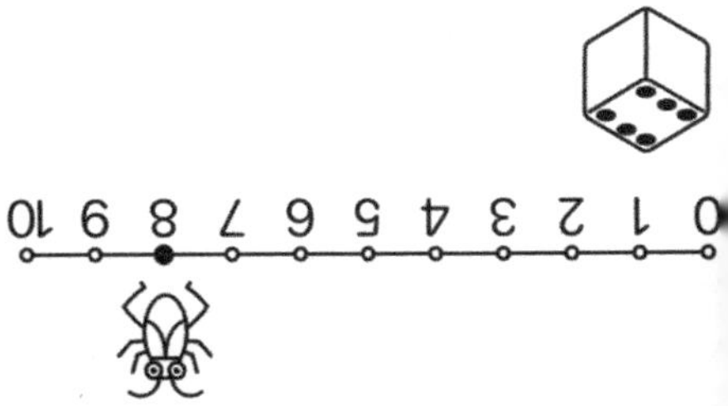

8 – 6 = ____

4

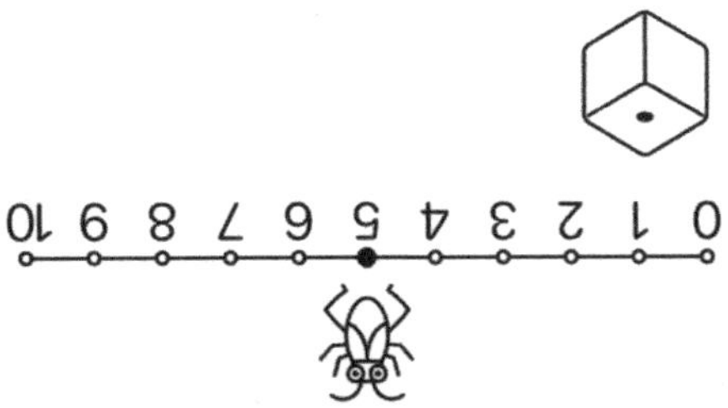

5 – 1 = ____

5

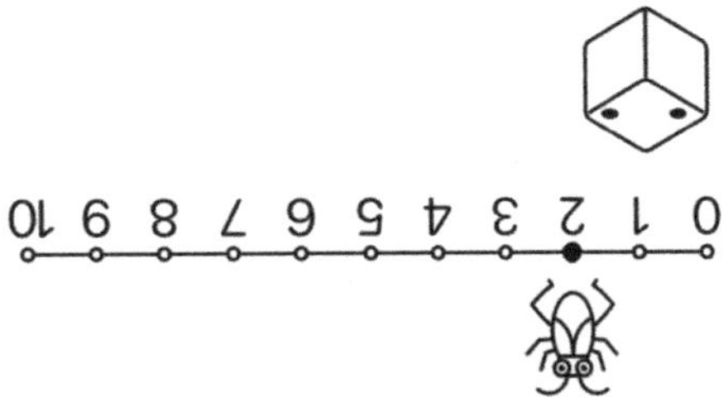

2 – 2 = ____

6

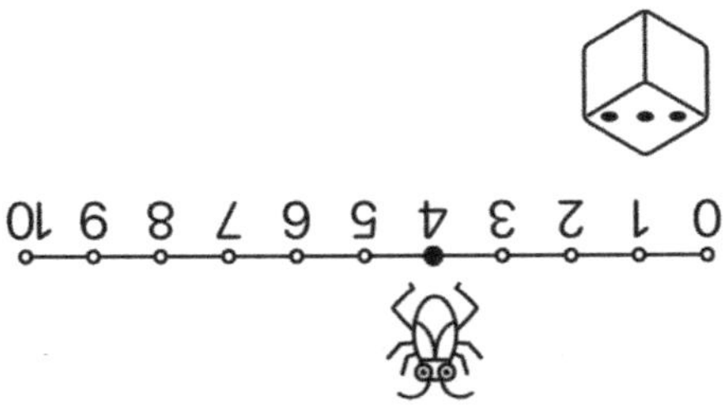

4 – 3 = ____

7

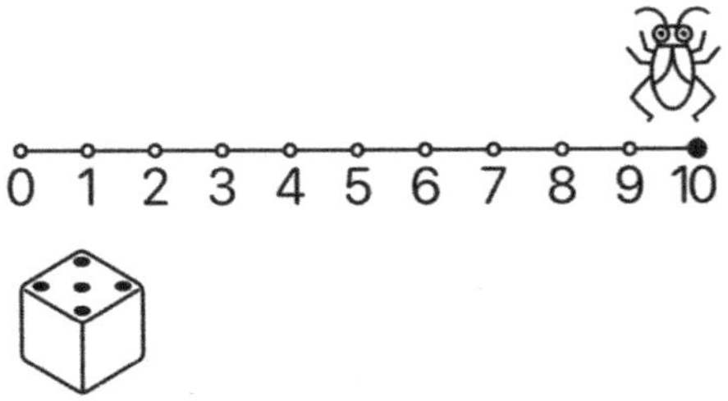

10 – 5 = ____

8

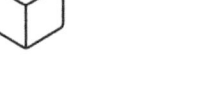

THE DIFFERENCE

Compare the 2 quantities on each page. Write down the difference between them.

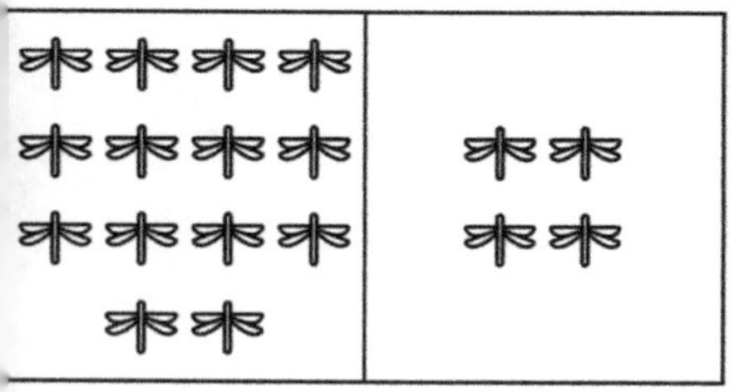

14 – 4 = ____

8

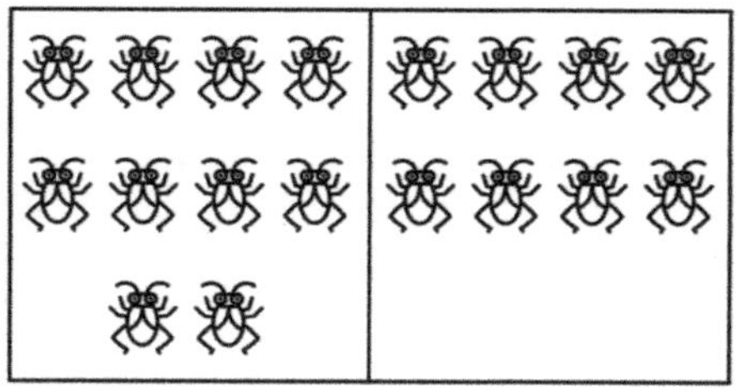

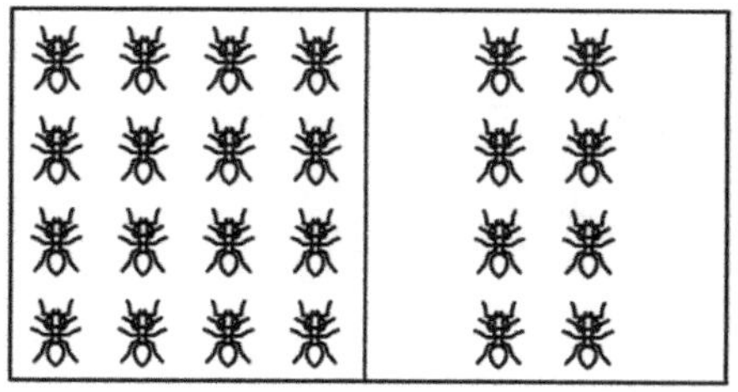

16 – 8 = ____

2

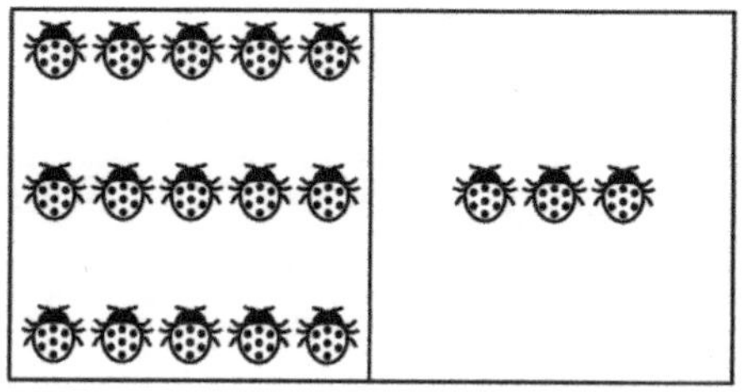

15 – 3 = ____

3

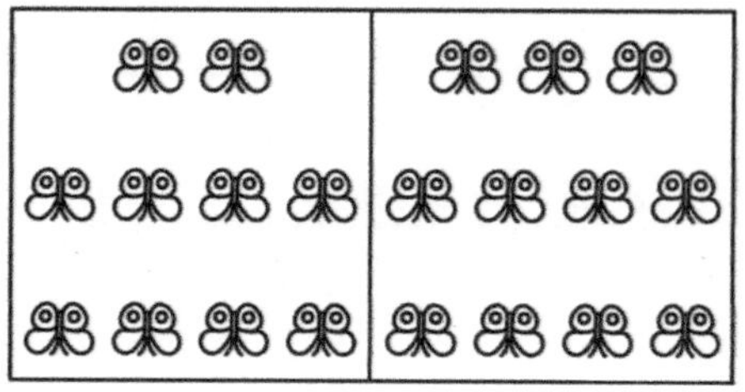

11 – 10 = ____

4

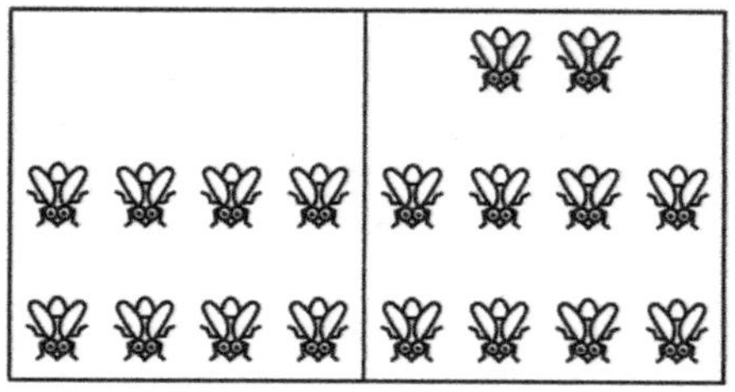

10 – 8 = ____

5

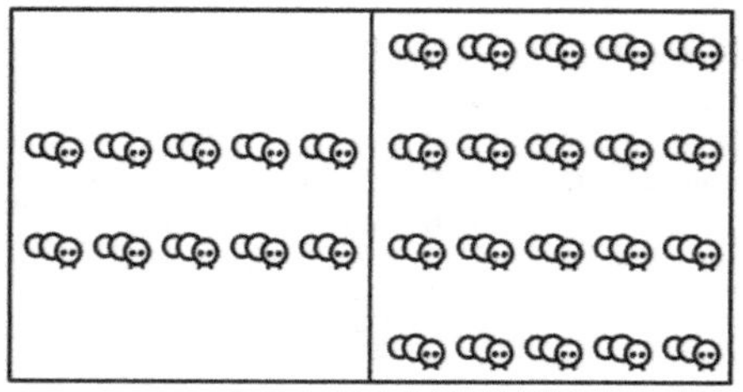

20 – 10 = ____

6

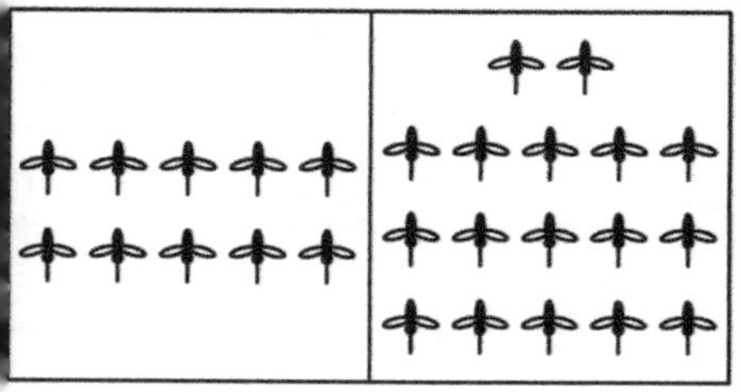

17 – 10 = ____

7

VEGETARIAN WOLF

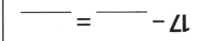

On each page count how many items the wolf has eaten and calculate how many items are left.

18 – 8 = ____

15 – ____ = ____

20 – ____ = ____

17 – ____ = ____

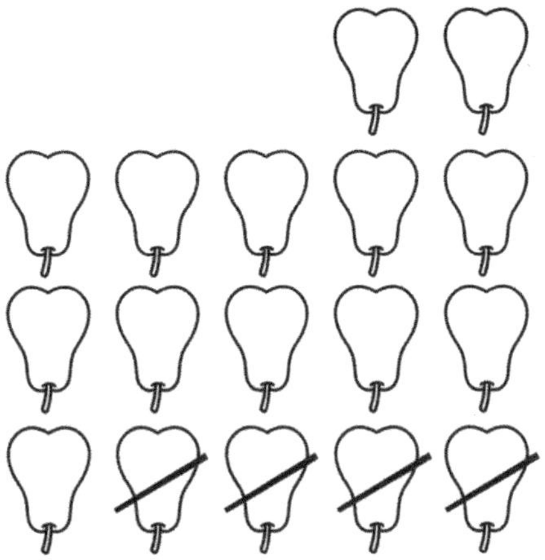

12 – ____ = ____

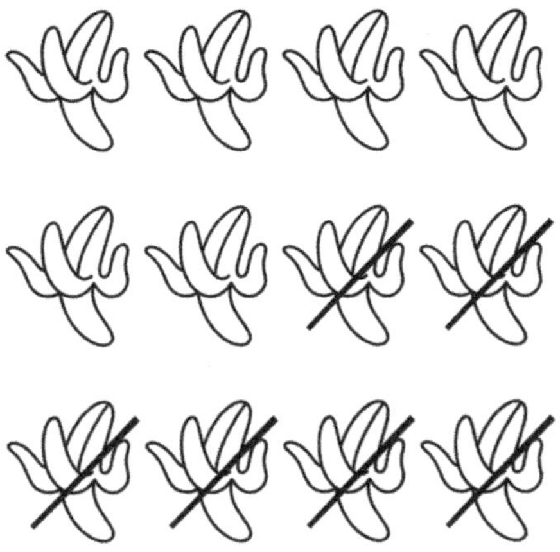

13 – ____ = ____

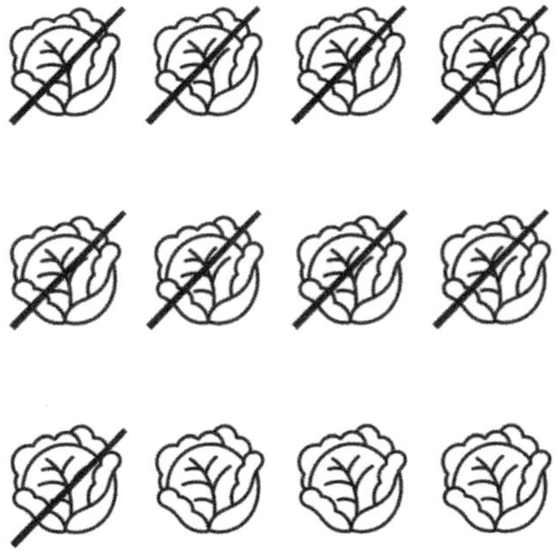

12 – ____ = ____

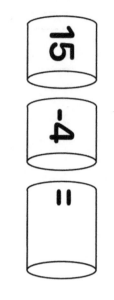

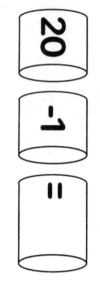

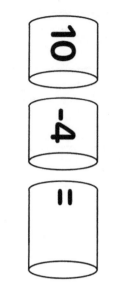

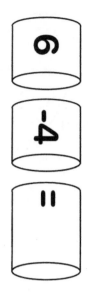

PATH BACKWARDS

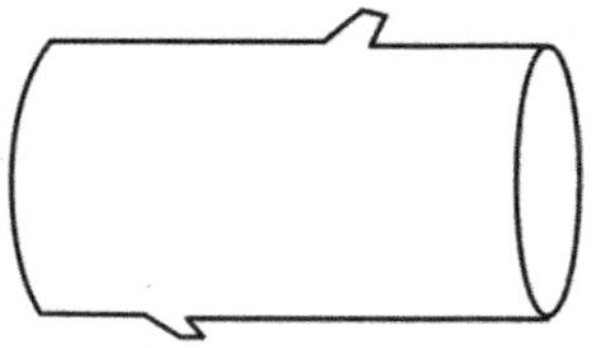

On each page solve the subtraction and write the result on the empty log.

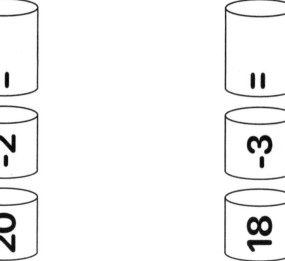

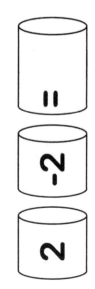

20 -2 =

2

18 -3 =

3

15 -4 =

4

20 -1 =

5

10 -4 =

6

6 -4 =

7

2 -2 =

8

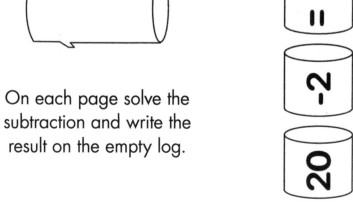

NUMBERS BEYOND 20

Numbers Beyond 20

Counting is an important skill as it is the stage during which children begin to associate the name of the number with a visual quantity. When children learn to count and visually quantify numbers, first up to 10 and then up to 20, a "photograph" is created in their mind and an understanding of place value begins to emerge (where the numbers repeat in the tens and ones place). This helps children more readily identify and read numbers. When they are helped through an orderly arrangement of symbols (e.g., squares, balls, stars), perceptually grouped by ten, counting becomes intuitive. This format then repeats itself as children move beyond 20. Knowing this format builds success, confidence, and motivation.

Within a number, each digit is characterized by not only where it is in the sequence 0 through 9, but also by the place value spot it occupies. For example, the digit 4 comes after 3 but is before 5 in the sequence 0 through 9. In terms of place value spot, the value represented by the digit changes. For example, the digit 4 in the ones place represents a value of 4. However, the digit 4 in the tens place represents a value of 40. This system is repeated throughout the number system, and this repetition enables students to see patterns in numbers and apply their numerical understanding as they continue to encounter larger numbers.

Mathematics is permeated with challenging elements where children can apply their knowledge to build solutions to new problem situations. It is a content area that exemplifies Vygotsky's famous zone of proximal development. Tackling counting with a practical, experiential, and visual approach facilitates participation.

NOTES FROM THE CLASSROOM

Like the previous section, this section supports and extends students' understanding of number. Students will have opportunities to explore numbers up to 100. Within this exploration, students will construct, deconstruct, compare, order, and sequence numbers.

Patterns students identified in the section Numbers to 20 can be adopted to Numbers Beyond 20. It is in this section that students develop a more solid understanding of place value. By working with groups of tens and ones, students can compare and order numbers.

Finally, this understanding of number and place value assists students in being able to apply a more sense-making approach to addition and subtraction, one that is not always reliant on counting.

Working with Numbers Beyond 20 encompasses many key learning areas. As support, you'll find a tracking form (pg 110) that highlights the key learning areas: counting principles; number sequence; comparing numbers (<, >, =); ordering numbers; and groups of ten. Teachers can use this form to monitor student learning within the key learning areas and can use the information gathered to guide instruction.

100 DAYS OF SCHOOL PARTY

Goal

Use a special occasion to start counting beyond 20.

Materials and Resources

- Bristol board
- 100 peel-off sticker dots

Directions

In the first phase, arrange children in a circle. Ask children to reflect on the days of school that have already passed and then prepare a poster where they can stick a dot for each day of school that has passed. If the 100 days have not yet passed, take care to meet with the class every day for a few minutes to dedicate to counting the remaining days, making any connections to previous dates and patterns on the board.
Share that there will be a celebration for "the first 100 days of school." Brainstorm ideas about what this celebration may look like. Given the importance of the 100th day celebration, the children will prepare a simple invitation letter for another class in the school.
This 100th day celebration constitutes an important moment of learning. On the day of celebration, ensure that all students have a role.

Numbers Beyond 20

STUDENT	NUMBERS BEYOND 20				
	Counting Principles	Number Sequence	Comparing Numbers (<, >, =)	Ordering Numbers	Groups of Ten

NUMBERS OVER 20

Hint: Each horizontal row contains 10 squares. You do not need to count them every time.

Look at the squares. How many are there?

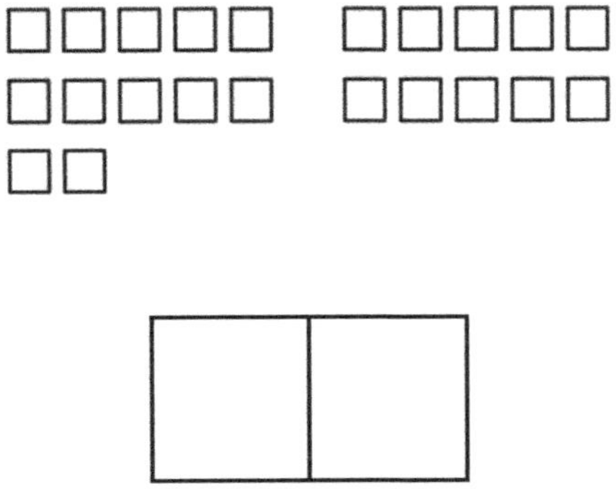

Complete as on the previous page.

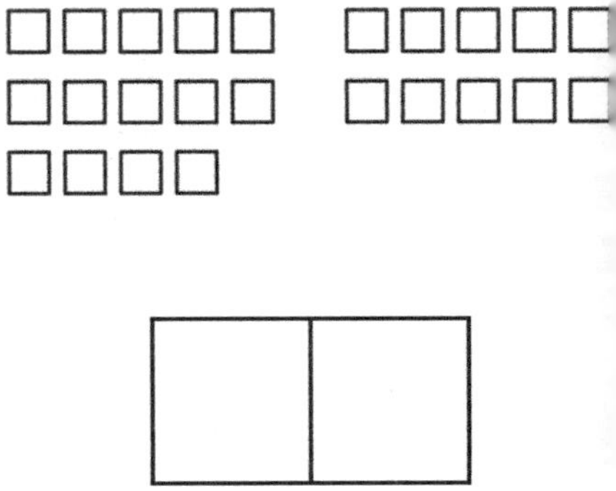

Complete as on the previous page.

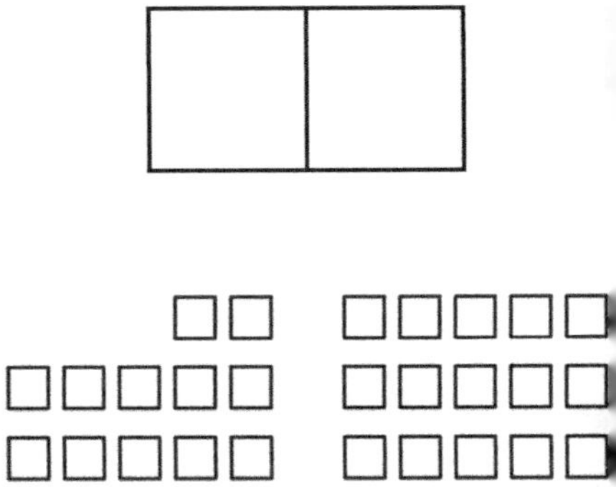

Complete as on the previous page.

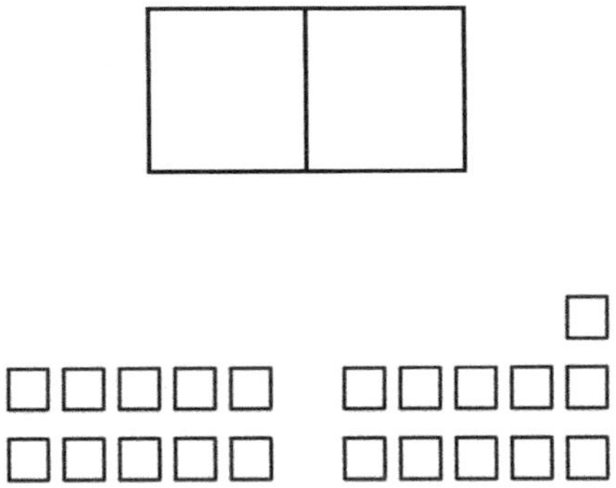

Complete as on the previous page.

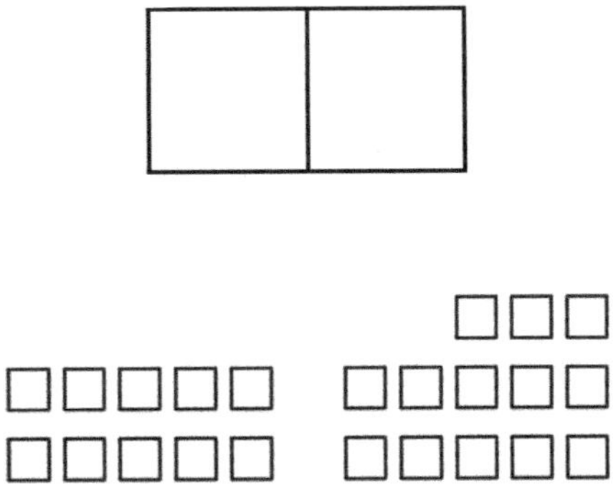

Complete as on the previous page.

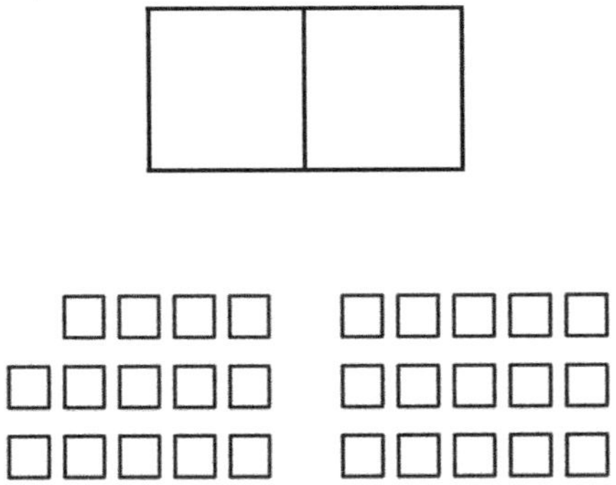

Have you been able to count the numbers beyond 20? Check your work with a classmate's. How did you feel?

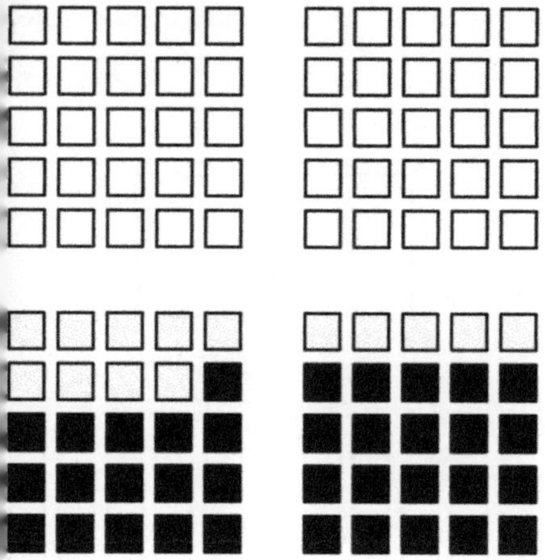

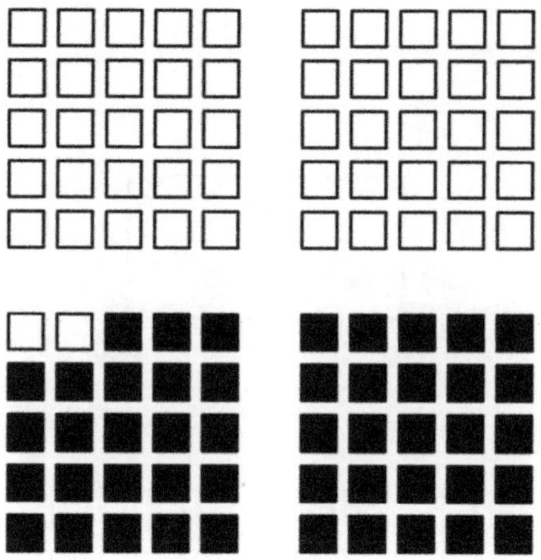

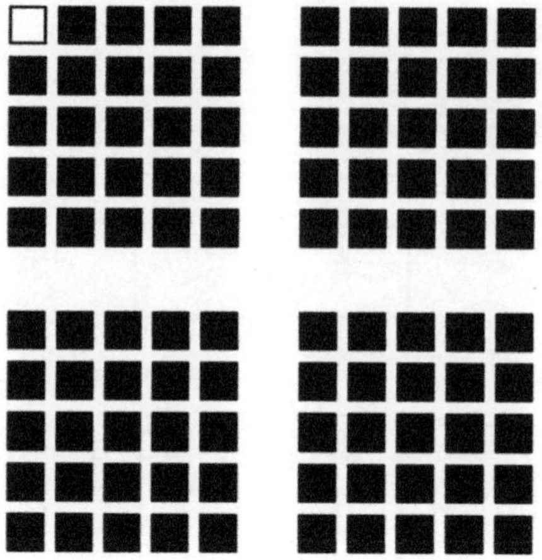

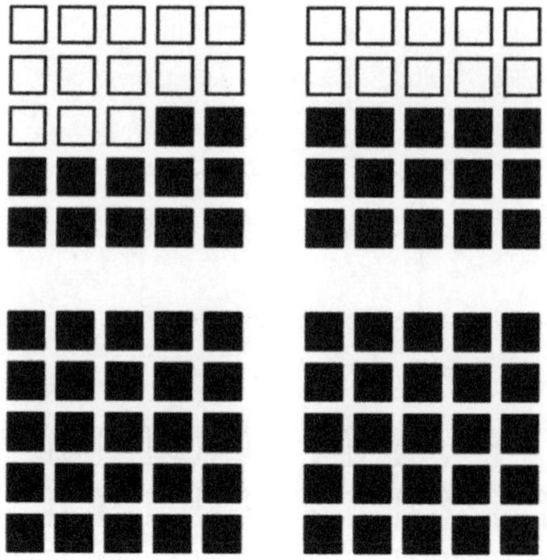

Black: ____
White: ____

Black: ____
White: ____

Black: ____
White: ____

Black: ____
White: ____

Black: ____
White: ____

LOTS OF SUMS

Count how many black squares and how many white squares there are and write down the numbers. Remember: 1 horizontal row = 10 squares!

Black: ____
White: ____

Black: ____
White: ____

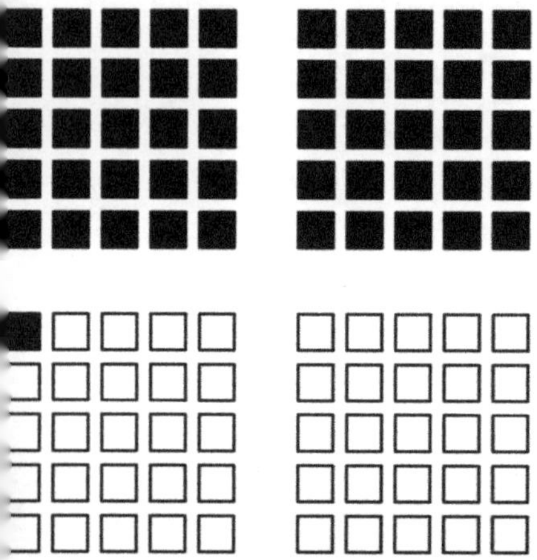

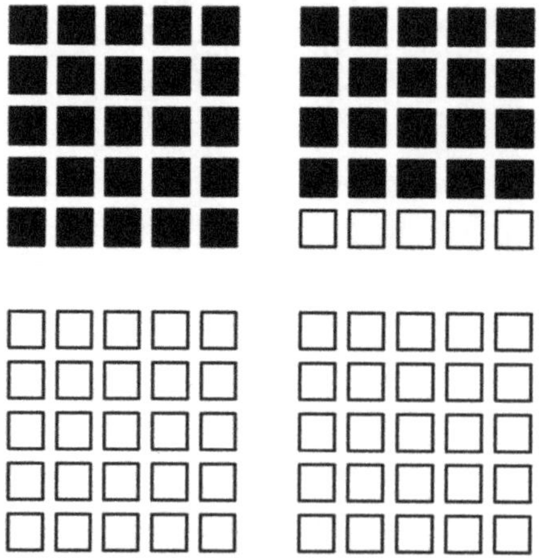

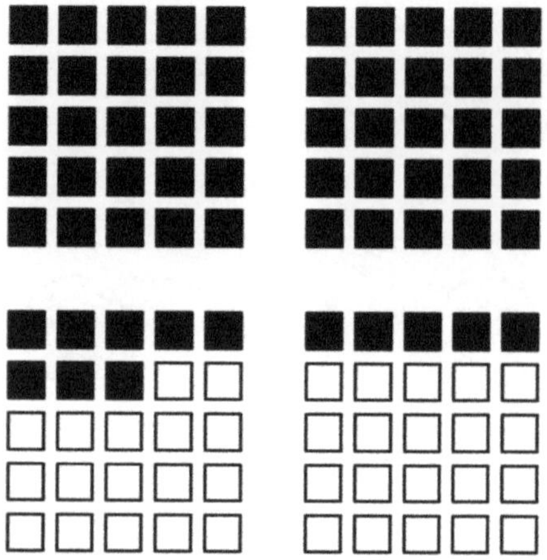

NUMBERS IN THE GRID

Complete the grids. Write the numbers in sequence, from left to right.

1		3			6		8		10
	12		14						20
				25		27		29	

21		23				27			30
			34				38		40
	42								50

41		43				47			50
			54				58		60
	62								70

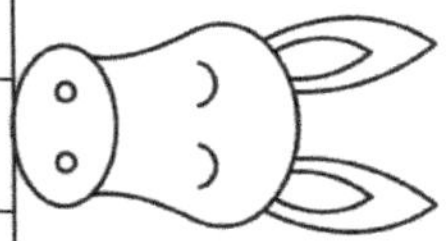

			54			57			60
	62						68		70
71			74						80

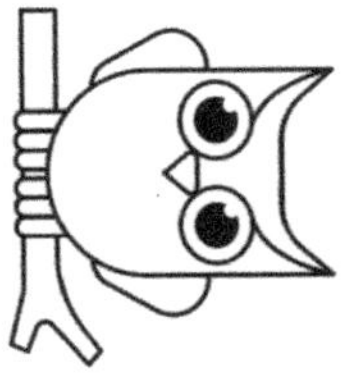

61									70
			74						
	82						88		90

71									80
			84			87			
	92			95					100

How did it go? Check your work with a classmate's. How did you feel?

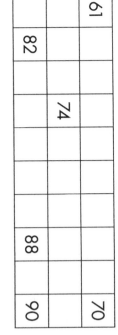

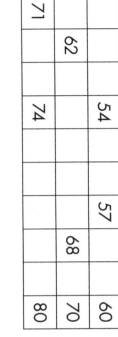

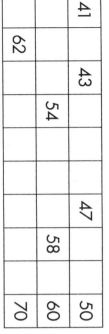

COLOR THE BOXES

Look carefully and color the number of boxes indicated.

2

Color **25** boxes.

3

Color **29** boxes.

4

Color **79** boxes.

5

Color **30** boxes.

6

Color **50** boxes.

7

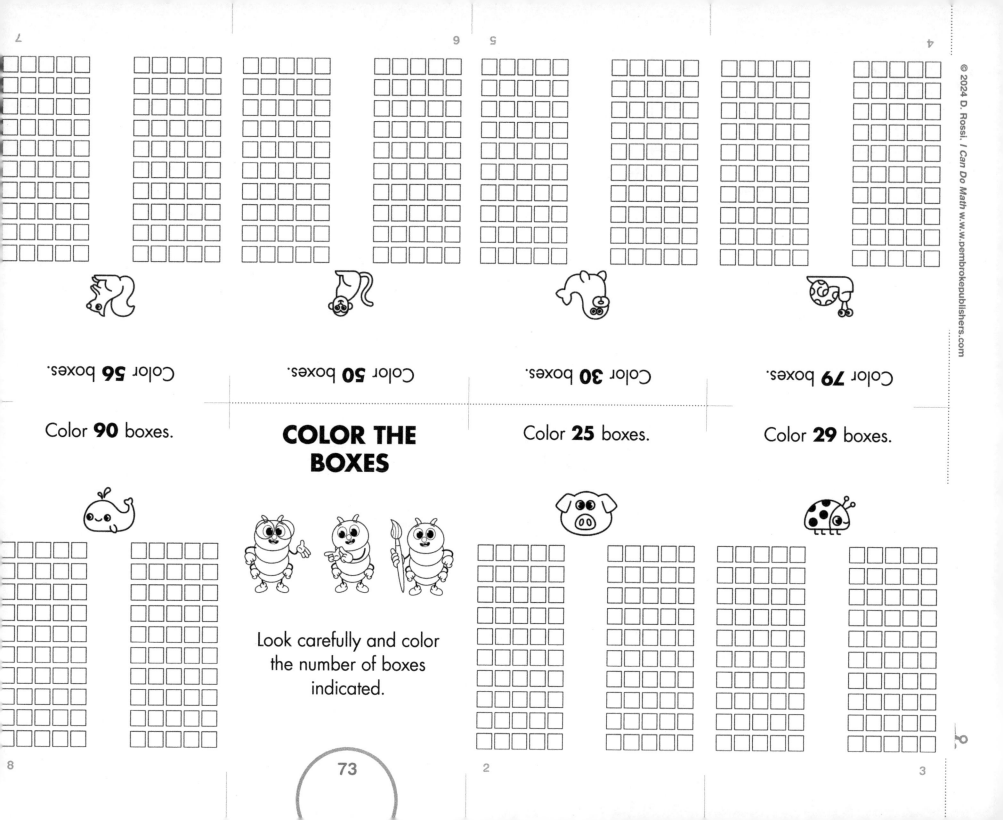

Color **56** boxes.

8

Color **90** boxes.

PROBLEM SOLVING

Problem Solving

Problem solving in the realm of math involves the ability to develop and apply mathematical thinking to solve situations and authentic and significant questions that we encounter in daily life. It involves both creative and critical thinking.

Consider the cognitive and metacognitive skills that underlie problem solving:

- *Understanding the problem situation*: identification of key information, cognitive representation of each piece of information, and integration of verbal and mathematical information into a unified representation.
- *Representation*: connection and relationship between all pieces of information present in the problem, guides towards the correct strategy for solving the problem.
- *Categorization of the problem structure*: recognition of similarities and differences in problem structure that allows recognition of similar problems that belong to the same category and that are solved in the same way.
- *Planning of operational procedures*: metacognitive competence that allows us to choose the sequence of strategies that will support a solution.
- *Monitoring and final evaluation* (Lucangeli et al., 2002).

Each resolution leads the student to build their competence and experience in the mathematical approach to problem solving that, in turn, has important effects in daily life. In an initial phase of learning to solve problems, it is important for children to focus on the problem situation in a concrete and controlled way (propose problems with numbers that are within their reach with respect to the operations that can be carried out).

Discuss with the children that problem solving occurs not only in mathematics but is a way of thinking in any academic area that stimulates creativity and curiosity. Problem solving competence is multilayered and complex, but the skills that compose it must be supported starting in Kindergarten so that it develops over time.

NOTES FROM THE CLASSROOM

The goal of much mathematical instruction is problem solving. Regardless of the grade level, we seek ways to encourage our students to be problem solvers, confident and capable math learners. Problem solving is a mathematical process that underpins all mathematics. And this important process is supported by critical and creative thinking.

As such, the workshops and minibooks within this section provide students with opportunities to further develop their problem-solving skills. You can choose tasks that best align with the learning needs of your students, and the outcome of those tasks will provide you with evidence of student problem-solving abilities and ways to further students' thinking.

The minibooks can be referenced later in the year as part of students' learning portfolios.

The instructional goal of most math teachers is for students to be confident and capable math learners who can problem solve novel situations. As a way to monitor student progress in terms of problem solving, you'll find a reproducible (pg 120) that highlights the key learning areas represented: understand the problem; distinguish relevant information; and solve problems.

Bibliography

Lucangeli D., Ianelli M., Franceschini E., Bommassar G. and Marchi S. (2002), *Laboratorio logica,* Trento, Erickson.

https://www.metodologiedidattiche.it/problem-solving/

THE ROUND OF NUMBERS

Goals

- Resolve small problematic situations to be able to proceed along the path and reach the finish line.
- Use motor skills in a controlled way in a learning context.
- Add quantities, carry out addition and subtraction operations, carry out classification and sequences, and associate two elements based on a relationship.

Materials and Resources

- Paper adhesive tape
- Gym hoops
- 5 red cardboard cards to mark unexpected events
- 5 blue cardboard cards to mark challenges
- 5 green cardboard cards to mark advantages.
- 20 white cardboard cards, numbered from 1 to 20
- Large dice
- 2 strips of paper, one labelled "Departure," the other, "Arrival"
- Materials for the chosen challenges

Directions

In a large space (e.g., gym, playground), arrange 20 cards with the numbers from 1 to 20 on the ground inside gym hoops. The numbers must be arranged sequentially.

Ask the children to color the Departure and Arrival strips. They place the Departure card beside the card marked 1 and the Arrival card beside the card marked 20. Decide as a group at which points to place the unexpected, challenge, and advantage cards. Encourage children to find some suggestions for completing the cards.

Opposite are some examples of how you could conduct this game. Remember to start with the definitions of unexpected, challenge, and advantage.

- UNEXPECTED: Situations that need to be resolved. They answer the questions: What do you use when...? What do you do when...? How do you dress to go...? What do you do before...? What items do you take if you have to...? What materials do you need to build...?
- CHALLENGES: Involve doing. They can be a motor challenge (e.g., filling a water bottle with a precise number of glasses by walking a short distance; doing a specific number of jumps with both feet together). An element of quantification must always be included in this type of challenge. Challenges can also be visual (e.g., you could create pieces of a giant tangram and ask children to use them to replicate an image represented on a small card).
- ADVANTAGES: Provide for an advancement of boxes following the passing of a test (which must be quite easy and feasible for children), for example, associations, groupings, or serializations with materials made available for the game or with materials naturally present in the school. Again, the challenge must contain quantification.

After writing the unexpected, challenges, and advantages cards and placing them along the route, divide the class into three groups, within which the children will be grouped in pairs. The pairs take turns rolling the die; the one with the highest number will be the first to play, and the others will follow respecting the decreasing order of the numbers obtained from the test roll. Pairs move forward by as many steps as the dice says. When they land on UNEXPECTED, CHALLENGES or ADVANTAGES boxes they will have to be successful to advance. The first pair to reach the finish line wins. The last roll of the die must give the exact number to reach the final square.

Problem Solving

STUDENT	PROBLEM SOLVING		
	Understand the Problem	Distinguish Relevant Information	Solve Problems

NAUGHTY FROGS

Color the number of frogs given in the instructions.

2

Color 2 frogs.

3

Color the 2nd frog.

4

Color 4 frogs.

5

Color frog number 4.

6

Color the 10th frog.

7

Color 10 frogs.

8

Color 6 frogs.

HEDGEHOGS IN A ROW

Color.

Color more than half of the hedgehogs.

Color some hedgehogs.

Color every hedgehog.

Color half of the hedgehogs.

Color each hedgehog.

Color 3 hedgehogs.

Color all the hedgehogs.

IN THE KITCHEN

Look at the pictures and answer the questions.

How many pies are there?

2

How many frosted pies are there?

3

How many sweets are there?

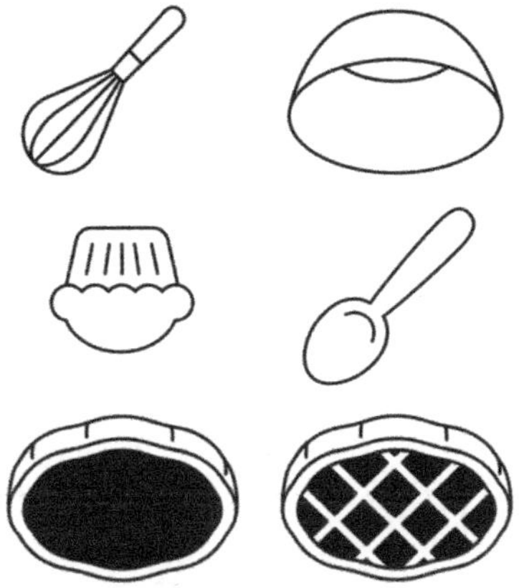

4

How many kitchen utensils are there?

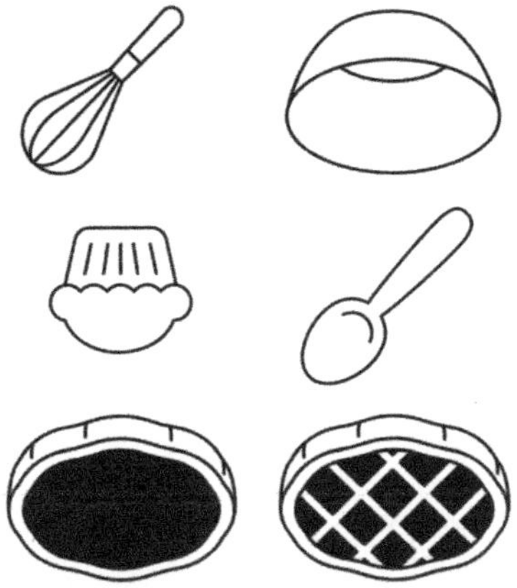

5

How many cupcakes are there?

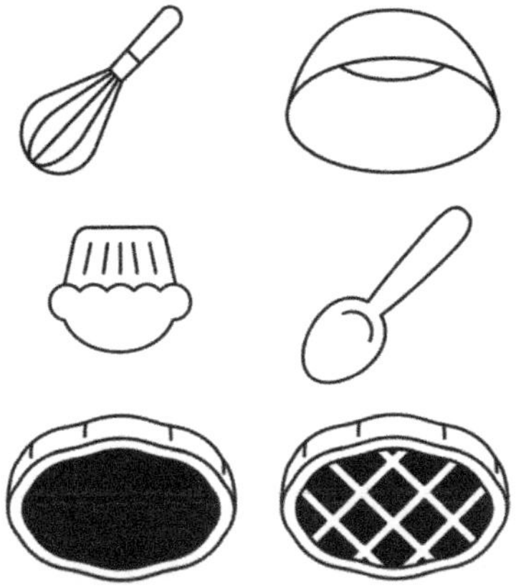

6

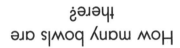

How many bowls are there?

7

How many items are there in total?

8

ON THE BEACH

Look at the pictures and answer the questions.

How many items are there in the picture?

2

How many items are made of paper?

3

How many items are not fruits?

4

How many items are fruits?

5

How many items can you use on the beach?

6

How many items have a round shape?

7

How many items are not games?

8

…they sleep outdoors?

…it gets dark?

…it is very sunny?

…they get lost in the forest?

…they climb a mountain?

WHAT DO EXPLORERS USE WHEN…

Color the item in the box that you may need in the situation.

…it is raining in the mountains?

…they are hungry?

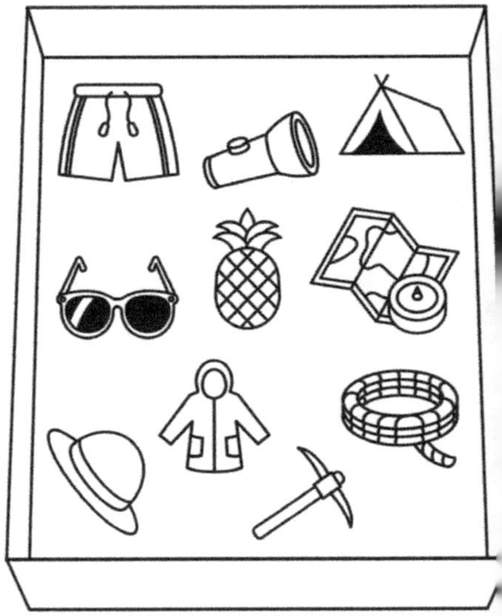

WHAT DO YOU DO BEFORE...

Choose and color the picture that is right for the activity described.

2

...you eat a sandwich?

3

...you go to school?

4

...you have dinner?

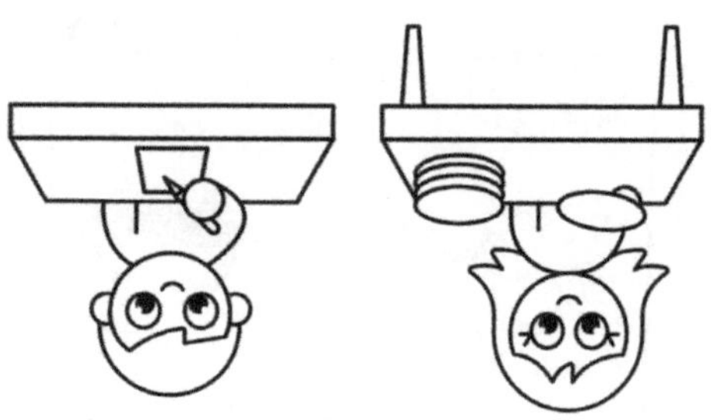

5

...you go running?

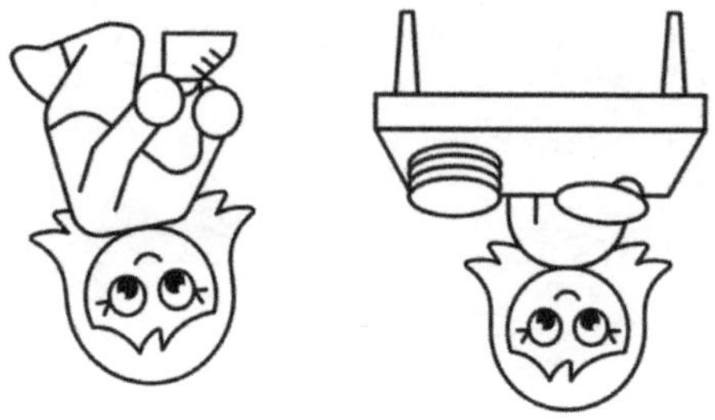

6

...you go to sleep?

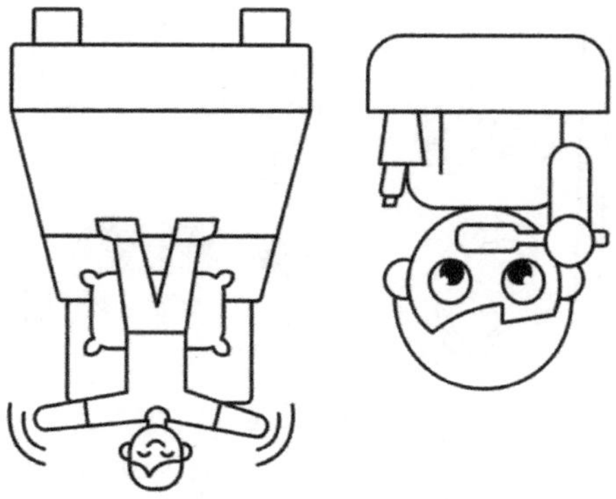

7

...you go to the beach?

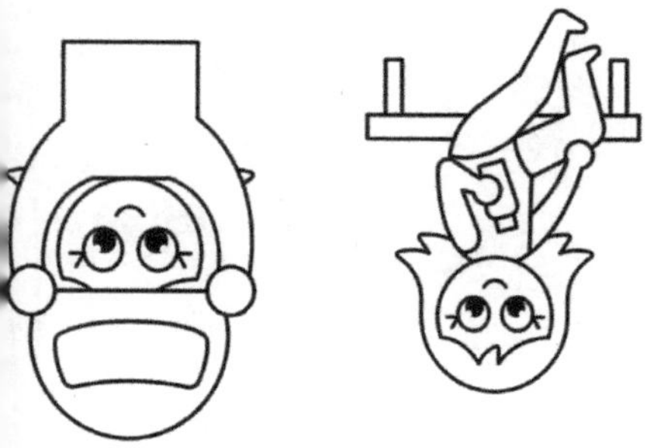

8

...you ride a bike?

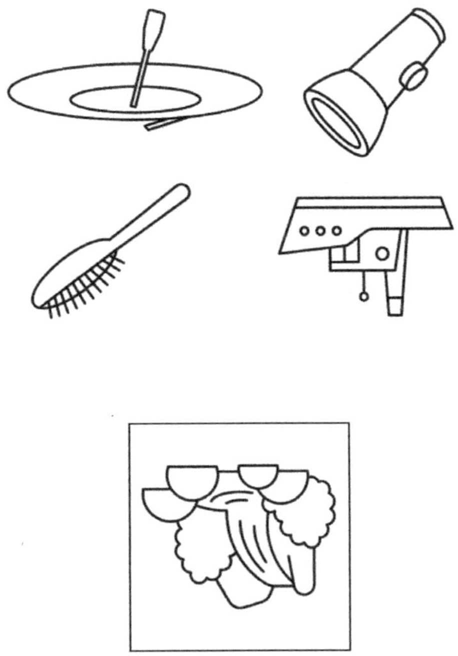

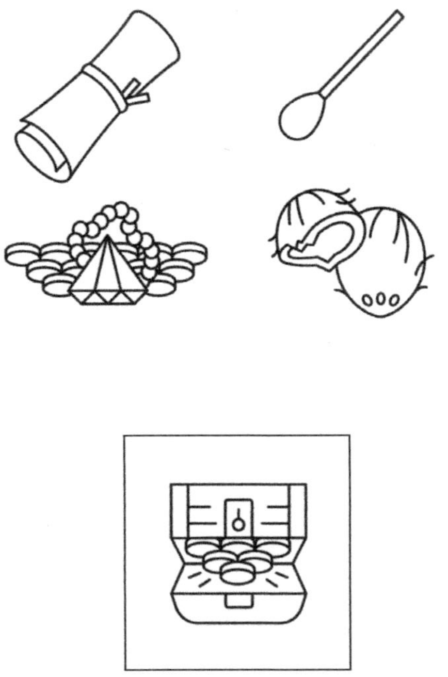

MAKE A MATCH

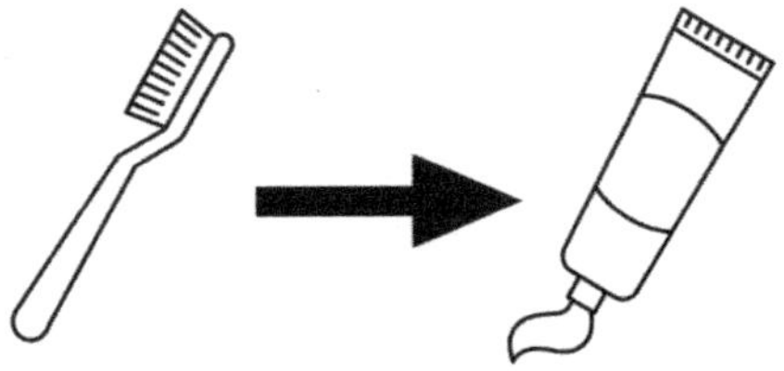

Look at the object in the box at the top of each page and match it to one of the items below.

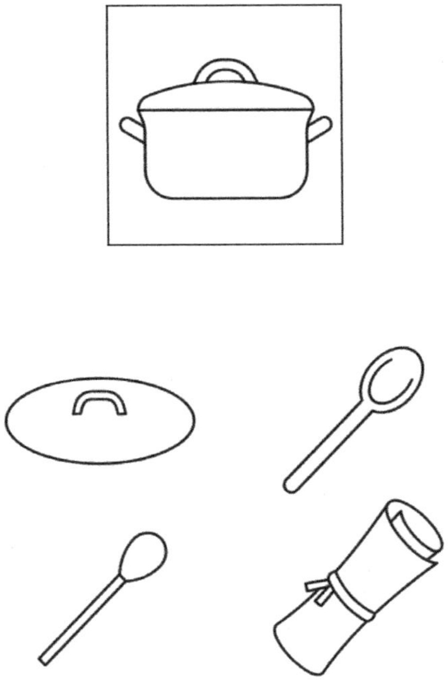

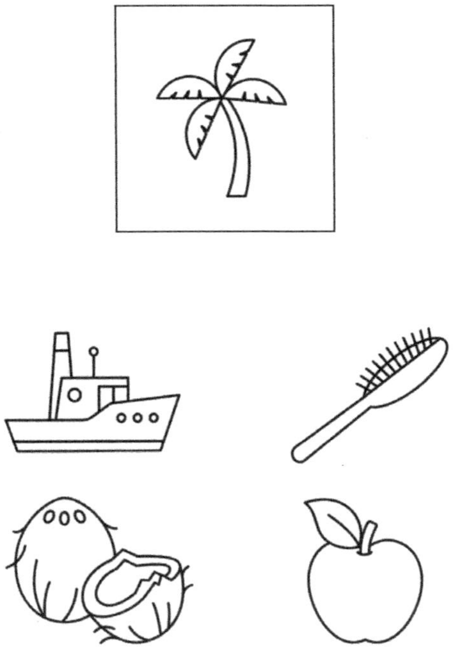

WHERE ARE THE ANIMALS?

Look at the map on the next page and write the coordinates (for example, A1) to find the missing animals. Color the found animals on the map.

Here is the map…

2

Where is my caterpillar?

3

Where is my ladybug?

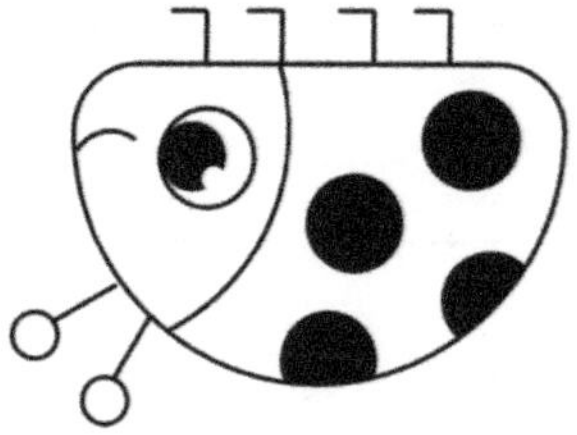

4

Where is my bumblebee?

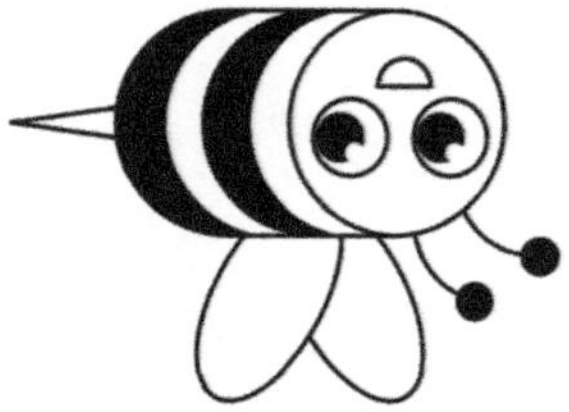

5

Where is my dragonfly?

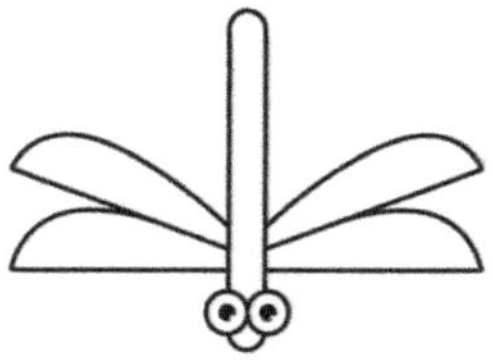

6

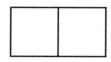

Where is my frog?

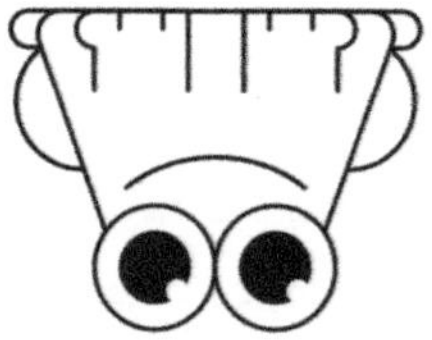

7

Where is my ant?

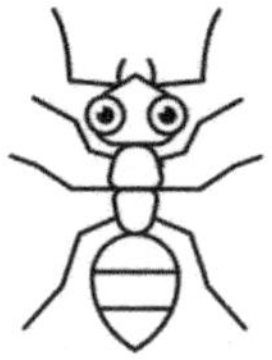

8

CANDY IN JARS

Complete or color the drawing on the next page. Answer the questions.

2

Here are the jars of candy...

- In the 1st jar there are 4 red candies.
- There are the same number of candies in the 2nd jar as in the 1st jar and the candies are yellow.

3

Read and complete the previous page.

- In the 3rd jar there are 2 green candies.
- There is 1 more candy in the 4th jar than in the 3rd jar and the candies are orange.

4

Read and fill in the page where the jars are.

- There is 1 less candy in the 5th jar than in the 4th jar and the candies are blue.
- In the 6th jar there are the same number of candies as in the 5th jar and the candies are green.

5

Answer the questions.

1. How many jars of candy are there?

____

2. How many candies are there in total?

____

6

Answer the questions.

3. How many red candies are there?

____

4. How many candies are not red?

____

7

Answer the questions.

5. How many jars have 2 candies?

____

6. How many candies are there in the 4th jar?

____

8

Answer the questions.

7. What color are most of the candies?

____

8. How many jars have green candies?

____

SOLVE

Use the pictures on the following pages to solve the problems.

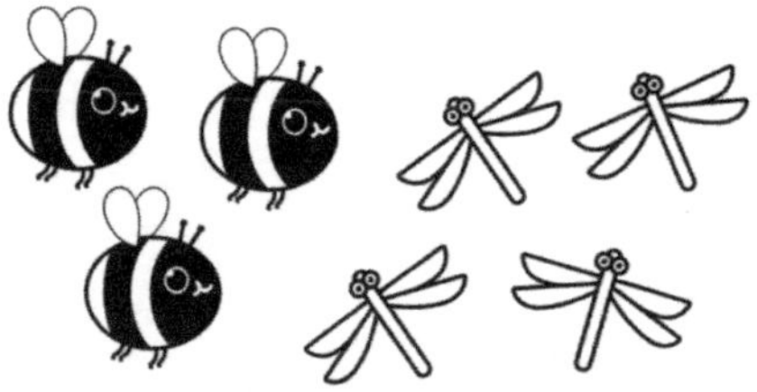

In the meadow there are 3 bumblebees and 4 dragonflies. How many insects are there in total?

____

2

In the meadow there are 5 butterflies and 5 ladybugs. How many insects are there in total?

____

3

In the pond there are 2 large frogs and 2 small frogs. How many frogs are there in total?

____

4

In the meadow there are 2 butterflies. After a short time 3 more arrive. How many butterflies are there in total?

____

5

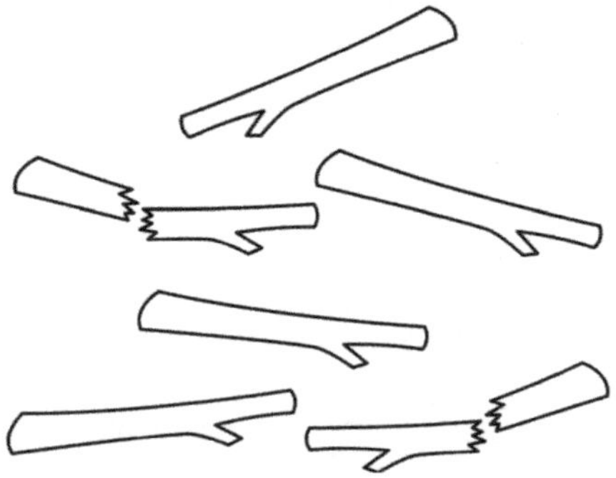

In the forest there are 4 whole sticks and 2 broken sticks. How many sticks are there in total?

____

6

In the meadow there are 3 black mice and 2 white mice. How many mice are there in total?

____

7

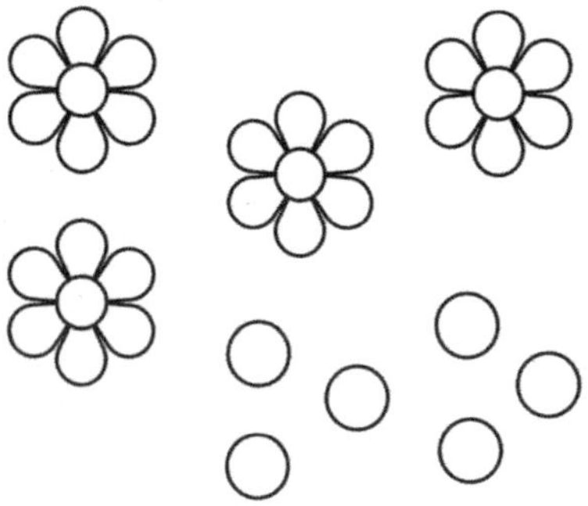

In the meadow there are 4 fresh flowers and 6 flowers that have lost their petals. How many flowers are there in total?

____

8

TRAINING FOR PROBLEMS

Use the pictures on the following pages to solve the problems.

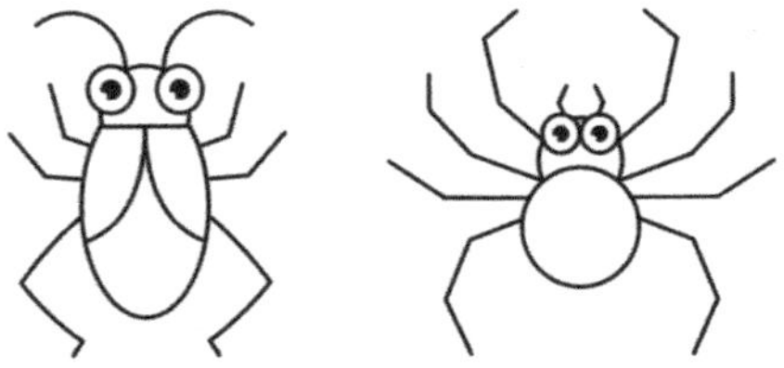

The cricket has 6 legs. The spider has 2 more legs. How many legs does the spider have?

____

2

The clover on the right has 4 leaves. The clover on the left has 1 less. How many leaves does the left clover have?

____

3

4

In the 1st pile there are 7 stones. In the 2nd pile there are 4 stones. How many more stones are there in the 1st pile than in the 2nd?

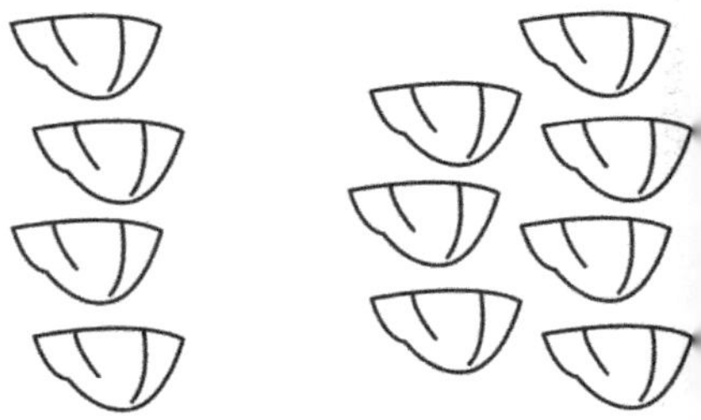

____

5

There are 5 butterflies in the meadow. 3 fly away. How many butterflies are left?

____

6

In the forest there are 6 sticks. 2 of these sticks are broken. How many sticks are not broken?

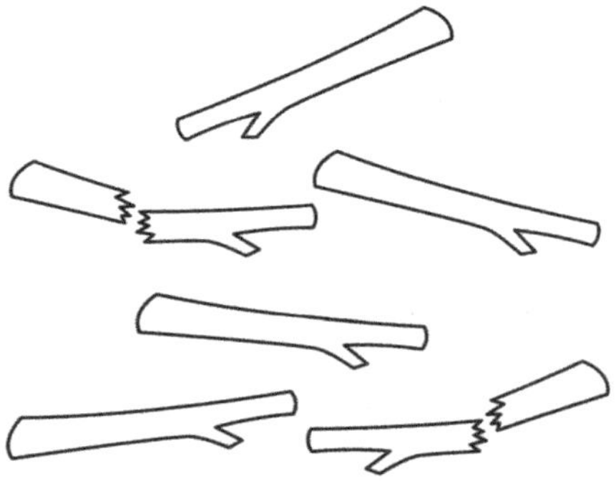

____

7

There are 10 trees. 2 have leaves. How many trees are there with no leaves?

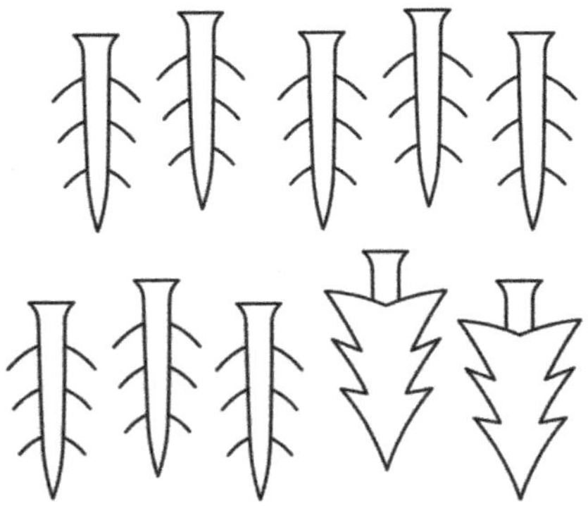

____

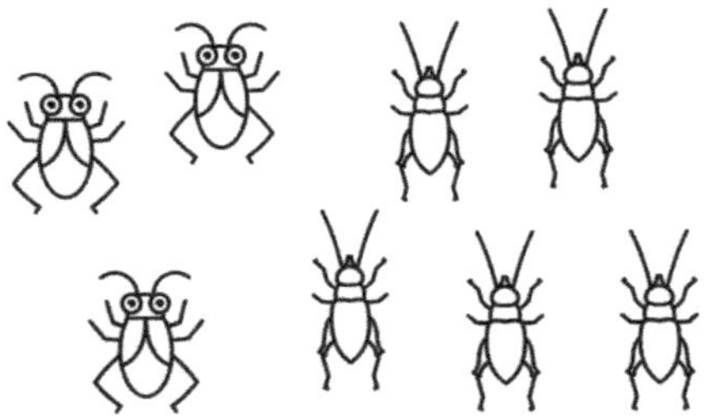

In the meadow there are 3 crickets and 5 grasshoppers. How many insects in total?

____

8

SUDOKU

In sudoku, all the numbers 1-4 must appear only once in each row and each column. Complete the diagrams.

	3	2	4
2	4	1	
	2	4	1
	1	3	2

1	2	3	
4	3		1
		4	
	4		3

	1		4
4		1	
1			2
2	4	3	1

	4		2
		4	3
		3	1
1	3		

4		2	
	2		4
		1	2
2	1	4	

3			4
1		2	3
2	3		1
	1	3	

Compare your work with a classmate's. How did you feel during the activity?

GEOMETRY

Geometry

Few psychology studies have explored how children recognize geometric shapes and develop learning in this field. It was only after Piaget and then Inhelder (1979) did so that other researchers begin to study the development of geometric cognition in aspects relating to topological, projective, and Euclidean relationships. What emerged is that the evolution of geometric cognition correlated to immersion in education and experiences carried out in this area, rather than to the chronological age of children.

To develop geometric skills, we need to provide opportunities for students to work on a practical manipulative level, focusing on visual aspects and leaving the verbal language in the background—definitions can come later. In teaching geometry, students must first pass through the visual and physical exploration path (e.g., folding, drawing, motor paths, searching for shapes in the environment), before arriving at the acquisition of the regularities that characterize geometric shapes.

Functions of the visual path and analysis are explored in activities and minibooks in the Foundational Knowledge section. Working in an in-depth and targeted manner on these aspects constitutes a fundamental starting point for the geometric area.

NOTES FROM THE CLASSROOM

Increasing attention is being paid to geometrical reasoning. Geometry offers students opportunities to experience mathematics within their lived experiences.

As teachers, we often search for tasks that will engage students and assist them in further developing their understanding of geometry. The workshops and minibooks within this section will support students in understanding how shapes are constructed and deconstructed, as well as how they can use reasoning to solve geometric problems.

Geometric reasoning serves as an important milestone in student mathematical understanding. As support, you'll find a tracking form (pg 142) that highlights the key learning areas within geometry: types of lines; open and closed shapes; and distinguishing shapes. Teachers can use this form to monitor student learning within the key learning areas and can use the information gathered to guide instruction.

The tracking form will support teachers in broadening their approach to geometry as they use the minibooks to support student understanding of its various aspects. The tracking form coincides closely with the minibooks and experiences offered within *I Can Do Math.*

Bibliography

Hershkowitz R. (1989), *Visualization in geometry: Two sides of the coin,* "Focus on Learning Problem in Mathematics", vol. 11, pp. 61-76.

Piaget J. and Inhelder B. (1979), *La rappresentazione dello spazio nel bambino,* Firenze, Giunti & Barbera.

HUNT FOR THE LINES

Goal

Recognize these geometric lines: curved, broken, straight, open, closed, dashed.

Materials and Resources

- Masking tape
- 14 index cards, labelled with different types of lines
- Pen, permanent markers, or wax crayons
- Digital camera
- Whiteboard

Directions

Preparation: Prepare the cards, each with a drawing of a type of line and an instruction to look for it (e.g., "Search for a curved line," "Search for a closed line," "Search for a dashed line"). Then identify a large place (e.g., the hall or corridor) and draw a series of different types of lines (like those used on cards) with masking tape. It is important that they are large and that they do not cross each other, so that they are clearly visible and distinguishable. Then photograph each line to record the work in the notebook and for self-correction on the interactive whiteboard. Finally, prepare a digital sheet with photos of the lines and the corresponding definitions.

The activity: Divide the class into pairs and give each child a card. Children will read their card, identify their line on the floor, and explain their thinking with their partner. Once found, ask children to go over it again with a marker or wax crayon, tracing the masking tape without ever taking their hand off. When everyone has finished, return to class and show the digital sheet with the images and definitions of the lines on the interactive whiteboard. Each pair will check their work against what is displayed on the interactive whiteboard.

HIDDEN FIGURES IN THE PAINTING

Goal

- Recognize flat geometric figures and associate the correct name of the figure.
- Use a double entry table.

Materials and Resources

- White cloth (approximately 1 m x 1 m)
- Dark covering cloth
- Images of various objects (e.g., leaves, branches, flowers, birds, animals, pinecones)
- Colored cardboard
- Scissors, pencil, eraser
- Geometric figures (rectangles, squares, triangles, circles) of different colors
- Some copies of the table illustrated in the example (one for each group of three children)

Directions

Preparation: In a large environment (e.g., gym, hall) spread the white cloth on the floor and place the images on it to create a scenario (e.g., a forest) while also inserting the geometric figures. The geometric figures can be partially hidden if they are still recognizable. Prepare the table to count the figures: associate a color with each row, a shape with each column. The children will have to write how many shapes of each color they see. Cover the painting with the dark cloth.

The activity: Place the children in a circle around the painting and explain to them that they will have to observe it and strain their eyes to find the hidden geometric figures. Show an example of the figures included in the painting and check that everyone knows the shapes and colors. Then divide the class into groups of three children and give each one a copy of the table, explaining how to use it.

Then uncover the painting and let the children work for a few minutes. When everyone has finished, share results as a large group.

TRACING LINES

Donkey and Goat have drawn lines in the grass. Trace each line with a colored pencil, and color the correct label.

2

Look, review, and color.

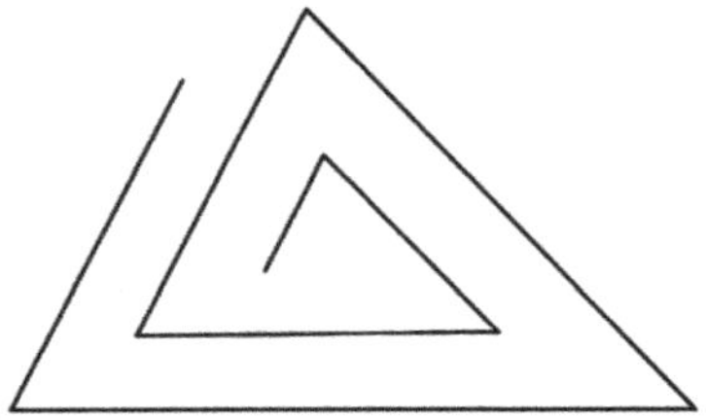

OPEN CURVED LINE	**OPEN ZIGZAG LINE**

3

Look, review, and color.

OPEN CURVED LINE	**OPEN TWISTED LINE**

4

Look, review, and color.

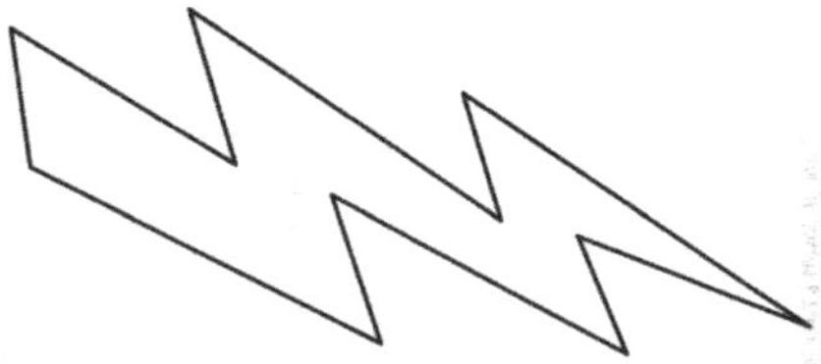

CLOSED CURVED LINE	**CLOSED ZIGZAG LINE**

5

Look, review, and color.

OPEN TWISTED CURVED LINE	**CLOSED TWISTED CURVED LINE**

6

Look, review, and color.

CLOSED ZIGZAG LINE	**OPEN ZIGZAG LINE**

7

Look, review, and color.

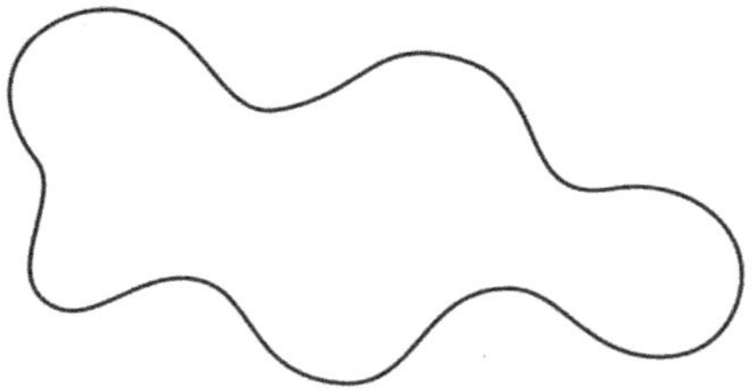

OPEN CURVED LINE	**CLOSED CURVED LINE**

8

Look, review, and color.

CLOSED MIXED LINE	**OPEN MIXED LINE**

THE SHORTEST WAY

Look at the lines that connect the two characters and choose the shortest one. Which line is it? Circle the correct answer.

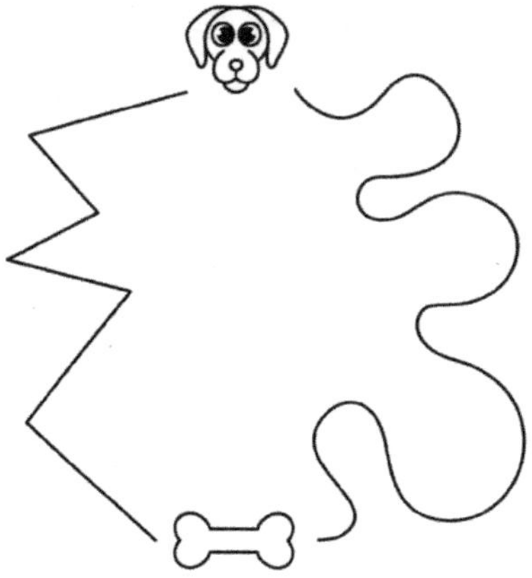

The shortest way is:

- the curved line.
- the zigzag line.

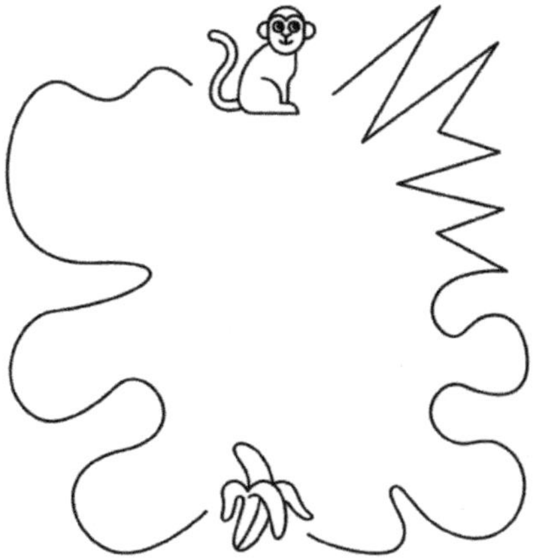

The shortest way is:

- the curved line.
- the mixed line.

The shortest way is:

- the twisted curved line.
- the curved line.

The shortest way is:

- the zigzag line.
- the curved line.

The shortest way is:

- the curved line.
- the twisted curved line.

The shortest way is:

- the zigzag line.
- the straight line.

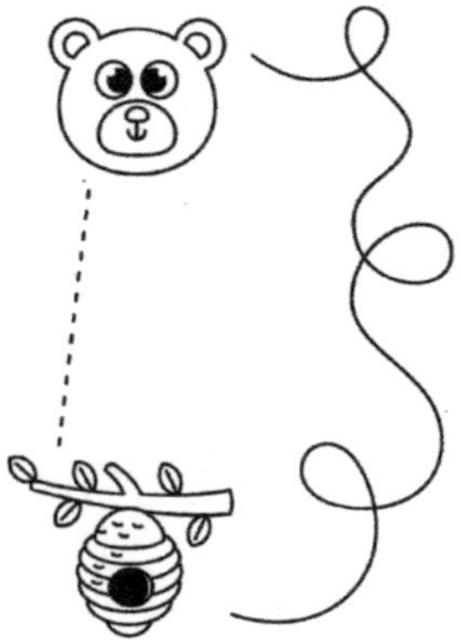

The shortest way is:

- the twisted curved line.
- the dashed straight line.

ANIMALS ALLOWED

What is shown in each picture? Color the correct answer.

Open space, frogs outside
Closed space, frogs inside
Open space, frogs inside

2

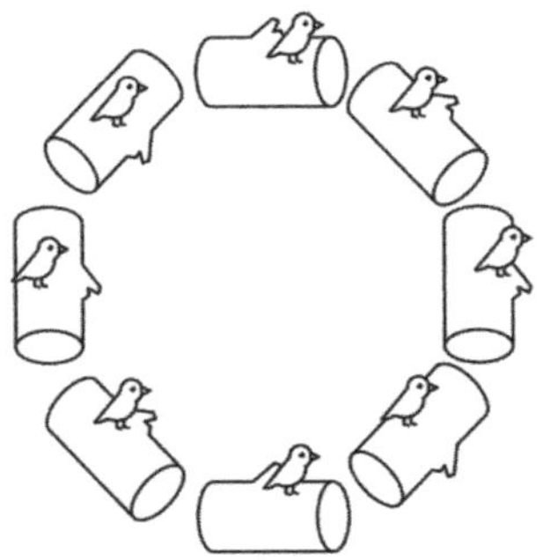

Closed space, birds outside
Open space, birds inside
Closed space, birds on border

3

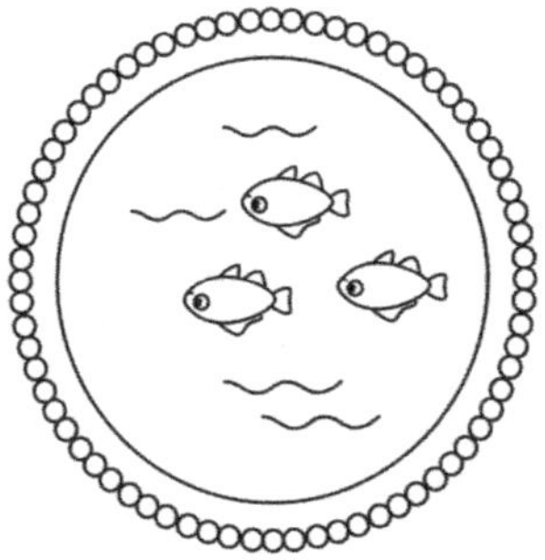

Open space, fish outside
Closed space, fish inside
Open space, fish inside

4

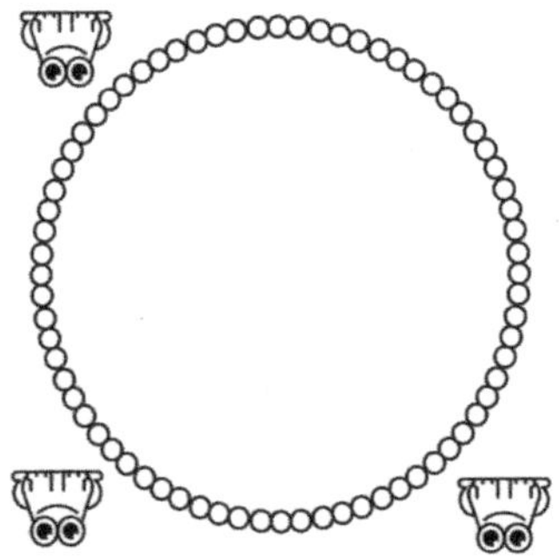

Closed space, frogs outside
Closed space, frogs inside
Open space, frogs outside

5

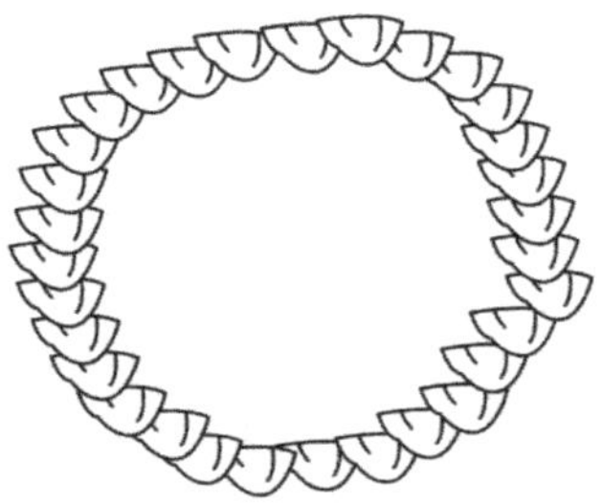

Closed space, animals outside
Closed space, no animals
Closed space, animals inside

6

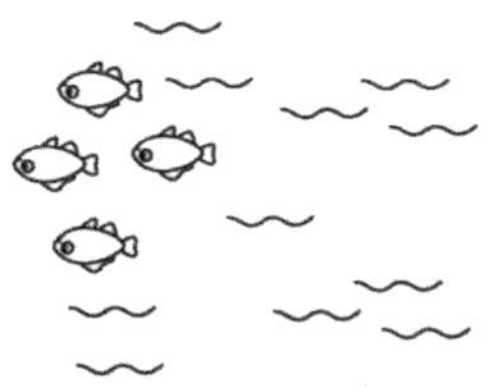

Closed space, fish outside
Closed space, no fish
Open space, fish in space

7

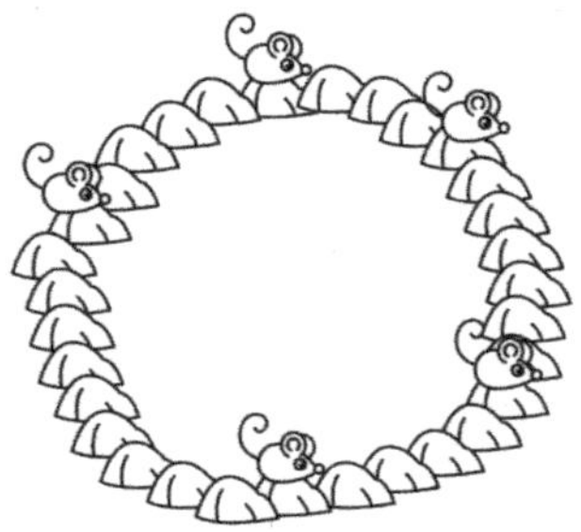

Closed space, mice on border
Closed space, mice inside
Open space, mice on border

8

GEOMETRIC FIGURES

Color the shapes as indicated.

2

Color the square blue and the circle orange.

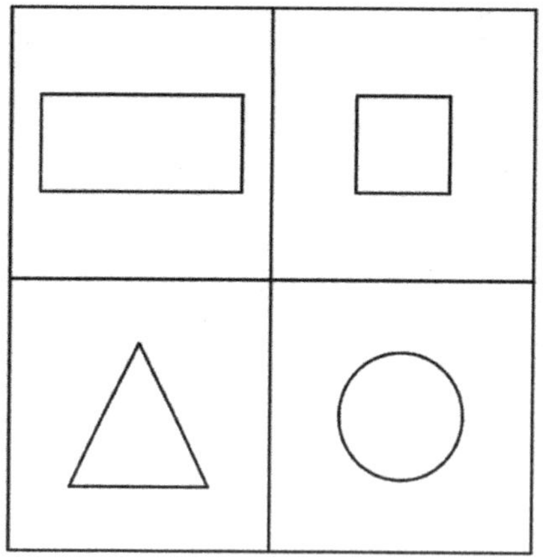

3

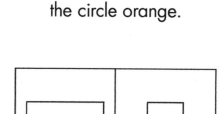

Color the triangle green and the rectangle purple.

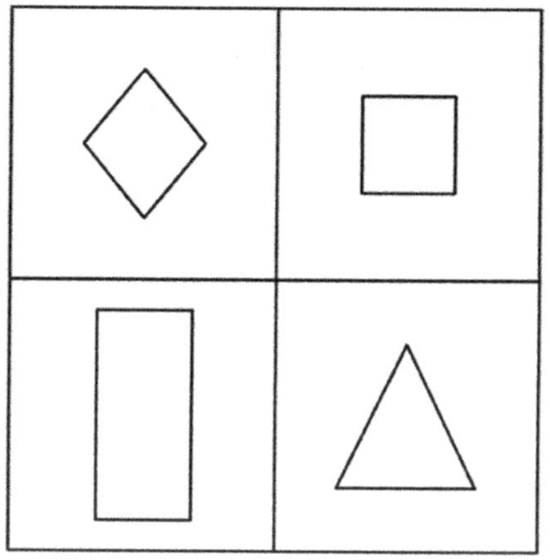

4

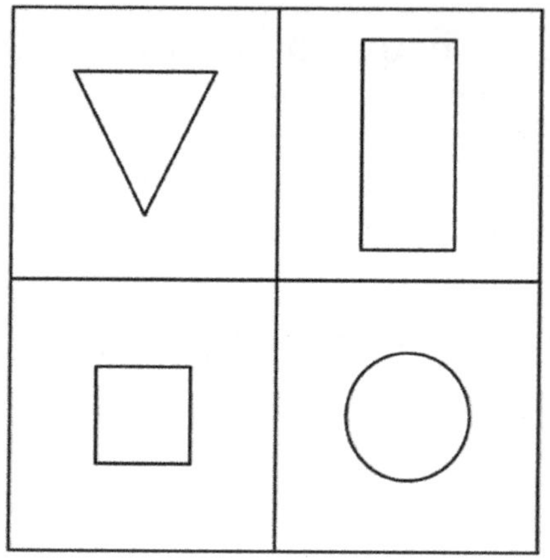

Color the triangle green.

5

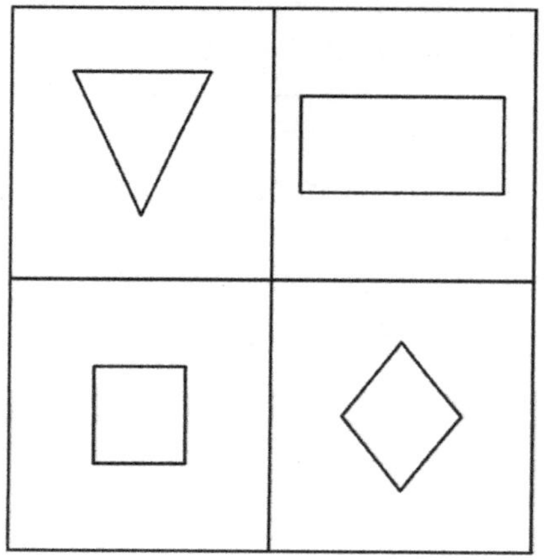

Color the rectangle purple.

6

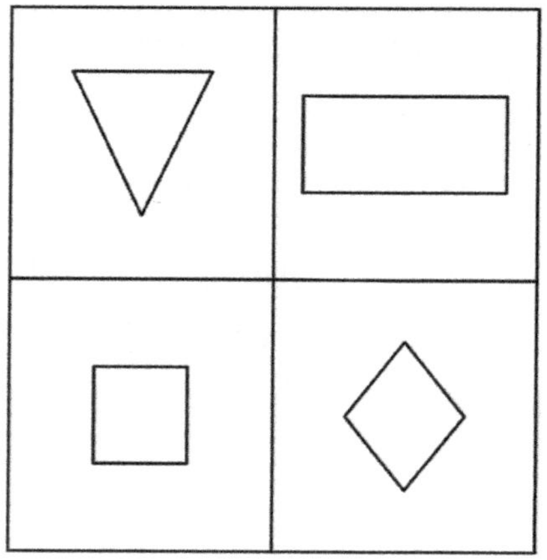

Color the square blue.

7

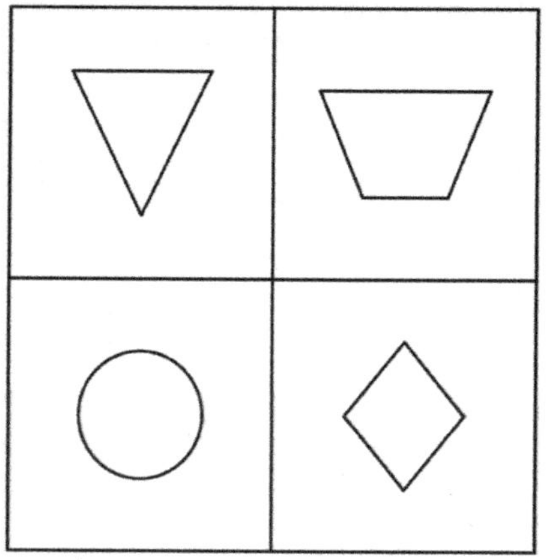

Color the circle orange.

8

Color the figures based on the colors assigned to each on the previous pages. Leave the other shapes white.

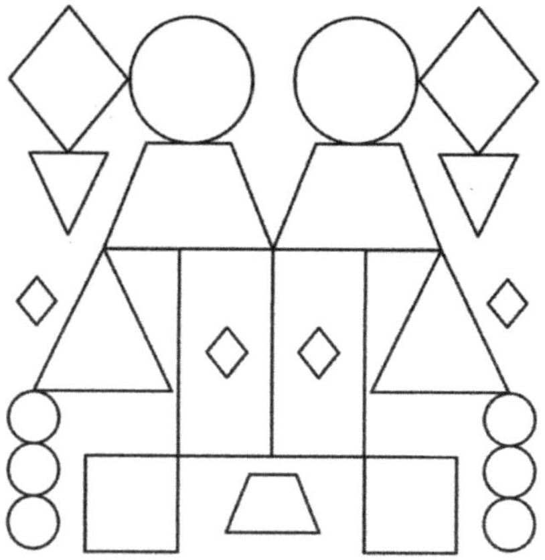

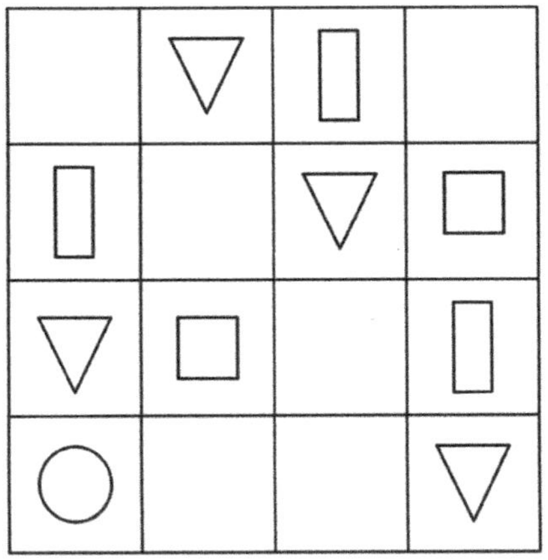

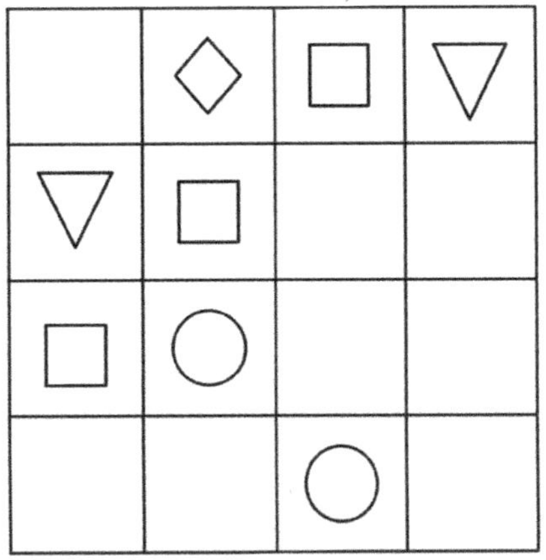

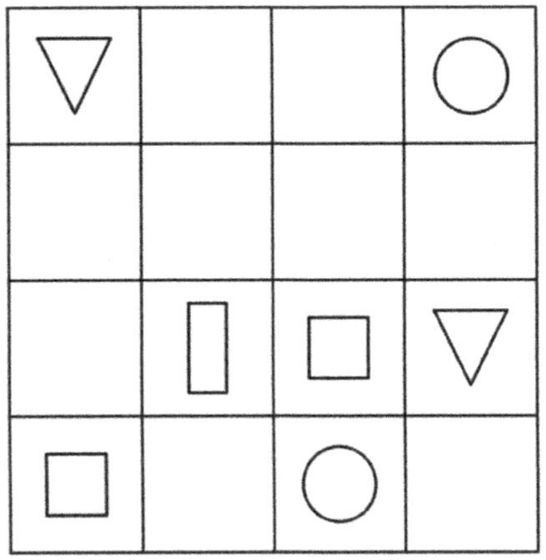

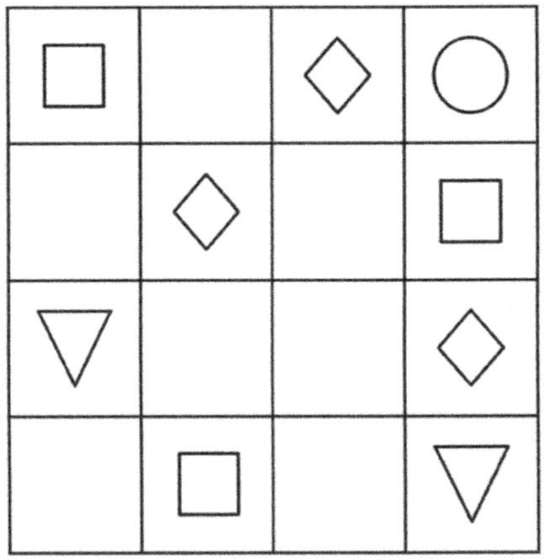

Compare your work with a classmate's. How did it go? How did you feel during the activity?

GEOMETRIC SUDOKU

Geometric figures must be in each row and each column without repeating any of them. Complete and color.

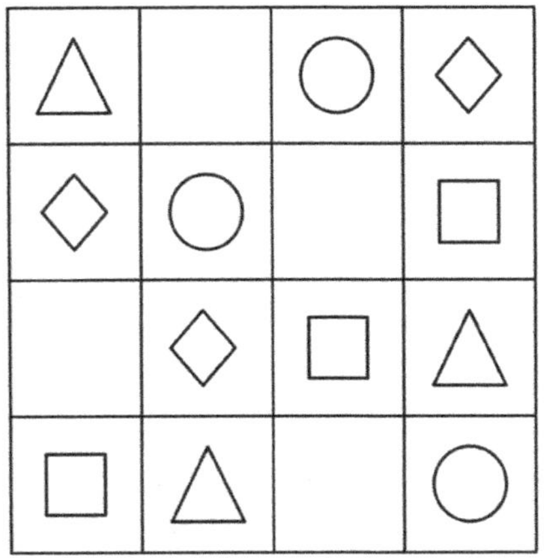

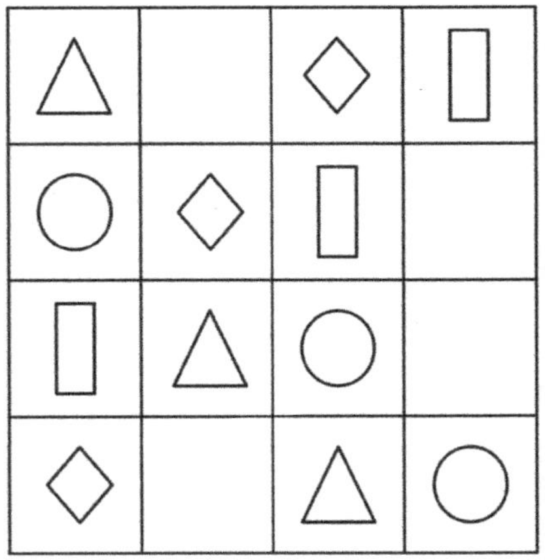

Geometry

STUDENT	GEOMETRY		
	Types of Lines	Open & Closed Shapes	Distinguishing Shapes

HOW DID IT GO?

Fill in the table at the end of each section. Did the minibooks seem difficult to you? How did you feel doing the exercises?

	How busy was I, from hardly at all (1) to extremely busy (5)? Color the box.	How hard was the work? Color the box from 0 (without difficulty) to 5 (very difficult).	How did I feel when reading the minibooks? Circle the emoji that fits your feeling.
Foundational Knowledge (minibook 2-10)	1 2 3 4 5	0 1 2 3 4 5	😀 😐 😢
Counting and numbers to 20 (minibook 11-57)	1 2 3 4 5	0 1 2 3 4 5	😀 😐 😢
Addition and subraction to 20 (minibook 58-69)	1 2 3 4 5	0 1 2 3 4 5	😀 😐 😢
Numbers beyond 20 (minibook 70-73)	1 2 3 4 5	0 1 2 3 4 5	😀 😐 😢
Problem solving (minibook 74-85)	1 2 3 4 5	0 1 2 3 4 5	😀 😐 😢
Geometry (minibook 86-90)	1 2 3 4 5	0 1 2 3 4 5	😀 😐 😢

Glossary

Abstraction: It does not matter what you count, how we count stays the same.
Automaticity: In math, the ability to recall a fact without computation.
Cardinality: The last number spoken in a counting sequence names the quantity for that set.
Logical-mathematical intelligence: The ability to think and process information in numerical terms and abstract relationships.
Numerical competency: The ability to understand, interpret, and work with numbers and to apply math concepts to problem-based scenarios.
One-to-One Correspondence: When saying the names of numbers, each item receives one count.
Order Irrelevance or Conservation: A group of objects has the same amount regardless of how objects are counted or any difference in size.
Stable Order: Numbers have a name and are said/written in a sequential order.
Subitize: The ability to accurately identify the number of items in a small set without counting.

Recommended Resources

Costello, D. (2021). *Making math stick: Classroom strategies that support the long-term understanding of math concepts.* Markham: Pembroke Publishers Ltd.

Costello, D. (2022). *Mathematizing student thinking: Connecting problem solving to everyday life and building capable and confident math learners.* Markham: Pembroke Publishers.

Costello, D. (2024). *Messing around with math: Ready-to-use problems that engage students in a better understanding of key math concepts.* Markham: Pembroke Publishers.

Franke, M. L., Kazemi, E., & Chan Turrou, A. (2018). *Choral counting and counting collections: Transforming the Pre K-5 math classroom.* Portland: Stenhouse Publishers.

Hintz, A., & Smith, A. T. (2022). *Mathematizing children's literature: Sparking connections, joy, and wonder through read-alouds and discussion.* Portland: Stenhouse Publishers.

Krpan, C. M. (2017). *Teaching math with meaning: Cultivating self-efficacy through learning competencies, grades K–8.* Toronto: Pearson Canada.

Pecaski McLennan, D. (2020). *Joyful math: Invitations to play and explore in the early childhood classroom.* Portland: Stenhouse Publishers.

Small, M. (2012). *Good questions: Great ways to differentiate mathematics instruction.* New York: Teachers College Press.

Small, M. (2013). *Making math meaningful to Canadian students, K-8.* Toronto: Nelson Education.

Van de Walle, J. A., Lovin, L. H., Karp, K. S., & Bay- Williams, J. M. (2014). *Teaching student-centred mathematics: Developmentally appropriate instruction for grades pre-K-2* (2nd., Vol. 1). Upper Saddle River: Pearson Education, Inc.